Praise for *Stop Sitting On Your Assets:*

From *New York Times* **best selling author,** television and film writer, RIDLEY PEARSON:

"There's plenty of great information in this well put together book. It's both readable and educational. I'm going to stop sitting on my assets and start sitting on the ideas expressed in this book." — RIDLEY PEARSON, CO-AUTHOR OF DISNEY FEATURE ANIMATION: *PETER AND THE STARCATCHERS*

From *New York Times* **best selling author,** ELLEN TANNER MARSH:

"… the effervescent Marian Snow, in her groundbreaking book, *Stop Sitting On Your Assets,* has set down a number of easy-to-implement solutions to take you from cash crunch to real riches.

Snow's advice is honest, informative, and downright revolutionary. So forget the money managers, whose costs and fees actually hurt investors, and instead grab a firm hold on Snow's timely book. Indeed, *Stop Sitting On Your Assets* is every bit as good as money in your bank." — ELLEN TANNER MARSH, AUTHOR

"Marian Snow's background as a scientist and underwriter creates a fresh new perspective on a recent financial formation called Home Equity Management. I suggest highly that you read Marian's book, make copious notes, and keep a copy of this at your bedside or in your personal library to reference on a regular basis to insure that you can live to experience the financial freedom that she outlines in *Stop Sitting On Your Assets.*" — JOHN BELL, FINANCIAL STRATEGIST *THE VALUE SHIELD SOLUTION SYSTEM*

"I have read dozens, if not hundreds, of financial books during my 16 years in the real estate industry and none of them have summed up such an easy to follow strategy for retiring wealthy as *Stop Sitting On Your Assets.* Ms. Snow lays out a methodical approach that is full of "inside secrets of the wealthy" in an easy to read format. Not only does she explain "why" you need to do this she describes "where" your money needs to go in order to retire wealthy. If you are concerned at all about being able to retire, this is the book for you." — DAVE MUTI, JD, RMA PRESIDENT, *FORGOTTENEQUITY.COM*

"In the mortgage industry, the key to helping homeowners achieve their "freedom point" faster is, first and foremost, to help them make the most informed decision possible. *Stop Sitting On Your Assets* does a great job of providing education, insight and clarity to help homeowners make informed decisions." — DAVE SAVAGE, CEO *THE MORTGAGE COACH*

"Do your HOMEwork! This book is not a conceptual or theoretical discussion, like so many other books about money. Instead, it's a practical step-by-step roadmap full of illustrations and explanation leading to a future of financial success that almost anyone can follow!" — BRADLEY S. BYRNE, ATTORNEY AT LAW

"Separation of equity is not a new concept to many Americans. The question has always been where you place the equity dollars so they are safe, liquid, and earn a rate of return that out performs the borrowing rate. *Stop Sitting On Your Assets* by Marian Snow addresses this important issue by detailing what financial instruments work and the precise way they should be funded. Marian delivers this message in an easy to follow format, that is a must-read for all homeowners." — SCOTT BERGMAN, PRESIDENT & MERLE GILLEY, VICE PRESIDENT *EQUITY FOR LIFE*

"*Stop Sitting On Your Assets* is not a book written on theory – it is written on reality! I can categorically make this statement because of my decades of actual financial planning experience. My files are overflowing with substantial numbers of clients that have already benefited from many of the facts and ideas expressed in Marian's book. I feel I can speak authoritatively because I have been a full-time financial planner for almost 30 years, a Certified Financial Planner for over 20 years, securities licensed for over 15 years and have written four personal finance books. Please believe me when I say, "This book is a MUST READ"."
— JAMES P. KRAISS CFP
AUTHOR, *MULTIPLY YOUR MONEY, MINIMIZE YOUR RISK*

"If you're 50-something and have been told that retirement is "not an option," you need this book. In *Stop Sitting On Your Assets,* Marian Snow explains why home equity is not the safety net we thought it was. She shows you how to move those dollars (which are getting a zero rate of return) into safe investments that will grow over time and help you achieve your financial goals. Be prepared to "think differently" and look forward to the retirement you thought was out of reach."   — MICHELE DEFILIPPO, OWNER, 1106 DESIGN

"Wow! I never expected a financial book to be so entertaining! I love how Marian presented her points to me as if just the two of us were having a conversation. I also liked how it wrapped up the points with a fictional story that applies all the principles presented. An excellent, inspiring and practical guide to financial success."
— BRIDGET FOX, *AMERICAN DREAMS REALTY*

"Quite simply the best book on equity management I've read. I offer a book to my clients to prepare them for our initial meeting. In the future, *Stop Sitting On Your Assets* will be my number one choice for client preparation because of the easy, conversational style and reading level. As icing on the cake, the non-technical illustrations, cartoons and stories clarify the concepts for true understanding!"   — GARY LEE, INSURANCE SPECIALIST

"Real estate ownership is an important element in true wealth creation and *Stop Sitting On Your Assets* shows the homeowner a different approach to maximizing and leveraging the assets that real estate creates in your lifetime. Whether you own multiple properties or just your primary home, you need to know about the wealth enhancement options and the tax benefits that real estate equity management can provide."
— JAMES POCKROSS, AUTHOR
CONFESSIONS OF A REAL ESTATE MINI-MOGUL

"Years ago, I understood that a mortgage is a power tool. I understood that the home and the mortgage generally represent the two largest numbers on the balance sheet of most homeowners. I also understood that mortgage payments, taxes, insurance and other home related expenses can easily consume as much as 60% of one's net spendable income. Therefore, to not integrate the mortgage into an overall financial strategy is simply a flawed plan. It's no wonder millions of Americans are so frustrated because they find it difficult to save and invest.

The equity management strategies researched and presented in this book simply work. What more can I say? I've personally implemented them. My clients have successfully implemented them. Every intelligent homeowner should investigate how using them can boost the success of their comprehensive overall financial plan."
— RANDALL A LUEBKE RMA, RFC
THE ACADEMY OF MORTGAGE PLANNING

STOP SITTING ON YOUR ASSETS

How to safely leverage the equity trapped in your home and transform it into a constant flow of wealth and security.

MARIAN SNOW

Ethan Madison Publishing
Chicago

PUBLISHING

Ethan Madison Publishing,
4890 N. Ashland Avenue, Suite 2N, Chicago, IL 60640
Phone: (800) 664-9713   Fax: (630) 563-6899
www.EmadisonPub.com   info@EmadisonPub.com

Printed in the United States of America on acid-free paper

Real Wealth Vision™, H.E.R.O. Solution™, S.A.F.E.T.Y. Fund™, C.O.F.F.E.E. Crisis™, Real Wealth L.A.W.™, Amazing Retirement Machine™ and Glasses of the Masses™ are all trademarks of HERO Solution, Inc.

Book Design: Michele DeFilippo, 1106 Design, LLC; Book Consultant: Ellen Reid

This publication is designed to provide competent and reliable information regarding the subject matter covered. It represents the opinions and viewpoints of the author and may not be applicable to all situations. It is sold with the understanding the author and publisher are not engaged in rendering legal, financial or other professional advice. Relevance of these principles may change, become outdated, or rendered incorrect by new legislation or official rulings. Laws and availability of products illustrated may vary from state to state.

Any performance data presented herein doesn't imply that similar results will be achieved in the future. All such data is provided merely for illustration of an underlying principle. All tables, charts and numbers shown were from prior time periods and are merely presented for discussion.

The information presented is accurate to the best of the author's knowledge. The reader is encouraged to verify the status of tax laws and other information before taking action. Neither the author nor the publisher assumes liability or responsibility for losses that may be sustained or alleged to be sustained, directly or indirectly, through actions taken by readers based upon the advice presented herein. Any liability is hereby expressly disclaimed.

None of the material illustrated is intended to serve as an entire basis for a financial decision. Caution should be taken in applying these principles to your specific situation and competent professional assistance should be sought before making any critical financial moves. Additionally, though having been trained and having acquired an insurance license, the author is not a professional insurance salesperson. Information provided herein should not be considered a solicitation to purchase insurance or financial products.

Please purchase only authorized electronic editions, and do not participate in or encourage electronic piracy of copyrighted materials. Your support of the author's rights is appreciated.

Publisher's Cataloguing-In-Publication Data

Snow, Marian.

    Stop sitting on your assets : how to safely leverage the equity
    trapped in your home and transform it into a constant flow of wealth
    and security / Marian Snow. -- Chicago, IL : Ethan Madison Publishing, 2007.

        p. ; cm.
        ISBN-13: 978-09790142-5-3
        ISBN-10: 0-9790142-5-5

     1. Asset allocation--United States. 2. Finance, Personal--United
States. 3. Financial security--United States. 4. Investments--United
States. I. Title.

HG4529.5 .S56 2007
332.024/010973--dc22   0612

To my dad, Bill Snow,
an extraordinary man who truly lived
a wonderful life and, in his own words,
"was surrounded by wonderful people."

Author's Note

What if I told you I'm about to share inside secrets that, before now, only the very wealthy among us knew? What if I told you these secrets will absolutely transform you into a millionaire? What if this proven system could be set up so that you could just implement it once to be wealthy? Then, what if I showed you how you could recycle it every three or five years to double or even triple your wealth? What if I said it doesn't involve effort, concentration or budgeting? Would you want to know more?

This book should carry a warning: "What you are about to read is contrary to what you've always been taught and what you may have previously believed about how money works."

Most likely, the largest chunk of your present belief system about wealth has probably been built upon information you received from unwealthy sources. What you've been taught or have heard about protecting, borrowing and accumulating money was presented to you by people without real wealth of their own. Isn't that true for you?

Stop Sitting On Your Assets reveals a revolutionary, yet easy, system for building riches that leaves most of the other plans out there in the dust. It simply shows you the secrets of how to take the assets you already have, lock-in their safety and turbocharge them the way the wealthy do. This solution can work for just about anybody — if you spend less than you make — no matter your wealth or income level.

I'm confident the revolutionary ideas presented will surprise you, possibly amaze you and, hopefully, benefit and liberate you. I've chosen to concentrate on the ideas and theories that can make you a fortune, rather than the technical and legal ramifications involved in the individual application of some of the products discussed. This will allow you, the reader, quicker access to information about the core concepts behind these wealth-optimizing approaches.

As you go through each chapter, please keep an open mind. While these strategies are different, they're still very conservative and safe methods for assured wealth building. Most financial professionals are unaware of these strategies ... but then, most financial professionals aren't wealthy.

Between 2000 and 2003, millions of average investors lost about nine trillion dollars, much of which was in their retirement accounts invested in the market via stocks or mutual funds. I'll show you how the convergence of three unrelated events in this fresh millennium has created a new financial solution that could have protected and prevented those losses.

As our aging society moves toward retirement, we need to shield our assets from loss, boost our wealth and look forward to self-sufficient older years beyond the age of 100, living with security and peace of mind.

We need a hero and the H.E.R.O. Solution™ may just be the answer.

Thank you,
Marian Snow

Contents

Foreword

If you had enough money to pay off your mortgage right now, would you? Many people would. In fact, the 'American Dream' is to own your own home, and to own it outright, with no mortgage. If this *dream* is so wonderful, how can we explain the fact that thousands of financially successful people, who have more than enough money to pay off their mortgage, refuse to do so?

The answer? Most of what we believe about mortgages and home equity, which we learned from our parents and grandparents, is wrong. They taught us to make a big down payment, get a fixed rate mortgage, and make extra principal payments in order to pay off your loan as early as you can. Mortgages, they said, are a necessary evil at best.

The problem with this rationale is it has become outdated. The rules of money have changed. Unlike our grandparents, we will no longer live in the same home for 30 years. Statistics show that the average homeowner lives in their home for only seven years. And unlike our grandparents, we will no longer keep the same mortgage for 30 years.

Marian Snow, a scientist by education, is a financial analyst and underwriter for a Chicago mortgage-banking firm. Her rare insider's view into the money activities of thousands of individuals for over fifteen years brought some interesting revelations to her attention. Many extremely wealthy people were not following the traditional conventional wisdom of the past.

Heuristic is a field of science that has been around since the fourth century. The word comes from the same Greek root as "eureka", which means, "I find". It has been used in the technical analysis of financial trends for decades. Often applied within the arena of the behavioral sciences, it can be utilized to study why people do what they do with their money. Knowing these methods, Marian wanted to discover the essence of what the wealthy were doing differently. To achieve this end, she gathered real numbers from thousands of mortgage application files that came across her desk.

In much the same fashion as the professor in the CBS Television show, *NUMB3RS*, who uses mathematical analysis to solve crimes, Marian, armed with an analytical mind and a scientific background; set out to drill-down to the details of what the wealthy were doing differently to achieve such successful financial results ... the results so illusive to the majority of Americans.

The methods she validated were so simple that almost anyone would be able to begin using the strategies right away to make a tremendous difference in the outlook for their family's future. In *Stop Sitting On Your Assets*, Marian reveals how to make immediate changes with your current holdings and then reposition the money that flows through your hands in the future to guarantee your life's financial success.

Wealthy Americans, those with the ability to pay off their mortgage but refuse to do so, understand how to make their mortgage work for them. They go against many of the beliefs of traditional thinking. They put very little money down, they keep their mortgage balance as high as possible, they choose adjustable rate interest-only mortgages, and most importantly they integrate their mortgage into their overall financial plan to continually increase their wealth. This is how the rich get richer.

Many people hate their mortgage because they know over the life of a 30-year loan they will spend more interest than the house cost them in the first place. To save money it becomes very tempting to make a bigger down payment, or make extra principal payments. Unfortunately, saving money is not the same as making money. Or, put another way, paying off debt is not the same as accumulating assets.

You know, it's funny, we all are using the same game board, but while most Americans are playing checkers, the affluent are playing chess. The good news is the strategies used by the wealthy work for the rest of America as well. Any homeowner can implement these strategies of the wealthy to increase their net worth.

Steven Marshall
Founder & CEO of Strategic Equity
and CEO, Bellevue Mutual Mortgage

Introduction

If you have read the *Foreword* section in this book, you already know I've been privy to the inside financial secrets of thousands of people, many of them extremely wealthy. The mysteries of much of their riches can be boiled down to a fascinatingly simple set of steps.

To create amazing, effortless, inevitable wealth for yourself, you must simply follow behind them down the path of life. How will you know the way? Once you get these secrets, you'll have acquired Real Wealth Vision™, their footprints left in the sand will become immediately visible to you. The rest is simple. Each step to take is laid out in clear view. Place one foot in front of the other and follow them. Your personal financial success will be unavoidable.

After you learn and comprehend the concepts revealed in this book, you will be able to see things through virtual lenses giving you Real Wealth Vision™. From that moment on, you'll exist, possessing the ability to see and understand round world concepts, but you'll be completely surrounded by people who only see a flat world.

This dilemma may be difficult for you. Until you are able to explain these new insights to others, I can guarantee you'll be up against some real resistance. Old beliefs are very ingrained. Financial planners, CPAs, parents and

MAKING SENSE OF CONFUSION

A teacher presented his student with a paper covered in what appeared to be a multitude of random dots. The student was asked to find the image that would emerge if the dots were connected. After fruitlessly trying to see the possible connections, the student returned to his teacher. He told him all he could see was just a bunch of dots on a page.

The teacher replied, "This is the way the financial world looks to most people. It is just a bunch of confusing choices with no rhyme or reason. They have no clue how to connect-the-dots to make sense out of it all. A multitude of experts give completely conflicting advice. Your relatives may tell you to make careful and safe choices; the personal banker tells you to put your money in their money market or a CD; brokers may say the answer is in stocks, mutual funds or tax-exempt bonds; some may tell you your pension plan or Social Security will be all you need. The average person is perplexed and puzzled at best, paralyzed at worst. In a haze, he rubs his temples and confusingly enters the ring, tries a couple of things with his money, gets burned and retreats to a corner, feeling like an idiot. Just as in Mark Twain's story, where the cat steps once on a hot stove and never steps on any stoves again—hot or cold."

The teacher asked the student if he had yet been able to see the image within the dots. Since the student could not make out any picture at all, the teacher produced a second page with the same dots, but they had been connected to produce the depiction of a man lounging in a hammock.

He put away the connected image and produced the original page, once again, without the dots connected. It was the same sheet he'd spent so long pondering upon with fruitless results.

The teacher asked the student what he saw when he looked at the dots. The student spoke without hesitation, saying, "I see a man in a hammock." The teacher said, "And from now on, whenever you see this image, instead of a confused mass of dots, you'll always see a man in a hammock. I changed your perception. I taught you how to make sense of the confusion."

relatives will all believe the traditional ways of thinking are the right ways.

Those who see through the "Glasses of the Masses," as I call it, say, "I want to be wealthy. That's why I save my money." But those who possess Real Wealth Vision™ know that just saving money has never made anyone wealthy. Accumulating assets that can continually create more assets is the secret to real wealth.

Most people think they are really saving money by ridding themselves of what they consider to be costly mortgage interest. That error in thinking is actually robbing them of a rich future for themselves and their families. Paying down mortgage debt is not the same as accumulating assets. The more cash you can put to work churning out more cash ... the more you can employ assets ... the wealthier you will become.

THIS BOOK WILL MAKE THE COMPLEX SIMPLE

Are you tired of all the confusing advice flying at you from all sides? Talking heads on the business and news channels. New financial books are out every week. Magazines and newspapers offer constant columns on money advice. Everyone promises they have the true way to make you rich.

There's a good chance you have bought books that offer you get-rich-quick schemes. Chances are they are sitting on your bookshelf gathering dust.

First, let me assure you, this book WILL fulfill its promise to show you the path to unavoidable riches. It will do so in a simple, workable and uncomplicated manner that anyone can follow. Your success will be determined by a plan you set in motion that is pretty much unstoppable.

Stop Sitting On Your Assets™ will:

- NOT tell you to automatically skip a cappuccino-a-day!
- NOT tell you what a *wealthy father* said that very few can actually use!
- NOT teach you to buy no-money-down investment real estate and flip it!
- NOT tell you to search for undervalued properties and become a landlord!
- NOT teach you to trade in the stock or futures markets!
- NOT tell you to quit your job, create legal entities and open a business that could fail!

This book will show you the secrets very wealthy people use everyday. But one thing is very important, once you know these secrets and are shown the path, you must follow it.

To allow you to see the way more clearly, you'll be introduced to three couples selected for an imaginary reality television show. The participants' experiences will demonstrate how each of them begins with the same income, same family size and same housing expenses, and yet, ends up with a totally different wealth outcome than the other two.

One of the participants will reveal basic Real Wealth Vision™ principles in action. Which couple will it be? Who'll become a millionaire? Which one will be left penniless? The principles they demonstrate should illuminate the path for you like switching on runway lights. You may discover traits, notions and habits they possess that are much like your own.

As the show begins, each of the participating couples will start at exactly the same place. They will each be given an equal opportunity to become millionaires. They'll be provided with the tools and the time to create real wealth for themselves. Without question, if they follow the show's plan as prescribed, they will all end up with riches. But what goes wrong?

The three surprisingly different outcomes will prove to be astounding and the lessons taught could be life changing for you. The simple path to take will be exposed for you. Its revelation will cause a true financial transformation in the way you look at every dollar from this day forward.

Once you are shown the secret of how money can actually work for you, it will be easy to absorb the lessons taught, apply these changes in your own thought processes and actually put yourself on track to, without question, acquire inevitable wealth. There is no way you will be able to go back to your old way of thinking.

HOW DO YOU KNOW IT WILL WORK FOR YOU?

I can assure you that many others have been successful using the secrets presented in this book and still more are currently practicing these techniques on their way to unstoppable riches. Most of these folks came upon this wisdom through having Real Wealth Vision™ passed on to them by others in their lives already possessing it. Many acquired it through their own inherent analysis. Lucky for them, they were somehow able to come upon these phenomenal secrets without this book. Lucky for you, this book is in your hands.

Let me warn you ... if you are currently carrying credit card or consumer debt, you may need to seek corrective financial help from other sources before you begin implementing the plan in this book. There are other remedial financial publications, radio and television shows out there (one does a complete financial makeover and one focuses on those who are broke but fabulous). You know the books.

The strategies presented in this book will work best for you if you spend less than you make and have a positive cash flow within your personal finances. This system provides real results if you have critical cash accumulated in your house and in your retirement accounts. If you are serious about turbocharging those accumulated assets you already have or being on your way to a positive monthly income position, then you should read on.

There's too much at stake for you to just skim through and stop at the end of the first chapter. You must forge ahead and continue until the concepts are crystal clear to you.

Imagine … in just a few hours you could possess the previously elusive secrets that may change your financial future. By then, you will have internalized Real Wealth Vision™ and made it part your own insight. Upon acquiring it, you'll immediately be able to see the footprints left in the sand ahead of you. After that, it's up to you to take that first step.

Once you see with Real Wealth Vision™ a fresh new day in your life will have dawned.

Stop and breathe in the fresh ocean air. Listen to the seagulls and the sound of the waves rolling onto the beach. Feel the cool pleasant breeze at your back. Stretch your arms up high and gaze into the fabulous morning sky. Wiggle your toes in the sand and feel its warmth beneath your feet.

Go ahead. Place your heel into the first footprint that has appeared on the beach of life directly in front of you. Roll forward to your toes and repeat with your other foot. You get the picture. Once you get going, you may even break into a jog. The steps will come easily and naturally. Your experience will be life changing. You'll become unstoppable as you start down the path laid out ahead. There'll be no going back, once you've been shown the secrets and possess Real Wealth Vision™, your future of personal wealth will be inevitable.

CHAPTER ONE

UNSEEN THIEVES
ARE ROBBING YOU
IN THE NIGHT

Installing a new security system won't help. Your bank's Internet firewall protections won't stop them. They are pervasive and rampant. You should be terrified. You are probably their target right now.

The culprits aren't a gang of international cat burglars that could be tracked and thwarted. They're not an identifiable bunch of computer hackers getting into your bank accounts. These robbers are a much larger group and extremely difficult to identify.

An organized ring of white-collar bandits has become ingrained into our society. Subtly and slowly, they're taking the largest part of the potential life savings of most working adults. Worse yet, they're doing their dastardly deeds disguised as trusted advisors, grandparents and teachers.

This diabolical and pervasive robbery system sucks the unknowing target into trust, brainwashes them and sets them up to have their money siphoned away gradually and without notice over years and years. The victims are totally unaware. It's a truly sinister plot.

Most likely you are being preyed upon as you read this page.

So, what will be the toll? The average victim is going to lose hundreds of thousands, possibly millions of dollars in their lifetimes.

"Wait a minute," you're probably thinking, "How can something this big be going on without me knowing? Why haven't I read about this in the news?"

As I said, people are unaware this is happening. The media isn't reporting it. You haven't heard about it on the *O'Reilly Factor*. CNBC's talking heads aren't sending out warnings. Clark Howard isn't announcing a "shark attack."

Why? Robber barons of old, corporate raiders and pension fund pirates all pale in comparison. Even though this devastation will be worse than the savings and loan debacle of the late 1980s and more crippling than the Enron scandal, it can't be captured neatly in a two-minute news segment!

Most victims will be older citizens, but people in all age groups are losing vast sums of money. In fact, more than half of Americans over age 45 are having millions taken away from them at this writing.

Combine this horror with our plummeting savings rate[1] and we look around to find ourselves seated on a runaway train headed for ultimate financial disaster, carrying our future security in the overhead bin.

---

[1] Economists at the Federal Reserve Board and the Bureau of Economic Analysts say our savings rate has dropped below 1%, the lowest since 1938. This drop has descended from a high of 11% in the 1980s.

Is The American Dream Really A Nightmare?

How is this travesty possible? 16.5 million homeowners sit in their homes today with 100% of their equity bricked up inside their walls. Each of them has gone about their plan with deliberation in their method. Compelled to complete their life-long goal to be mortgage free. Ever consistent and depend-able, yes. But, they planned their financial actions based on unfounded fear, outdated assumptions and bad advice. Sadly, **every dime of their largest asset[2] is now receiving a zero rate of return** for their future.

For many, it may be their only asset. According to an online pension and retirement resource firm, one of every four workers in America that is offered a retirement program through their employer does not even enroll in the plan. This means a large por-tion of our population is just not planning or saving at all.

> **Equity** is the difference between the current market value of a property and the amount the owner still owes on the mortgage.

Worse yet, when they are going to really need their money, many will be unable to get to it. Jobs will be lost, disabilities will occur, financial tragedies will pounce upon them when least expected, and they'll have no recourse. A large number will ultimately lose their homes.

What is at stake? Safety. Long-term financial security. Stability and well-being in retirement. All potentially at risk. This horrific mistake is literally stealing away the chance for richer lives and comfortable enjoyment into what will inevitably be longer and longer lifetimes.

---

[2] Per the Federal Reserve Board publication entitled, *Home Equity Lines of Credit*, "... the home is likely to be a consumer's largest asset."

Alan Greenspan, former chairman of the Federal Reserve Board, tallied the total value of Americans' homes to be over 16 trillion dollars, but went on to say only 7 trillion dollars exists in mortgage debt against those homes.[3]

What does this tell us? We keep obscene portions of cash lying dormant. As a whole, our country has 9 trillion idle dollars trapped inside the walls of our houses. That's not millions, not billions, but trillions of dollars bricked into the hearths, stuffed in the mattress and, otherwise, buried in the backyards of our American homes.

I Thought Building Equity Was Good. How Can It Be Bad?

> *That's not millions, not billions, but trillions ...*

Idle home equity is the largest unemployment crisis imaginable! We've got over 9 trillion dollars in non-producing capital tied up in the equity in our homes, yet we have entire generations approaching retirement with little or no savings.

Why do we do it? We are giving ourselves a false sense of security by keeping the majority of our assets inside our walls. When illness, disability, unemployment or other such events strike us, most people are left unable to get a loan to access their cash. Most banks and mortgage companies require evidence of a monthly income in order to obtain a loan. If we're left with no income, even temporarily, getting a loan becomes extremely difficult, expensive or even impossible for many of us. Do you see how this puts a wall, so to speak, between us and our cash? We are left exposed. In that

---

[3] Source: Alan Greenspan's testimony before the House Financial Services Committee in 2005.

vulnerable position, the possibility of losing our home through foreclosure or sale becomes very real.

Adding to the liquidity risks and lack of safety, vast fortunes have been lost and will continue to vanish because of missed opportunity costs. The cash buried in home equity could instead be working to earn a compounded return, dramatically changing our lives. Millions of Americans live under the poverty line yet have homes that are paid off. What relief, assistance and comfort those assets could have provided if home equity had only been managed more effectively.

The majority of homeowners, financial planners and even personal finance authors falsely believe borrowing money and then investing it at the same or a lower rate holds no potential for improvement of your personal wealth. **They don't know what they don't know.**

I met with a financial planner/mortgage consultant who is on the staff of one of Chicago's largest trust banks. When I began to explain to him how most people should be keeping the largest mortgage they can afford and investing their equity in a safe and compounding side account, he immediately said, "You can't do that! It won't work!"

Then I said, "But look at the real numbers in black and white. The results are unequivocally proven to be true."

He refused to even look at the spreadsheets. Again, he simply replied, "That can't be done and I won't even consider it!"

Not only was he completely closed minded about the successful strategies. He wouldn't even listen to an explanation or hear anything that wasn't what he had always been told was the way things should be done.

Securing your critical cash in a protected, side account to earn a tax-sheltered and compounding return holds the potential for tremendous profits. The relative interest rates of the times do not affect the success of this strategy. When mortgage rates are high, interest yields are high. When mortgage rates are low, the relative earnings move in lockstep. It works in all market situations.

How Can So Many Be Losing So Much?

Outdated guidance. Pure and simple. Most of us receive direction from well-meaning parents, lacking yet concerned advisors and volumes of published advice from ill-informed gurus and media warriors out to protect the little guy. Where do these soothsayers get their information? History.

Ancient wisdom. That's it. It's just a reliance on what they learned from their own well-intentioned parents, conventionally trained advisors and textbooks of supposed traditional knowledge. They are going through life, all too often, failing to look beyond the accepted way of accomplishing a goal. This causes them to overlook and miss out on even better methods of achieving the desired end. They're simply oblivious to the reality that innovations in the financial community bring new and improved ways to accomplish wealth success.

Copyright 2006 HERO Solution, Inc.

Why Do We Let This Continue To Happen?

Fear is the main culprit. We are like little children who are afraid of the dark or the monster under the bed. 99% of financial advisors have the same fears and, in an attempt to protect you, guide you based upon those fears. But — are those fears based in reality?

What are we actually afraid of?

- We fear we're losing money in mortgage interest.
- We fear we'll lose our home.
- We fear we'll lose our job.
- We fear we'll lose our cash in a risky stock market or some other investment.
- We fear we'll waste the money on something frivolous if we don't put it away.

FEAR =
False Education Appearing Real

Have you heard any of those small voices in your head? Maybe they sound faintly familiar? So what do we do to diminish our fears? We squirrel our money away in our mattress by paying down our mortgage. Out of sight, out of mind. Right? Maybe we are operating on deliberate, yet bad advice from a trusted source fearing for our safety. Perhaps we have no plan and just want to be less afraid, but we don't know of a better place to put the money.

Want to know what's worse? Those fears are only child's play. They are pebbles or grains of sand compared to the boulder of alarm you should be concerned about. They are tiny unfounded worries in the scheme of the bigger picture.

"What could be a bigger fear?" you say.

How about the unthinkable ... outlasting your money? How about the horror that you'll be financially unprepared for living to age 100? Sure you'll have a roof over your head, but your Social Security will go to property taxes. Picture yourself then, unable to pay the heating bill, crouching at your small kitchen table with the oven door open for warmth. You'll be nibbling away at your dinner of cat food on a cracker.

That could be where traditional wisdom is leading us. It's literally causing us to lose millions through our ignorance. But, there is a better way.

The Wealthy Can Pay Cash For Their House But They Don't. Think There Might Be A Better Way?

Wow! Why would you suppose the wealthy among us don't operate using the old conventional wisdom everybody else uses? What do they know that 99% of us don't?

Do you think they may have discovered the fallacies inherent in the outdated ways of our parents? Who knows how it came to be, but the numbers prove this fact: **The wealthy get big mortgages and don't pay them down or pay them off.**

> "*Many people engaged in financial planning are **Victims of Conventional Wisdom**.*"
> — Chairman of Forbes

These folks have lots of liquid assets. Most can pay cash for the real estate they buy. But they don't. When this fact jumped out of the numbers at me from my data evaluation, I set out to discover why.

My research validated that the wealthy know there is a better way. They detest idle cash and have better uses for their money than to bury it away, sentenced to a life of non-productivity. They also know mortgage money is the cheapest form of borrowing and has the potential for tax benefits that could make it an even more inexpensive source of capital.

Their own safety is another reason. Wealthy homeowners realize they are just farther out of harm's way when their money is accessible. The ups and downs of daily life can be more easily weathered when short-term cash needs are met. You can make less pressured decisions and take advantage of opportunities that present themselves in a timely manner. Keeping assets working continuously puts a person way ahead in the financial race of life. It's just a smarter, less stressful way to live.

Large equity positions can actually hurt us in the long run. The risk of losses from natural disasters, lawsuits and housing markets are increased when all our cash is buried in that single asset. Tax benefits are reduced with every payment we make to our mortgage principal. And, of course, who in their right mind would put a large chunk of their money in an investment that is yielding a zero rate of return? Return on capital is extremely important over time, since the magic of compounding works for us on investment accounts while the mortgage balance stays the same or reduces.

The wealthy have come to recognize that **accumulating large amounts of equity in real estate is simply a losing proposition.** It's something most of them would never get trapped into if they have the ability to steer clear of it. Avoiding equity build-up is a pretty easy thing to do in today's world with the plethora of choices for using other people's money. Other people's money, or OPM, as it is often referred to, is simply borrowed money. Using OPM to tap our accumulated equity creates an advanced financial strategy called arbitrage. We'll talk about that later on.

How did they determine the old way was no longer a viable system to own a house? Who's to say? Perhaps they had privileged access to extremely astute planners. Maybe their own parents were also wealthy and gave them these pearls of wisdom. Maybe they did the research and discovered it on their own. Whatever the method, they've discovered the evidence and they've proven by their financial success that several factors in the financial world have come together to create a new highway to wealth. The sad thing is most of us are headed through life using the old, outdated map.

Are You Getting a Zero Rate of Return on Your Largest Single Investment?

> *Equity in your house earns a zero rate of return.*

Let me give you an example. There are two men who accept different jobs and move their families to a new town. Their prior homes were in more expensive areas so they both netted $250,000 from the sale of those houses. The new city offers less expensive housing, so they decide to buy homes for the same price.

Let's say Tom Today buys his house for $250,000 and gets a $200,000 mortgage. The remaining $50,000 of his purchase price comes from the profit on his previous home. Tom has $200,000 cash left, but he chooses to put it in another investment. Harry Historic buys the house next door for exactly the same price. Harry also netted $250,000 from his prior home, but he feels that a mortgage is expensive and he will save money by not paying a lender mortgage interest. With this in mind, he decides to just pay cash for the house.

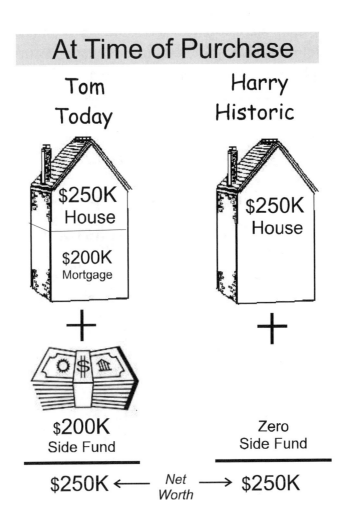

At Time of Purchase

Tom Today — Harry Historic

$250K House / $200K Mortgage + $200K Side Fund

$250K House + Zero Side Fund

$250K ← Net Worth → $250K

So lets see where we are:

At Time of Purchase:

	Tom Today	Harry Historic
House Values:	$250,000	$250,000
Cash Account:	$200,000	0
Total Assets:	$450,000	$250,000
Mortgage balance:	−$200,000	0
Net Worth:	$250,000	$250,000

OK. So they start out with the same net positions. We'll assume Tom has an 8% interest-only mortgage, to make the math simple, and Tom is able to earn 8% on his cash investment account. Let's say homes values are appreciating at an average rate of 5% where they live.

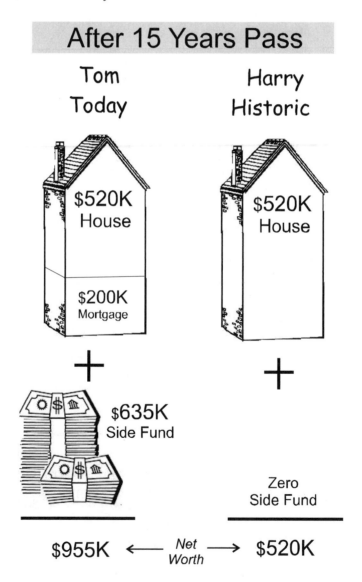

After 15 Years Pass

Tom
Today

Harry
Historic

$520K House

$200K Mortgage

$520K House

+

+

$635K Side Fund

Zero Side Fund

$955K ⟵ *Net Worth* ⟶ $520K

You would immediately think Tom is going to get nowhere by paying 8% on his mortgage and only earning 8% on his investment. Well let's see how the numbers have progressed after 15 years?

After 15 Years Pass:

	Tom Today	**Harry Historic**
House Values @ 5%	$520,000	$520,000
Cash Account @ 8%	$635,000	0
Total Assets:	$1,155,000	$520,000
Mortgage balance:	–$200,000	– $0
Net Worth:	$955,000	$520,000

Equity Has a Zero Rate of Return

Clearly both houses grew to $520,000[4] in 15 years regardless of their mortgage balance. The amount of equity had no bearing on the growth. Harry's $250,000 in initial equity compared to Tom's $50,000 made no difference at all to property values.

The two men had different equity positions, yet both houses grew to the same value in 15 years. Tom's $200,000 side account, kept in a secure investment and separated from his house's equity, grew at 8% to $635,000. If he paid his mortgage balance off now, using his cash account, he would still be $435,000 ahead.

But, Wait! — There Were Payments

"Yes, wait just a minute," you say. "Tom had mortgage payments to make. That's not all we should consider."

---

[4] Per the 2003 Census Report, the average U.S. home is experiencing an across-the-board annual increase of 5.33%.

OK. Let's pay him back every single interest-only payment out of his net side cash account that remains and lets also give him credit for the tax refunds he got along the way. We will assume he is in a 33% combined federal and state tax bracket to make the math easy.

Wow! A Quarter-of-a-Million Dollars Ahead After 15 Years

Tom Today is over a quarter-of-a-million dollars ahead of Harry Historic, even after he got back all his house payments! That's only after 15 years.

After 15 Years Pass:

	Tom Today	Harry Historic
Net Worth from above:	$955,000	$520,000
180 Payments Made @ 8%:	$240,000	$0
15 Tax Refunds received:	−$80,000	− 0
Total Net Payments Made:	$160,000	$0
Net Worth less Payments:	$795,000	$520,000

So, how will their financial positions look in 30 years? Are you curious? Well, let's take a look.

1.5 Million Dollars Ahead After 30 Years!

Yes, fast forward another fifteen years and Tom Today is worth 1.5 million dollars more than Harry Historic! Do you see how the wealthy have found the secret to easy financial success? Do you also see their different equity positions had no bearing whatsoever to the growth of their perspective properties? The magic is in maximizing time and utilizing compounding interest. We'll delve deeper into compound interest later on.

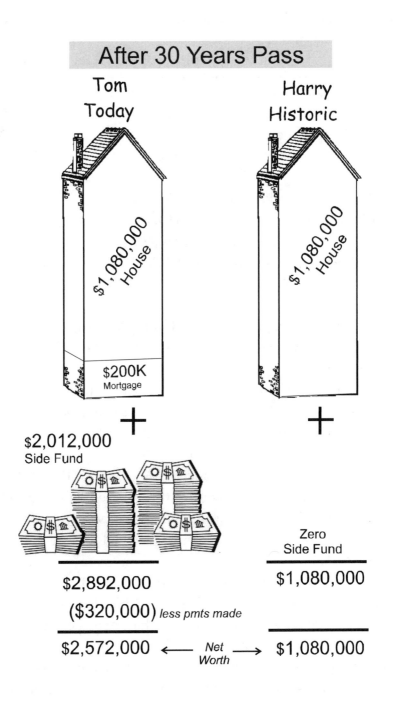

After 30 Years Pass

Tom
Today

Harry
Historic

$1,080,000 House

$1,080,000 House

$200K
Mortgage

+

+

$2,012,000
Side Fund

Zero
Side Fund

$2,892,000

$1,080,000

($320,000) *less pmts made*

$2,572,000 ⟵ *Net* ⟶ $1,080,000
Worth

After 30 Years Pass:

	Tom Today	Harry Historic
House Values @ 5%:	$1,080,000	$1,080,000
Cash Account @ 8%:	$2,012,000	0
Less Mortgage Balance:	−$200,000	0
Net Worth:	$2,892,000	$1,080,000
360 Payments Made @ 8%:	$480,000	$0
30 Tax Refunds received:	−$160,000	− 0
Net Payments:	$320,000	$0
Net Worth less Payments:	$2,572,000	$1,080,000

But I've Always Heard The Money You Pay Down On Real Estate Is Leveraged By That Real Estate

Again, you are speaking the language of outdated wisdom. If you buy a property with zero money down, it will grow in value just the same as if you put 10% down, 25% down or pay cash. Your equity really has nothing to do with the so-called "leveraging effect." Old financial advice said, "Pay $10,000 down on a $100,000, then your return is based on the growth of the entire house, not just your down-payment. If your property grows by 10%, you have received a 100% gain on your $10,000."

That's a *bunch of baloney* ... an old sales line. It sounds really good if you are trying to sell a house. It's also a good point to bring up to lure investors into purchasing real estate. Don't get me wrong. Real estate is an excellent investment. I own multiple properties myself. But the truth is, any money you pay into real estate is receiving zero return. Once you acquire a piece of property, it will appreciate or depreciate based on its own merits, not on your cash investment.

Money paid down on real estate is also cash forfeited that could have been redirected into other investments. Once paid into equity, it's pretty much gone. It is really difficult and sometimes costly to retrieve that dollar back. Great care should be taken when determining whether cash in hand should ever be exiled to an idle life by being thrown into your house.

What Do You Think Of Traditional Financial Advice Now?

Well, let's recap. Most of us are being robbed of fortunes by following traditional financial wisdom. We are missing out on potential millions in unearned compounding future earnings and systematically chopping away at valuable tax deductions. These deductions will disappear every year we don't take them.

You should always consider the future value of a dollar today and what it could become over time.

To add insult to injury, as you will see in Chapter Nine, we are placing ourselves at risk for financial loss by systematically moving away from a position of safety and putting our cash farther and farther out of reach. We're increasingly exposing our assets to lawsuit liability and loss from events out of our control. Every dollar we pay into our equity moves us further away from safety and financial security.

And some of us are even paying professional advisors for this so-called financial wisdom? Talk about being robbed ...

CHAPTER TWO

THE C.O.F.F.E.E. CRISIS™ ... ARE WE FORFEITING A FORTUNE UNKNOWINGLY?

Time Won't Wait

What is our most precious commodity? Aside from our family, time probably holds the number one spot. Whether you are a billionaire or penniless, time is something we all have in equal amounts. What we do with our time can make all the difference in our lives. Were we to consider how time can change our assets, we might come to realize time is truly a precious wealth.

Time certainly won't wait for us. Many people put off planning or saving for the future, thinking, "Someday I'll start." If we could truly understand how time has the potential to heap value upon our money, we would begin to look at time in a whole new way. We'd wonder what we were waiting for. We've all heard, "Time is money," and nothing could be truer. For when time has slipped away, making up for its loss is very difficult.

> "Compound interest is the Eighth Wonder of the World."
> — Albert Einstein

The largest expenditure most of us make in our lifetimes is our house purchase. It only follows that our housing or our mortgage payment is going to be our largest monthly expense. In the mortgage industry, the portion of a family's monthly cash considered prudent for this expense is between 25% and 40% of their gross income. In addition to being the largest expenditure made, it usually requires a very long-term commitment on the part of the homeowner.

POWER OF COMPOUNDING

Which would you choose? 1¢ doubling every day or $10,000 per week?

To illustrate the power of the doubling effect, suppose you were offered a job that would last only one month. You were to choose between being paid $10,000 per week or being given a penny the first day, which would subsequently be doubled every day for the remainder of the month. This sounds like a pretty easy choice. Which would you pick?

At $10,000 per week, you would end your job with a check for $40,000. If the other payment method is chosen, you would receive a penny the first day, two cents the second, four cents the third, eight cents the fourth, and so on. The second choice would pay you over **$5,000,000** (yes, 5 million dollars) by the 30th day. If you worked in a month with 31 days, you'd have over 10 million dollars! Wow, the power of compounding is absolutely amazing!

Because so many of us feel negatively about mortgages and what we mistakenly think they are costing us, we often make large down payments on our homes in order to reduce the mortgage we need to get. In an attempt to improve our situation, we are actually condemning ourselves to tremendous financial losses over time.

Hopefully you understand by now, equity has no rate of return. So what have we done? We've taken massive chunks of money and bricked them up into the walls of our house. After that money has been sentenced to a life of futility, our largest asset begins to grow in value, heaping more and more idle cash into the bowels of the basement and caverns of the crawlspaces. As we learned in the first chapter, the more equity that grows senselessly inside our house, the less safe our family's position becomes.

What Is Opportunity Cost?

As related to money, opportunity cost is the benefit forfeited by using your money in a particular way. It's the idea of what must be given up as a result of a decision. Many people see the concept of opportunity cost as one of the few profound "eternal truths of economics." It's a result of the universal nature of scarcity.

Any road taken … any decision made … abandons many other choices not taken. When you apply this to dollars and the future value a dollar can represent if utilized in alternative ways, the differences in the opportunities not taken can be huge.

To illustrate this idea, let's say you spend $100 and several hours of your time going out for the evening. You could go to a play, attend a sports event, do dinner and a movie. Whatever. (I know there's not a lot you can do for $100 anymore, but humor me.) The time you use comes with an opportunity cost, the lost time that could have been invested in reading a good book or taking a pottery class. You get the idea. There are a multitude of choices for those hours and how you could use them.

Now, what about the money part of the evening? Because time affects the value of money, the $100 is a more complicated subject. You probably wouldn't think about it this way, but the opportunity cost of that $100 bill is different according to your age on the night you spend it.

"How can my age have any bearing on the money I spend?" you ask. "Isn't a dollar a dollar on any given day?"

The answer is definitely NO. Your dollar is worth much more to you the younger you are. To illustrate my point, let's say you don't spend that night out and you take your $100 and put it into a conservative investment that pays you an 8% compounded return. We'll also assume you're going to live to be 80 years old. With that in mind, take a look at the future value of $100 in your hand at different ages in your life.

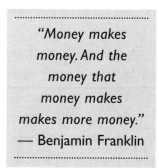

"Money makes money. And the money that money makes makes more money."
— Benjamin Franklin

If you are 80 years old, $100 is pretty much a hundred bucks. But, if you're only 15 years old, that single Ben Franklin[5] is worth over 17 grand! That's right, if you keep that money and let conservative compound interest do its magic, you'll create over $17,500 for your life's wealth.

---

[5] Benjamin Franklin's picture appears on the $100 bill in U.S. currency.

Before You Spend That $100 ...
What Could It Be Worth Later?

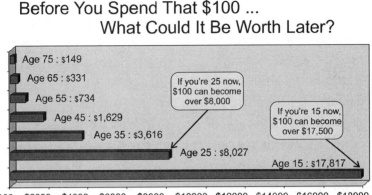

Age 75 : $149
Age 65 : $331
Age 55 : $734
Age 45 : $1,629
Age 35 : $3,616
Age 25 : $8,027
Age 15 : $17,817

If you're 25 now, $100 can become over $8,000

If you're 15 now, $100 can become over $17,500

$100 $2000 $4000 $6000 $8000 $10000 $12000 $14000 $16000 $18000

Future value of $100 earning 8% compounded until age 80.

How's that for a whole new view? If you spend that $100, you forego much more than the $100. You also forfeit the interest that you could have earned on that money for years into the future.

Let's say you don't spend it and you put it away. In your first year, you will have made an extra $8 on top of your $100. In the 2nd year, the return will be earned not only on the principal of $100, but also on the $8 of earnings. So, by the end of the second year, there will be $8 more in interest earned from the principal added to the account, plus 64 cents earned from the previous year's interest of $8. Therefore, at the end of the 2nd year there will be $108 + $8 + $.64 = $116.64 total in the account. This is an example of compounding interest or interest paid on interest already earned.

This process can be repeated and repeated for any number of years into the future. The results are quite astounding. The table above shows the lost opportunities created by that single evening out. Find your age and your own future value

> "Time is the greatest ally when it comes to saving for retirement. A worker who saves $1,000 a year from age 20 through age 30 and then stops, will have more at retirement than someone that starts at age 30 and saves the same amount for 35 years straight."
>
> — Elaine L. Chao,
> U.S. Secretary of Labor

figure for an eye-opening jolt. If you're younger than your life expectancy, $100 is much more than a hundred bucks!

C.O.F.F.E.E.™ — Cost Of Forfeiting Future Equity Earnings

Now let's take the concept of opportunity cost and put it on a bigger stage. Think of it as moving the discussion from a little community theater to the Millennium Dome.[6] Does this illustrate my point? We're talking about a lot more money than $100 here. Your entire life's wealth could be at stake.

Since your home is probably the largest purchase you'll likely make, I want you to think, for a moment, of this gigantic transaction in a different light. Most of us don't realize there are loads of choices to be made when we buy a home. Most of us know the basic decisions. You find your house. You put down as much cash as you can scrape together. You acquire a mortgage at the lowest rate you can negotiate on the smallest mortgage amount possible. You walk through these decisions robotically.

Why? Why do we automatically do this? It's because these steps are ingrained in our minds. Everyone else does it. We're all told to do it this way. Conservative planners advise us,

---

[6] Millennium Dome, built on the prime meridian of the world in Greenwich, England, is the largest dome concert venue structure on earth.

parents guide us, books and magazine articles preach to us and our friends all do exactly the same.

Nobody ever stops to say, "Wait a minute! Maybe there's a better use for the money I'm about to plop onto the table at the title company or attorney's office when I sign the papers and get the keys?"

A Double Mocha Extra Whip Cappuccino

Picture yourself sitting at a large table in the impressive conference room of a real estate closing agent. The walls are lined with shelves filled with law books and brass accents. You've just signed the last paper. All done with the closing on the purchase of your new house, you hand the closer a crisp bank certified check for the down payment. The finished documents are stacked in a neat pile and, as you reach for the keys to your new front door, your elbow brushes by the white paper cup sporting the recognizable and familiar green logo. At that moment, you realize there is nothing you can do. The entire contents of the double mocha extra whip cappuccino is about to drench every piece of paper on the table. You cry out, "No!" But it is too late. "Coffee" is all over the documents. "Coffee" permeates the entire transaction. Oh, what a waste!

It truly is a waste. Every dollar you paid down on that house represented an opportunity not taken. Every dollar departed your hand with a cost ... an opportunity lost. Probably the largest opportunity cost you'll face in your life. I call it C.O.F.F.E.E.™ which is the *cost of forfeiting future equity earnings*.

In fact, each of the following represents practices many of us make regarding the equity in our home without considering the possible opportunity costs we're giving up.

Where are your equity dollars hiding, forfeiting their earning opportunities?

- Excessive down payments
- Principal component of amortized payments
- Extra principal payments
- Bi-weekly mortgage payments
- Untapped equity from real estate appreciation

To better understand what is actually at stake here, take a look at the illustration of what a down payment of $100,000 could have represented over the thirty-year life of a mortgage if it had been relocated into a conservative side account earning an 8% compounding return. When it is put into your equity, it automatically begins receiving a zero rate of return inside the walls of a house.

Forfeited Future Loss on $100,000 Idle Equity	
Years to Compound	At 8% Money Grows To
5	$146,933
10	$215,893
15	$317,218
20	$466,097
25	$684,849
30	$1,006,267

This is only a simplistic illustration of the power of time, compound interest and larger dollar amounts. Many other components of C.O.F.F.E.E.™ also come into play. What about the opportunity cost of the dollars you refuse when you slash your tax deductions by taking a smaller mortgage?

Your first reflex answer to this would be "But a lower mortgage balance costs me less. I'm saving interest."

Are you really saving anything? Aren't you forfeiting the opportunity to deduct more interest that year? What about the future earnings on the cash from that tax refund check you just tore into little pieces? Those dollars you refuse represent great mounds of potential wealth for your future, greater security for your family and increased choices in your golden years. Opportunities lost. Earnings forfeited. But can they be retrieved? Is there a way to regain those opportunities?

C.O.F.F.E.E.™ Recovered Could Be
Worth More Than A Million Dollars!

"How can that be?" you question, "If I don't pay that cash down, I'll have to get a bigger mortgage. Won't that expense wipe out any earnings I'll gain from investing my cash instead?"

Most people mistakenly believe that. You are being deceived if you are told that borrowing and investing are going to be equal on a balance sheet. The story of Tom Today and Harry Historic in the last chapter illustrated how handling the same home purchase situation in two different manners can have real impact on your life's wealth.

Idle Equity Liberated and Invested at 8%

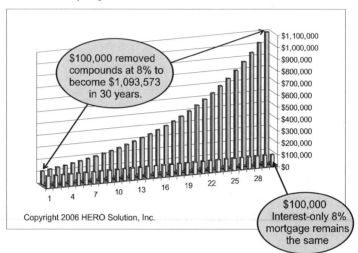

$100,000 removed compounds at 8% to become $1,093,573 in 30 years.

$100,000 Interest-only 8% mortgage remains the same

Copyright 2006 HERO Solution, Inc.

Borrowing money at simple interest and locking in the amount owed at today's value can never balance with investing your highly valued present dollars to receive compounding returns for up to 30 years into the future. Even if the interest rate paid and the interest rate received are equal, you're going to come out better. The invested side of your balance sheet pulls ahead and leaves the debt side in the dust. Time, and how it can transform money through compound interest, makes all the difference. Any financial balance sheet that equates those two transactions has a problem with its math.

"What about the additional mortgage payment I have to make to get this $100,000 mortgage?" you are probably thinking. "What if I obediently invested that same amount every month instead?"

Investing Those Same Monthly Dollars
Just Doesn't Create The Magic

By comparison, your results would be dismal with the savings-only method. But let's be honest. Would you even have the discipline to keep investing that monthly payment for 30 years? Assuming you followed through, you'd need to put away $467 per month (if you were in a combined 30% tax bracket.) This would be the after-tax cost of your mortgage payment at 8%. Your investment account would grow to $666,568 in thirty years. Had you gone the first route, borrowed the $100,000 and put it immediately to work, your wealth would have grown to $1,093,573. That's **64% more!**

Equity Liberated vs Saving Monthly
Both Compounding at 8%

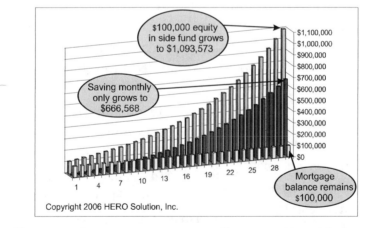

Copyright 2006 HERO Solution, Inc.

If you subtract your outstanding mortgage balance of $100,000, you'd be left with nearly $327,000 extra cash! Look at this illustration graphically. The difference is pretty dramatic.

Let's Cross The Street To The Other C.O.F.F.E.E.™ Shop

Now let's look at C.O.F.F.E.E.™, or *cost of forfeiting future equity earnings*, from a completely different point of view. Let's say that a few years back you sold your house and took all your profits and put them down on your current home. For sake of our illustration, we'll assume you netted $75,000 from selling back then and you bought your current house for $300,000. You put down the entire amount and got a mortgage for $225,000.

Fast-forward 10 years and you now wish to sell your house and move again. Your appreciation rate has been about 5% annually (which is the national average), so you are expecting to sell for about $485,000. You sit down with your calculator, subtract your $225,000 interest-only mortgage and figure you'll have a profit of about $230,000 from the sale (after your Realtor commissions and closing expenses.) Then, after taking back your $75,000 invested, you come out with a $155,000 net profit. "Wow," you say, "Not too shabby a profit for just ten years!"

> *With every dollar of cash used as a down payment, you forfeit your future earnings on that money.*

But, you're forgetting something — when you put down $75,000 of your own cash as a down payment, you forfeited ALL your future earnings on that money. Had you invested that cash and received a conservative 8% return, it would have grown to $166,475. This was an opportunity cost you didn't consider. With this fact in mind, go back and recalculate how much you actually made.

This next illustration shows the bottom line you thought you were making and then subtracts the lost earnings not made.

Do you now see the lost dollars that C.O.F.F.E.E.™, or *cost of forfeiting future equity earnings,* represents? The impact of this concept on the huge amounts of equity most Americans have sitting idly in their homes propels this to crisis proportions.

C.O.F.F.E.E. Effect On Profits From Selling a $485,000 House

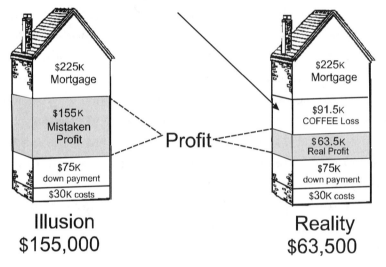

Illusion	Reality
$155,000	**$63,500**

$75,000 down payment on $300,000 house became useless equity which could have earned $91,500 more, if invested at 8% for 10 years. These were forfeited earnings.

C.O.F.F.E.E.™ = *Cost of Forfeiting Future Equity Earnings*

Had that $75,000 been invested and working, your total profit would have truly been $155,000. Since you lost $91,500 over those 10 years, your true net profit was slashed down to only $63,500. That's 60% less!

Handling your home and managing your equity the traditional way can cost you a fortune. Buying your home with a large down payment could truly be the most costly mistake of your life.

OK, I See The Error of Big Down Payments, But The Traditional Wisdom Of Getting An Old Fashioned 15-Year Amortizing Mortgage Is A Good Thing. Right?

C.O.F.F.E.E.™ losses and tax deductions are sacrificed every time you make a payment if you have a standard amortized mortgage. Over time this loss increases making your shortfall more and more. With a 15-year mortgage, your losses occur faster than with the better choice, a 30-year mortgage. The best strategy is to eliminate principal reduction altogether and choose an interest-only mortgage.

If you make additional payments to principal, you lose more earning potential and tax refunds. If you make a large down payment when you buy a house, you have immediately abandoned future earnings and cut your tax refund for that year and every one thereafter.

Now, consider this. What is the biggest down payment you can make? That's right. Paying cash for your house. When you do this, you give up huge amounts of future income, lost to forfeited future earnings and abandoned potential tax refunds. Once a tax year passes without earning on an investment or maximizing your potential for tax deductions, it's gone forever. We can't turn back the clock.

Want to see how the wealthy make time their partner? What do they see that 99% of us don't? Their secrets to massive wealth creation are simpler than you may think. Let's take a peek …

CHAPTER THREE

DO YOU SEE WITH REAL WEALTH VISION™ OR THROUGH THE "GLASSES OF THE MASSES"?

Why do some people seem to get rich very easily, while so many struggle their entire life and never achieve financial success? Does it seem the charmed elite live a relaxed and abundant retirement, while others are scrimping and surviving below the poverty line in their golden years? What special ability or vision do those few possess that is lacking in most everyone else?

The insightful people who possess Real Wealth Vision™ carry themselves with confidence. They have an extra twinkle in their eye. It's like they've come upon a secret that most others haven't and it's changed their lives. They look at the same markets, mortgages, income and financial world seen by everyone else, but they're able to see what others can't. The visionary methods they've discovered and now employ in the handling of their wealth propel them far ahead of others who still see the world through the "Glasses of the Masses." These shrewd folks are highly future oriented and know the value of a dollar as it passes through their hands today. They have a plan and their long-term success is locked-in.

So, How Do You Acquire Real Wealth Vision™?

Perhaps you get it from wealthy parents or friends. Maybe it's accessible from elite advisors who are also financially successful. You could use your own shrewd intelligence and apply some intense personal investigation. Whatever the mode of discovery, you need a way to come upon the secret to creating real personal wealth.

> *"The real voyage of discovery consists not in seeking new landscapes but in having new eyes."*
> — Marcel Proust, French novelist and author, 1871–1922

Sadly, simple fear and ignorance seems to be the motivation for most people … those who see through the "Glasses of the Masses." Traditional advisors believe they have your best interest at heart, but they remain ignorant to the best wealth strategies. They continue to give advice based on fear that you'll lose your house. You know, the old Depression-era thinking. Most advisors today will tell you to save your money monthly, pay down your mortgage and just keep plodding along until you either retire with whatever you may have accumulated or you die. Whichever comes first.

These advisors are looking at your finances through the "Glasses of the Masses." What about all that equity you are bricking up inside your walls? What about the fact that your largest asset is getting a zero return? They're simply ignoring your biggest source of potential wealth like it isn't even there!

Do You Wear The "Glasses of the Masses"?

Are you in need of a visit to the wealth optometrist? Are you also seeing your finances through Coke-bottle thick "Glasses of the Masses"? Maybe you just like the old way of doing things. Do you think your comfort zone is more important than your family's security or your personal well-being into your golden years? Could you be today oriented instead of future oriented? Fear of loss may grip you because of the recent stock market devastation and you mistrust anything but zero debt and a few dollars in the bank.

"Coke-bottle glasses" — *a pair of glasses, with lenses as thick as the bottom of a soft drink bottle.*

What about your friends and family? Do they see the same way? Maybe they doubt anything that might be different than the norm. Well, the "norm" by definition will give you mediocrity in your results. Isn't normal just kind of average, anyway? It's closed-minded thinking and lack of innovation that will keep all the lemmings following the guys in front of them right over the cliff.

LEMMINGS WITH THEIR ADVISORS

Copyright 2006 HERO Solution, Inc.

Does Your Advisor Wear The "Glasses of the Masses"?

Tell me ... how can an everyday, hang-out-your-shingle, nine-to-five, possibly struggling, or even mature and seasoned financial advisor know the inside secrets of the wealthy? Unless your CPA, attorney, financial planner or insurance agent is independently wealthy in their own right, how could they be familiar with what the rich really do to be so successful with their money? 98% of the time, your financial professional will advise you to do what they were taught by their college professors, sales trainers, textbooks and company manuals or their parents. They will pass on the same old traditional wisdom that trickled down from their own mentors ... never anything new.

How many independently wealthy people do you personally know who would give you financial advice? Probably not too many. Since about 1% of the population is considered wealthy, then it would follow that about 1% of financial advisors would be wealthy. Lets give them a benefit of the doubt, since they do live in the world of money, and say they exist at double the national average. Then 2% of them are financially independent. What is the chance that your advisor is not one of the other 98% out there? It's pretty slim.

PARABLE OF THE BLIND MEN AND THE ELEPHANT

Once upon a time there was a certain raja who called to his servant and said, "Come, good fellow, go and gather together in one place all the men who were born blind ... and show them an elephant." "Very good, sir," replied the servant, and he did as he was told. He said to the blind men assembled there, "Here is an elephant," and to one man he presented the head of the elephant, to another its ears, to another a tusk, to another the trunk, the foot, side, tail and tuft of the tail, saying to each one that that was the elephant.

When the blind men had felt the elephant, the raja went to each of them and said, "Well, blind man, have you seen the elephant? Tell me, what sort of thing is an elephant?"

Thereupon the men who were presented with the head answered, "Sir, an elephant is like a pot." And the men who had observed the side replied, "An elephant is like a wall." Those who had been presented with a tusk said it was a ploughshare. Those who knew only the trunk said it was a snake; others said the foot was a pillar; the ear, a fan; the tail, a rope; the tuft of the tail, a brush.

Their curiosity satisfied the six blind men began disputing loud and long. Each now had his own opinion, firmly based on his own experience, of what an elephant is really like. For after all, each had felt the elephant for himself and knew that he was right!

And so indeed he was. For depending on how the elephant is seen, each blind man was partly right, though all were in the wrong.

For, quarreling, each to his view they cling.
Such folk see only one side of a thing.

A well-known Indian tale from the Buddhist canon

Mainstream financial planners, CPAs and insurance agents acquired their training through standardized CFP classes required for their professional designation, traditional textbooks at college, professor's guidance and their personal upbringing.

Most financial advisors are like the blind men describing the elephant in the age-old story most of us heard when we were children. One man thought an elephant was like a snake, one like a wall and one like a brush. Each advisor sees your finances from their own professional perspective, their own point of view and their own experience. The broad picture of your wealth involves asset management, risk management and debt management. Very few individual planners are able to step back enough to see your entire big picture.

Of course, a financial planner or a CFP[7] does not give you tax or legal advice. They have been trained in selling and explaining securities, stocks, bonds, mutual funds and fixed investments.

> I remember having a college professor clarify the distinction between accounting and finance majors ... accountancy deals with the past of money, while finance deals with the future of money.

They know about asset allocation, but only as it applies to your cash accounts. Most chant the mantra to save monthly, max out your retirement account, pay down your mortgage and eliminate debt. They're also unknowledgeable about debt management or the mortgage industry in general.

Tax advisors and CPAs aren't trained to give you financial or legal advice. Their specialty is minimizing your taxes, preparing your federal and state returns, handling your books and accounting. Most do not feel comfortable with investment advice, nor are they particularly well versed in handling mortgages or your debt management. Attorneys

---

[7] Certified Financial Planner is a designation given to financial planning professionals who have completed the coursework and passed required examinations. CFPs are also subject to continuing education to maintain their designation.

don't give you financial or tax advice, unless they are tax attorneys. Your average attorney specializes in compliance with the law, protecting you from legal liability, securing your legal ownership of assets and protecting your wealth from attachment or confiscation through lawsuits. They are not investment advisors and seldom know much at all about debt management or mortgages.

Finally, insurance agents are trained in risk management and liability protection and are not, usually, trained to provide financial or tax advice. You may find a financial planner with CFP designations, securities licenses and an insurance license. This individual would be able to provide you with two points of view regarding insurance and investing. But just because your planner is versed in insurance does not necessarily mean they understand how these Real Wealth Vision™ strategies work. I would venture to guess that less than 10% of life insurance agents have the ability to explain these concepts. Also, they wouldn't understand how to put these complex strategies together for you. This is mainly because few understand debt management, mortgages or tax reduction strategies.

You Need An Enlightened Financial Planner With Real Wealth Vision™

A financial planner or advisor with Real Wealth Vision™ sees how a mortgage has a proper role in the broader context of appropriate financial planning. They understand you will need a strategic plan that incorporates both debt management and asset management. In order to maximize the growth of your assets, it is imperative for you to have safe vehicles that provide tax-advantaged growth.

The professional who possesses Real Wealth Vision™ does the research, understands the importance of the plan as a whole and suggests innovative mortgage strategies to complement and nurture your wealth.

To keep you on track in all aspects of building real wealth, it takes a Real Wealth Vision™ team of professionals who understand how all the components of a strategic plan work in synergy. While a professional mortgage planner is not an investment advisor, he or she does see more aspects of a person's finances as a whole picture. This is why my position as a mortgage underwriter allowed me to see beyond what other financial professionals see and put the pieces of this puzzle together to discover these insider wealth secrets.

> *"The greatest discoveries have come from people who have looked at a standard situation and seen it differently."*
> — Ira Erwin

If your mortgage planner is experienced, knows the mortgage business and the innovative products that work best with this plan, he or she becomes an extremely important part of your wealth-building team. A mortgage planner can also refer you to a skilled investment advisor who understands these concepts.

Innovative Thinkers Are Difficult To Find

This is especially true in the conservative fields of financial planning, accountancy, insurance and mortgage lending. You must seek out only those advisors who have acquired Real Wealth Vision™ and will assist you in formulating your strategic plan.

While your Real Wealth Vision™ plan can be successful once it is put into place, it never hurts to check in on it periodically. Your advisors are important to keep you on track when you have changes in your life. To truly become rich and secure for the rest of your life using this plan, all your advisors should have discarded their old "Glasses of the Masses."

North Pole or Bust!

GOING MY WAY?

You can eventually get north by going due south, but it's just a lot easier and less stressful if you actually head in the direction leading to where you want to go.

Following "Glasses of the Masses" advice is about the same as trudging south to get to the North Pole. Chances are — you'll get lost in the Amazon jungle, wear out your shoes or see the inside of a giant alligator before you see any snow.

CHAPTER FOUR

DEPRESSION-ERA THINKING IN THE 21ST CENTURY

Are We Haunted By "The Ghost of Mortgages Past"

It was only a little over 80 years ago, in the 1920s, that residential mortgage lending by banks even began to be popular. Prior to that time, most house lending was from private sources and was mainly done on the underlying farmland.

Early residential mortgage lending was primitive. You had to save your dollars and put down 50% of your purchase price. Interest payments were made twice a year and the entire balance was usually due in three to five years. Mortgages with those specific repayment terms don't exist today, but if they did, we would describe them as an interest-only 3-year or 5-year balloon.

Since borrowers didn't usually have the money to pay off the loan in that short time period, most mortgages were refinanced when they came due. The usual terms upon purchase were to pay between 1% and 3% of the loan amount to the bank. Thereafter, every time a refinance was done, the homeowner paid another 1% for the transaction.

When a borrower entered into these property lien arrangements, they were given none of the modern consumer protections that come with mortgages today. A bank or lender could call the home loan due at any time for whatever reason. Shortly after residential lending by banks had begun, just at the end of the decade, the stock market crash occurred.

Enter The Depression

You know the story. Depositors were demanding their money from banks on a grand scale. The institutions, in need of quick cash, began to call mortgages "due in full" immediately. As you can imagine, most homeowners didn't have the cash and subsequently lost their homes to foreclosure. Banks everywhere were putting newly acquired properties up for sale to raise cash. By 1935, banks owned over 20% of all the real estate in the country that had been mortgaged.

Since money had been lost in the market, businesses failed, millions of jobs were lost and there were just no buyers for these properties. People who had mortgages lost their homes. Those who had paid cash for their house weren't on the street, but they still didn't have a job or any income.

So, what was the lesson learned and pounded into the heads of all Americans young and old? *"Mortgages are bad." "Pay off your loan as soon as you can." "Always own your home free and clear."* This is why, even today, you hear these old words of wisdom.

Now, Fast Forward To The 21st Century

In the 30 years that followed that troubled time, several evolutions occurred in the residential lending industry that drastically improved things for the consumer.

In response to the housing crisis experienced by millions, the Federal Housing Administration (FHA) and the Federal National Mortgage Association (FNMA or Fannie Mae) were created in the mid-1930s. FHA created the concepts of mortgage insurance and amortized loans. Government-backed creation of more liquid sources for mortgage financing money was the job of Fannie Mae.

Ten years later, the Veterans Administration began insuring mortgages for the soldiers returning from World War II. Then, in 1965, the U.S. Department of Housing and Urban Development (HUD) was born to oversee all real estate and mortgage lending.

So with the institutional and structural supports that evolved in residential finance, the prior risky environment that surrounded mortgages no longer exists.

Today, things are quite different:

- Banks are no longer able to "call" your mortgage at their discretion.
- The risk of a sudden demand for accelerated payments has been eliminated.
- The borrower has the power to keep, pay down or payoff any amount borrowed.
- Consumer protections are in place as long as monthly payments are made.

How Can So Many Modern People
Still Have Such Archaic Points Of View?

Isn't it funny to see? The old wisdom is pervasive. Most people have heard the same old mantra from history their entire lives. It comes from every nook and cranny, from parents, grandparents, professors, advisors and just about every personal finance book out there. All these people want to give you good advice. Most of them are really concerned about your well-being and are telling you what they believe to be true. In their own way, they want you to be safe. It's just that they've all got it wrong!

"It was from simple 'Depression-era thinking,' that I inherited my father's mindset about mortgages. He had owned a grocery store and a house back in the 1920s. During the depression, he lost both his home and his business because the mortgages were called. He sold cans of food left from his store inventory on the street corner for his family to survive through the hard times. He did eventually get a job and later re-entered the grocery business, but that experience echoed in the advice he gave the entire family over the years.

So what did I do? I paid cash for my most recent house when I bought it in 1982. ***That was the biggest mistake I ever made!***

I need money now and I'm going to have to go through the lengthy, difficult and costly reverse mortgage process to get to my own money!"

— Doris Fox, age 74

The fear of history repeating itself permeates the thinking of most old wisdom. Just about everyone out there is a simple "broken record" of what they've heard in their lifetimes. Most sources of supposed conventional and traditional advice are simply parrots hawking memorized sounds. Very few have any helpful ideas based on a panoramic view of what the real financial big picture might be in today's modern environment.

Since our financial world is so different now, why do you suppose many people still think mortgages should be paid off?

As I said earlier, it's like a child's **fear of the dark.** They're still afraid of something that really isn't even there.

Your grandpa always said, "The best mortgage is no mortgage!"

Copyright 2006
HERO Solution, Inc.

Remember, we are in a different world. A world based on protections for the consumer. Banks can't call loans anymore and the mortgage market is extremely competitive and liquid.

Mortgage money is readily available and the secondary market for mortgage cash is traded worldwide. Events from the 1930s simply won't happen in today's world.

Why Are Modern Financial Advisors Still Afraid You'll Lose Your Home?

I would venture a guess that many advisors are not even aware of changes in our economy compared to the markets back then. The training most professional advisors receive may include some history, but very few financial planners have much insight into modern mortgage markets, governmental protections or the system for originating and servicing home loans. Most cannot see a big picture for you due to the compartmentalizing[8] done in their specialties.

Most financial advisors probably truly believe you are safer with a paid-off house. They are completely unaware of the dangers you face and the wealth you are losing by handling your finances as they advise. No one has ever pointed it out to them.

Maybe They Think Your Mortgage Is Costing You Money

Another misunderstanding. As you will see in later chapters of this book, not having a mortgage actually costs you much more than having one. Additionally, because of the

---

[8] To *compartmentalize* is to see a matter, address it individually and move on the next one, not realizing how different issues may work together or affect other components.

unique benefits the IRS provides for home lending, you will see that having a mortgage will actually make you wealthy over time.

You have a much larger chance of losing your job or becoming disabled than of losing your house. If you have a paid-off mortgage when that happens, where will you get the cash to support you through tough times? You certainly can't get another mortgage without an income.

Truthfully, your safety position is exponentially increased if you keep your cash in a safe side fund and stop paying off your mortgage. You'll see proof in later chapters.

If Traditional Wisdom Is So Fiscally Sound, Then Why Do The Wealthy Carry Big Mortgages?

So your financial advisor and all those around you are telling you that paying off your mortgage is the smartest thing to do. Right? If it's so smart, then why do those with piles of ready cash to pay off their houses carry big mortgages? If it's such fiscally sound advice, then why do the financially successful not follow it?

Those with Real Wealth Vision™ want 1) ready access to their funds, 2) to lock-in security of those assets and 3) to get assets working elsewhere. These three tenants of Real Wealth L.A.W.™ will be covered in Chapter Seven.

The wealthy are all grown up. They know there's no monster under the bed and nothing to fear. They understand the importance of maintaining control of their own cash and their own wealth outcome. Awareness of consumer protections makes them extremely confident in their safety when borrowing against their personal and secondary residences. The

Washington watchdogs[9] are on their side. The competitive and liquid mortgage market will always make their home loan borrowing the cheapest money available anywhere.

The Old Risks Have Simply Been Removed For Today's Homeowner

Tell all those around you. Tell your friends, your relatives and your advisors. "There's nothing in the dark to be afraid of!" Give them a flashlight or, better yet, give them this book!

Today, we have RESPA[10] laws that protect the consumer from unscrupulous lenders and prosecute those who take advantage of borrowers. We have HUD[11] to oversee protections for the homeowner. The government-backed agencies like FHA[12] and VA[13] streamline and standardize lending for first-time buyers, veterans and those who need assistance in buying their homes.

The GSEs,[14] like Freddie Mac[15] and Fannie Mae,[16] have reduced the cost of borrowing by standardizing mortgage lending and creating liquidity in the secondary mortgage market. These entities are now 45% larger than the nation's biggest bank.

---

[9] By this, I mean Congress, HUD, FHA, VA and RESPA regulations, etc.
[10] Real Estate Settlement Procedures Act
[11] U.S. Department of Housing and Urban Development
[12] Federal Housing Administration
[13] Veteran's Administration
[14] Government Sponsored Entities
[15] The Federal Home Loan Mortgage Corporation (Freddie Mac) is a stockholder-owned corporation chartered by Congress.
[16] Federal National Mortgage Association

The Agencies Provide Lower Rates
And Higher Safety In Mortgage Lending

As I said earlier, Fannie Mae came into existence in the 1930s. More recently, Freddie Mac was created by the congress in 1970 to also provide a continuous and low-cost source of credit to finance housing in America.

Freddie Mac and Fannie Mae, the two GSEs, have the same charters, which are mandated by congress, and they operate under the same regulatory system. In 1992 the Federal Housing Enterprises Financial Safety and Soundness Act created a regulatory oversight structure for Freddie Mac and Fannie Mae.

According to the Office of Management and Budget (OMB), "mortgage rates are 25–50 basis points lower because Fannie Mae and Freddie Mac exist in the form and size they do." Because the secondary mortgage market saves homebuyers up to $\frac{1}{2}$% on their mortgage, borrowers nationwide save an average of nearly 23.5 billion dollars annually.

These are the main reasons why mortgages are more affordable today. Additionally, the evolution of zero-point mortgages in the late 1980s made borrowing and refinancing a no-brainer activity. And even more recently, zero-cost loans have come on the market.

Often, a mortgage can be acquired with no cost to the borrower whatsoever. These types of loans offer no points, no fees and no expenses. This doesn't mean the costs are simply financed, it means they are never charged. Of course, the rate on your loan will be slightly higher than a loan with costs charged, but the option allows for cleaner decisions when getting a new mortgage.

Now that adjustable-rate mortgages and interest-only mortgages are available, the cost of borrowing is, again, reduced. I know traditional wisdom says to get a 15-year amortized mortgage, but that is probably the most expensive lending you can get for several reasons. There'll be more about that later on.

Bottom Line? Mortgages Shouldn't Be Feared Or Avoided

The archaic thinking of the past still has a lock grip around the neck of the financial advice community — even 75 years after the depression. Traditional wisdom, when it advises us to eliminate our mortgage, isn't seeing the entire wealth picture. Not having a home loan actually costs a homeowner in many ways.

It may take several generations to overcome this backward thinking. Until then, we must do our own due diligence, be open-minded and evaluate the actual numbers to see the real truth.

In the end, we are responsible for our own destiny and the success of our wealth creation. This book is a step in the right direction.

In the next chapter, you'll see how to take the mortgage payment you already make, tweak your monthly financial picture and arrive at the position to pay off your house years sooner with the plan you are about to see. Often, you can do it using the same payment you're currently making. Just about everyone has a monthly mortgage payment already (and if you don't have one — you should). Why not turn it into a tool for becoming rich and secure for the rest of your life? The steps are ahead …

CHAPTER FIVE

THE H.E.R.O. SOLUTION™

Use Your Home To Turbocharge Your Wealth

The plan I'm about to reveal to you can literally add millions of dollars to your life's fortune. It can systematically explode your riches by maximizing your largest asset and transforming it into a wealth creation tool. You can make this happen by using just the monthly cash flow you already have. I've named this wealth-creating method of debt and asset management the *Home Equity Riches Optimizer,* or H.E.R.O. Solution™,[17] to make it easier to remember. If you are tuned into saving for your retirement, it could also be called the *Home Equity Retirement Optimizer.* Either is an effective description for this revolutionary plan.

> This is the first of the 3 Simple Money Secrets Millionaires use.

While it's most effective for long-term wealth building, like planning

---

[17] H.E.R.O.™ and H.E.R.O. Solution™ are trademarked acronyms for the *Home Equity Riches Optimizer* and the *Home Equity Retirement Optimizer.*

for your retirement income, it also cranks out cash for college expenses and allows you to become your own bank by replacing traditional financing you might have used in the past. You'll no longer need to talk to the finance guy at the auto dealership or to the bank manager when you need to buy a big-ticket item like a boat or vehicle. You can just go home, speak into the mirror and ask the smiling loan officer at your *Bank of Me* to arrange your financing.

One of the most dramatic results you can accomplish with the H.E.R.O. Solution™ is to achieve a financial position where you could pay off your mortgage years ahead of schedule. This system actually taps non-functioning cash, applies the magic of compound interest and creates a leverage situation identical to financial arbitrage,[18] which is the lifeblood of the banking industry.

In just the last few years, there has been a significant shift in the way people with Real Wealth Vision™ manage their assets to create wealth. Much of this shift has involved techniques of cash-flow management on the liability or debt side of their balance sheets producing financial leverage. Most of us don't tend to think we can use our debts to create more assets. Because the natural flow of human thought is to compartmentalize (or think of things in neat little packages and not as a whole), most financial planners never even contemplate utilizing your debts to enhance your wealth. 98% of them will simply tell you to eliminate your debt, not teach you how to transform borrowing into a money-making power tool. They should be advising you on how the two sides of your balance sheet can work together to create magic for your bottom line.

---

[18] The purchase of securities in one market to make gains on the sale in another. Also known as "riskless profit."

Ultra-conservative arbitrage, the system banks use every-day, is created within your own finances by the H.E.R.O. Solution™. So, how does it work? You acquire other people's money at simple interest and invest that cash in a principal-protected and extremely safe vehicle that nurtures it in a tax-favored and compound interest environment.

The results will amaze you. The H.E.R.O. Solution™ puts you in a position to pay off your mortgage years earlier than you could have using traditional methods. And what's more miraculous, the investing rate doesn't even have to be higher than the borrowing rate to achieve success. This means you can reach your goal no matter what mortgage rates are doing.

Pay Off My Mortgage Years Ahead Of Schedule? How?

"So, how can I accomplish this years sooner using just what I'm spending now?" you ask. "It's pretty hard to believe I could get this fabulous outcome without spending any more."

Through the magic of leverage, maximized tax benefits, compound interest and time, huge strides can be made toward accomplishing challenges we thought were impossible. I've seen some mortgage holders reach **payoff status in as little as 8 years!** The more equity you have in your home, the faster you can reach this goal.

If you are currently trying to pay off your mortgage using a 15-year amortized loan, the H.E.R.O. Solution™ can take the same monthly payment you are currently making and allow you to actually have the ability to pay off your mortgage years ahead of schedule. Want to see this in black and white? Take a look at this illustration.

Payoff Years Sooner with H.E.R.O. Solution™

$180,000 Mortgage

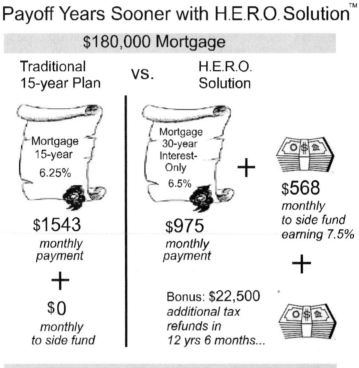

Traditional
15-year Plan **vs.**

H.E.R.O.
Solution

Mortgage
15-year
6.25%

$1543
*monthly
payment*

+

$0
*monthly
to side fund*

Mortgage
30-year
Interest-
Only
6.5%

$975
*monthly
payment*

Bonus: $22,500
*additional tax
refunds in
12 yrs 6 months...*

+

$568
*monthly
to side fund
earning 7.5%*

+

Same $1543 monthly for 12 years 6 months

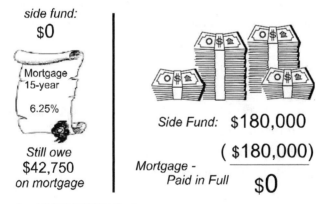

side fund:
$0

Mortgage
15-year

6.25%

Still owe
$42,750
on mortgage

Side Fund: **$180,000**

Mortgage -
Paid in Full

(**$180,000**)

$0

In this illustration, you have a mortgage balance of $180,000 and are paying a standard amortized 15-year monthly payment of $1543. If you employ the H.E.R.O. Solution™, you have the same monthly expenditure but you're able to **pay off your mortgage balance in just twelve and a half (12½) years** without a dime more. **That's 30 months earlier with no extra cash outlay!**

It's truly amazing to reach your goal years ahead of schedule with the same monthly cash you were paying for your 15-year plan. The additional tax refund received over and above the old refund is placed into the account each year to achieve the maximum wealth results.

Anytime after your side fund equals your mortgage balance, you can just wipe out your loan. In other words, take the cash from your right pocket and put it in your left one. **But, why would you want to stop there?**

What if you decided your H.E.R.O. Solution™ method was working so well you wanted to keep it producing cash for you?

You could continue on until your original fifteen years was up and you would have a nice cash account bonus.

After the original 15 years, you'd have a paid off mortgage Plus you are left with a side fund balance of **$59,578.**

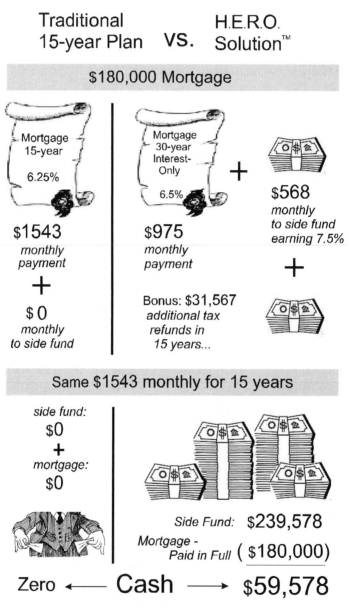

Traditional 15-year Plan **VS.** H.E.R.O. Solution™

$180,000 Mortgage

Mortgage 15-year
6.25%

$1543
monthly payment

+

$0
monthly to side fund

Mortgage 30-year Interest-Only
6.5%

$975
monthly payment

Bonus: $31,567 *additional tax refunds in 15 years...*

+

$568
monthly to side fund earning 7.5%

+

Same $1543 monthly for 15 years

side fund:
$0
+
mortgage:
$0

Side Fund: **$239,578**
Mortgage - Paid in Full **($180,000)**

Zero ⟵ **Cash** ⟶ **$59,578**

But why end the magical cash machine just short of $60,000 at 15 years? Couldn't you keep churning out tax-favored cash and continue to reap tax-deduction income from Uncle Sam? Let's see what would happen ...

Why Stop the H.E.R.O. Solution™ at 15 years?

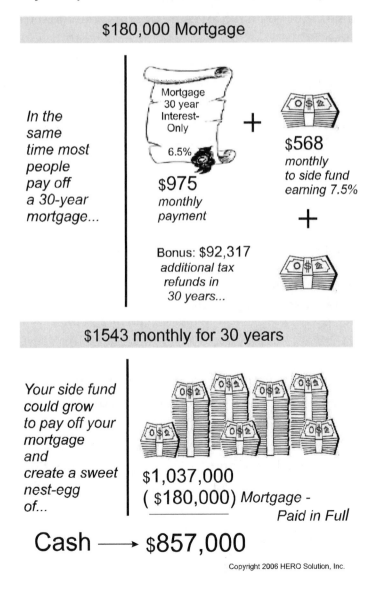

$180,000 Mortgage

In the same time most people pay off a 30-year mortgage...

Mortgage 30 year Interest-Only

6.5%

$975 monthly payment

Bonus: $92,317 additional tax refunds in 30 years...

\+

$568 monthly to side fund earning 7.5%

\+

$1543 monthly for 30 years

Your side fund could grow to pay off your mortgage and create a sweet nest-egg of...

$1,037,000
($180,000) *Mortgage -*
Paid in Full

Cash ⟶ $857,000

Should you decide to continue for another 15 years, you could end up with a huge balance of over a million dollars! Then, if you wanted, you could pay off the mortgage and keep a side fund nest-egg balance of $857,000 to enjoy.

Yes, if you have a larger mortgage, you can increase these figures. You can do it with your primary residence and your second home. If you have investment properties, do the same with them.

If you are currently using a *bi-weekly* payment plan ... stop. The H.E.R.O. Solution™ can take that same monthly cash and accomplish your goal in record speed. I won't use yet another diagram here, but the box below shows how the numbers work out against a 15-year bi-weekly schedule:

15-YR BI-WEEKLY VS.
H.E.R.O. SOLUTION™ WITH S.A.F.E.T.Y. FUND™

Loan Payoff in . . . . .11 years and 6 months
Cash at 15th Year $99,483
Cash at 30th Year $1,015,087
Monthly Income . . . .$6,344 for life without touching
the million-dollar balance

The truth is, if you have a regular amortized mortgage, if you have any equity in your home or if you have both, the H.E.R.O. Solution™ can dramatically improve your wealth. In a later chapter, you'll see how to take the equity you have trapped in your house and turbo-boost your separated side account (S.A.F.E.T.Y.[19] Fund™) to achieve amazing results.

---

[19] S.A.F.E.T.Y. Fund™ and S.A.F.E.T.Y.™ are trademarked acronyms for *Side Account Faithfully Earning Tax-favored Yields.*

But What If You Already Have A 30-year Mortgage? What Can The H.E.R.O. Solution™ Do For You?

Truthfully, the more idle equity you have in your house, the greater your wealth can explode. Let's say you have a $300,000 house with a $140,000 mortgage. That means you have $160,000 of non-producing equity built up inside it.

Let's look at an example where we liberate the equity up to 80% of the house's value. So, we would take out $100,000 and get it working inside your S.A.F.E.T.Y. Fund™. To be conservative, we'll say you borrow at 7.5% and you also earn at 7.5%. Since this scenario is quite cautious, I'm sure you can imagine how your account would grow if you earned an even higher rate.

The following illustration shows how your compounding side account grows while your mortgage balance stays fixed. After 30 years, your original $100,000 and your additional tax savings, compared to your old amortizing loan, compounds to well over a MILLION DOLLARS!

$100,000 HERO Solution
Borrowing at 7.5% and Earning at 7.5%

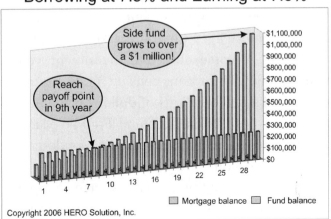

Copyright 2006 HERO Solution, Inc.

$300,000 house with $140,000 30-year mortgage is refinanced at 7.5% to liberate $100,000 in idle equity. The equity is placed into your S.A.F.E.T.Y. Fund™ and grows tax-favored at 7.5% over the life of the loan.

A paid-off house AND income for life!

After 30 years, you pay off your mortgage from your S.A.F.E.T.Y. Fund™ balance. You're left with $860,108. At 7.5%, this account could pay you a spendable $64,508 annually for life without ever touching your million bucks.

What If You Had More Equity To Liberate?
What If You Did It More Than Once?

Now your brain is really working! Larger chunks of equity can explode your riches. Increasing your rate of earnings can super charge your wealth creation. In Chapter Thirteen, *"Want To Recycle Into Multi-Million Dollar Riches? Why Not Take The Stairs?"* you will see illustrations of how you can systematically remove your equity as it grows and get it working for you in your S.A.F.E.T.Y. Fund™. The results shown will absolutely amaze you.

What Makes Mortgage Money The Deal Of The Century?

Mortgage money is the cheapest borrowing you can get today. Because the quasi-government agencies standardize the huge pools of mortgages on the market, mortgage-backed securities (MBS) become attractive investment vehicles for institutional money. This means pension funds, insurance companies and banks make billions of dollars available for mortgages. The agencies, Fannie Mae and Freddie Mac, carry an implied guarantee of safety through their pseudo-government sponsorship connection.

Liquidity created by this massive source of money along with a competitive marketplace make this type of borrowing extremely cheap compared to any other kind of financing you could ever acquire. The home loan market created in our modern mortgage industry provides readily available money that is traded just like stocks and bonds. This highly liquid environment is the reason for such low rates. With cheap money so easy to get, the consumer is the winner. It's sad that so many of us don't recognize this powerful opportunity when it's dropped right in our lap.

Let's say you are in a combined federal and state tax bracket of 33% and your mortgage interest paid in one year is $10,000. That money spent on interest didn't cost you $10,000. When the smoke cleared, you really paid only $6,667 because the IRS sent you a refund for 33% of it. Our government encourages homeownership so the cost of mortgage borrowing can be deducted from your income at tax time. No other personal borrowing you do will give such a marvelous benefit.

> *What is one reason mortgage borrowing leaves all other forms of financing in the dust? It's the great tax advantages offered by good old Uncle Sam.*

Deductibility can be HUGE (or *'uge* as Donald Trump[20] would say) in your quest for wealth. There are even mortgages out there where the entire payment can be deducted. These are called interest-only loans. Combine tax deductibility with low market rates and the availability of mortgage instruments where your entire payment can be deducted from your income ... you end up with a sure bet for the triple-crown[21] in wealth creation.

---

[20] Billionaire businessman and creator of a popular network television series.
[21] A championship title given to a horse that wins the three traditional top races.

Those with Real Wealth Vision™ use all tools available to create and enhance their life's wealth. By becoming their own bank, they can leverage other people's money to turbocharge their own. Just follow the business plan of the entire banking industry. They take depositor's money, which is really borrowing at low simple interest. Then they lend out that money at a slightly higher rate, which is really investing their cash. The profit from the difference in those two activities is called the spread or arbitrage. Many banks operate profitably on as little as one-half a percent spread.

Arbitrage Is Like Oxygen To A Bank

Without this basic strategy, banks would not exist. Profitable arbitrage applied to the large amounts of money controlled in the banking world is what gives life to the entire system. You would think that paying a 4% interest rate and investing that money at 4.5% wouldn't be very exciting. But take 200 million dollars in CD deposits and buy mortgage-backed securities with that money, and you just made the bank a cool million dollars in one year! That's if the spread is only ½%.

Mortgage As A Wealth Tool

• Lowest Cost Borrowing
• Tax Deductible
• Easy to Acquire
• OPM (other people's money)

What if they use a larger pool of borrowed money? What if they invest in an instrument that pays them compounded interest? What if they increased the spread between the borrowing and investing? What if they let time and compounding work its steady magic to snowball their profits?

Do you see why there are so many giant skyscrapers with bank's names on them? It isn't hard to amass fortunes for bank owners and stockholders using this simple finance strategy.

"That's great for big banks," you say, "but let's be real. I don't have that kind of cash lying around."

It's true. Most of us don't have access to hundreds of millions to create our own wealth. Surprisingly, though, we do have access to lots more of other people's money (OPM) than we realize. The wealthy have discovered this secret and have found a way to do the same with their personal finances.

We can tap tens of thousands, perhaps hundreds of thousands, and create our own arbitrage. Using compound interest on the investing side, our wealth can really take off. This magic can make our banking work, even when the borrowing rates and the lending rates are equal. I know it's hard to believe, but money borrowed at a simple interest rate and then invested at the same compounded rate can make you a millionaire over time.

> *"Some advisors say to pay off your mortgage. We say leverage up and invest."*
> — Forbes.com, 2005 Investment Guide, December 13, 2004

Those with Real Wealth Vision™ use heavy-duty equipment to build their fortune. Their number one tool is a mortgage. Why? Mortgage money is readily available and fairly easy to get. The extremely liquid market for home financing also offers highly competitive rates compared to any other lending. There's no better place to get large amounts of attractive cash for your *Bank of Me*. The tax deductibility of the interest paid is simply icing on the cake.

Isn't It Hard To Get A Safe Return
That's Better Than My Cost of Borrowing?

So you think you won't be able to find a secure place to put your borrowed money that'll give you a profitable spread for your personal bank? What if I told you the H.E.R.O. Solution™ works even when the spread is zero? In other words, the arbitrage works when the borrowing rate is the same as the investing rate. Let's go one step farther ... believe it or not, it works even if the borrowing rate is HIGHER than the investing rate.

Oh, so you're skeptical? Well, the numbers prove it and we've all heard that "seeing is believing," right? So lets see how it works.

Over the course of your life, you'll probably experience times with high rates and with low rates. This is because interest-rate markets are cyclical. By now, from your own experience, you may have noticed that when the interest you're receiving is high, the borrowing rates are also high. Conversely, when interest income is low, borrowing rates are low. Since these two sides of the equation mirror each other, the H.E.R.O. Solution™ will work pretty much all the time.

It's always easy to refinance when borrowing gets cheaper. Let's say you set up your H.E.R.O. Solution™ plan and, after a few years, mortgage rates fall. It's quite simple to refinance your balance into a lower rate and, possibly, pull out even more equity. In fact, refinancing and getting your idle cash out every few years is a good strategy, but we'll talk about that in a later chapter.

If the borrowing rates go up and you are locked into your loan rate for a decent amount of time, you'll have the chance of receiving higher yields and experiencing a nice spread on your arbitrage. Either way, because interest-rate markets on the borrowing side and the lending side move in lock step over time, your H.E.R.O. Solution™ plan should continue to work well for you in all environments.

A small difference can be gigantic over time.

Why Now? The New Millennium H.E.R.O Solution™ Trilogy — Three Opportunities Converge

In this third millennium, three things have come together that make the H.E.R.O. Solution™ an idea whose time has come. These evolutions emerged at the end of the last century and, taken individually, were each quite revolutionary in their own arenas. But when combined, a synergy has been created producing real wealth magic. Lets look at each component of the H.E.R.O Solution™ Trilogy, individually:

Opportunity # 1 — New Tax-Free Source of Big Bucks

Do you know how HUGE it is to get tax-free income? Think about it. Just about every dollar you make in your life comes to you with a big chunk of it sliced off for the government's cut. Each paycheck arrives as 60–65% money, because it must be shared with the federal, state and, sometimes, city governments. Wouldn't it be great to get a whole dollar for once? Most of us don't even know we have a readily available source of absolutely tax-free cash right under our noses. If we could get our hands on 100% dollars and put them to work earning compounded yields, just think of the results.

Wouldn't it be great to get a WHOLE dollar for once?

Since the *Taxpayer Relief Act of 1997*, we no longer have to buy a more expensive home to protect our gains from taxes. These strategies went into effect in 1998 and, prior to then, we were limited to a once-in-a-lifetime $125,000 exclusion if we were over age 55. Under the new law when a primary residence is sold for more than it cost you, the gain is not taxed as long as it's less than $500,000 for married taxpayers and $250,000 for a single taxpayer.

This means you can now take all your gains, cash them in and use them completely tax-free within those limits. You won't be able to do this more often than once every two years, because you must have lived in the house for at least that long.

Historically, most people have mistakenly thought they had to put all the cash they earned from the sale of their last house into the next one, every time they moved. This has never been true. If you wanted to avoid paying capital gains taxes, you were required to keep buying houses that were equal in value or more expensive each time, unless you took that one-time move down after you turned age 55.

The truth is, you never had to park your cash into the bigger house each time you moved up. You could have always taken your gains and gotten 100% financing on the new home. This fact is still true. You can actually sell your old house, take the gains, buy a new house every two years and never have to pay a penny down on the new one.

"But, what if I don't want to sell my house?" you ask.

Because loans are never taxed as income, you can pull out those future gains now with a new mortgage any time you want. Get that money working for you — churning out wealth. As long as your house isn't exceeding the $500,000 or $250,000 equity growth and you aren't selling more often than every two years, you are home free. Pardon the pun ...

Opportunity # 2 — A Type Of Mortgage That Puts You In Control Of Your Cash Flow, Lowers Your Payments and Gives You Bigger Tax Deductions

There's a type of loan program that can provide all these magical benefits: control of your cash flow, lower payments and bigger tax deductions. What if this loan could also let you borrow more when you purchase or refinance? What if it could even allow you to buy a more expensive house than you could get with a standard amortized loan?

"Sounds interesting," you say, "So, what kind of loan can do this?"

Collectively, these are referred to as "interest-only" mortgages[22]. (Yes, the type I keep referring to in all my examples.) They offer the ability to pay only the interest in the beginning years, which means you have lower monthly payments. Because the payments are lower, you often qualify

---

[22] Do not confuse "interest-only" mortgages with "Option ARM" mortgages. The interest-only mortgages recommended here have rates fixed for definite periods of time and don't allow negative amortization. Option ARMs are advanced-strategy adjustable-rate products for sophisticated borrowers. The additional risks inherent in Option ARMs, which allow negative amortization, can increase cash flow, but should be carefully evaluated with competent assistance.

for a larger mortgage amount. These programs began to emerge in the 1990s as a variation of regular amortized adjustable-rate loans. You could get them with your interest fixed for periods that ranged from 6 months to 10 years.

In the beginning, these mortgages were portfolio loans that banks created and serviced for themselves. As time has passed, more people have come to realize the benefits of these loans, so they've become readily available. The agencies, Fannie Mae and Freddie Mac, now offer them in many variations for loans within their loan size limits.[23] With agency money behind them, they are now highly competitive and broadly accepted.

> Fannie Mae's website says interest-only loans offer:
> *"… many years of lower monthly payments and the ability to use your money for other expenses or investments."*

Now, these pure-genius loans are available in 30-year fixed versions offered by Fannie Mae and Freddie Mac. With an InterestFirst[SM] loan, which is the name given to Fannie Mae's program, you can pay interest-only for the first 15 years!

Some portfolio lenders now offer 30-year fixed-rate loans that are interest-only over the entire 360 months. This is colossal benefit for anyone who wants to maintain control of cash flow.

---

[23] The conforming loan limit is the maximum loan size accepted by Fannie Mae and Freddie Mac. It usually increases each year and is currently $417,000 for a single-unit residence (50% higher in Alaska and Hawaii). It's hard to believe it was only $153,100 when I first started in the lending industry in 1988. Loans above this amount would be categorized as jumbo loans.

Interest-only loans also provide the borrower with a lower monthly payment. Since there is no part of your payment going into your equity, this frees up this monthly cash to put into other investments or utilize in some other wealth-building vehicle.

Of course, we all want more tax deductions. Right? With these loans, your deduction is the entire payment. You can't get much better than that. Traditional amortized loans begin with a larger part going to interest and, over time, gradually transition, reducing your interest as your loan balance goes down.

"So, if my interest charges are going down each month," you're thinking, "then, wouldn't that be a good thing?"

Wrong! Your interest paid gives you tax deductions. If your mortgage payment is the same every month but

> *Your annual tax benefit is steadily dribbling away — slipping right through your fingers like grains of sand.*

your interest charges are going down, what does that do to your bottom line each year? As time goes by, you are dumping more and more money each month into your idle equity. At the same time, you are cutting your annual tax benefit.

What can you do to stop this madness? Get an interest-only mortgage and take back control over where your monthly cash is directed.

Opportunity # 3 — A Vehicle That Locks-In Stock Market Gains In Good Years And Avoids Losses In Bad Years

"Wait a minute ... this sounds like a fantasy!" you're thinking. "How can any vehicle give me the gains of the market when it's up and never let me lose when it's down?"

This third component boosts the success of our H.E.R.O. Solution™. Those with Real Wealth Vision™ have discovered the secret and, now, I'm letting you in on it. Not only does this vehicle lock-in stock market gains and avoid losses but it allows your cash to accumulate these gains in a tax-deferred environment.

That's right, you get:

- Tax-favored growth
- No loss of principal
- Participation in stock market gains

In Chapter Seven, we'll discuss many of the specifics about these wonderful discoveries made by those with Real Wealth Vision™, discoveries that nurture and explode your life's wealth.

H.E.R.O. Solution™ Trilogy
Converges To Create Real Wealth

The 21st Century is the right time for our H.E.R.O. Solution™. The synergy created by these **three significant components** can now dramatically multiply your wealth:

1. Huge source of tax-free money now available
2. New lending that accesses more equity, lowers your payment and increases your tax deduction
3. Wealth can receive stock market gains, downside protection and tax-favored growth

By now, I hope you are beginning to see that getting the biggest mortgage you can possibly handle and applying the H.E.R.O. Solution™ can make you wealthy. The cash you extract from your equity provides a large, tax-free source of initial cash you can put to work. This huge asset produces a much greater yield than you could get by simply saving monthly.

In response to a ubiquitous personal finance guru's advice to become mortgage-free as soon as possible:

"If you struggle to pay your bills, [her] advice is sound. But if you are in a high tax bracket and your main concern is investing for the future, ignore her. So long as you have the self-discipline to invest the extra money you borrow rather than fritter it away, you're likely to come out ahead by carrying a big mortgage."
— Forbes.com, The 2005 investment Guide

Maximizing tax deductions using an interest-only mortgage gives you more cash for reducing your cost of borrowing or for reinvesting to receive more compound asset growth. Of course, the H.E.R.O. Solution™ works with standard 30-year fixed loans, too, but interest-only loans really boost your results. These loans allow you to control your cash flow, exploit the tax code and clear the way for your assets to feel the power of pure growth.

By seeking out tax-favored vehicles for your extracted cash, you'll avoid the erosion that happens when you invest in standard-taxed accounts. Frankly, you'll see an exponential difference in your account balance if it is allowed to grow tax-favored.

Repositioning your current assets and cash flow by properly using the H.E.R.O. Solution™ can actually increase your monthly retirement cash-to-spend by up to 50%! You'll see, in Chapter Twelve, how the combination of tax-favored initial cash, tax-favored growth and, ultimately, tax-favored access to monthly income produces spectacular results for your future.

Why Is The H.E.R.O. Solution™ Not For Everyone?

You must be disciplined not to tap into your accumulated cash. It is imperative for you to understand that the money extracted from your equity is considered critical cash and simply cannot be consumed.

In other words, removing your equity and using for any purpose other than strategic asset growth would be disastrous for your financial health. You must nurture this asset and place it where the principal is always protected.

Spending this critical cash on depreciating assets or everyday consumption would destroy the success of your conservative plan for becoming rich and secure for the rest of your life.

Once you have decided to implement the H.E.R.O. Solution™ to exponentially grow your wealth, you must commit to stick with the strategy over time. Of course, life happens, so you'll need to make adjustments as your financial situation evolves through the years.

You should rethink your plan when you move, get a new job, add family members or have any financially impacting event. While it's a fairly autopilot system, you'll need to check the flight plan periodically.

Now, what can you do with your harvested equity to protect it and explode its growth? In the next chapter, we'll talk about creating a safe and nurturing environment for your critical cash. The wealthy have discovered some amazing secrets that allow you to easily become a millionaire and they are so much easier than you could imagine. Want to know more? First, glance at this quick short story about two farmers, and then read on …

Tale Of Two Farmers

Many years ago, there were two farmers who lived just down the road from each other. Early in his life, Farmer White had married and left the home of his father, who had given him a milk cow along with these words of wisdom:

"Son, nice glass bottles are hard to come by. If you save up every bottle you find over the years, you will be able to fill them with milk from this cow and sell them to your neighbors. As the milk is used up, the neighbors will return the bottles to be filled. Then you will be able to replenish and sell them again to your neighbors. Over time, as you collect more bottles and keep filling them, you will never have to worry about feeding your family."

Farmer Hunter, the neighbor, had also received advice from his father. The words of wisdom he received as he left home to set out into the world were:

"Son, nice glass bottles shine and reflect. You can see them from a great distance. You can make them a tool if you put them to good use. As you come across bottles in your life, you

should gather up every one and utilize them to increase your family's security. You can use these bottles to sharpen your marksmanship skills. Each bottle you get should be lined up on a fence. Then practice and hone your sharp-shooting abilities by shooting the bottles as targets. As the years go by, move farther and farther away from the targets and keep improving your skills. Your ability to develop a true aim will become better and better with each bottle you shoot. After you have used the bottles, gather up the broken pieces of glass and place the pieces into mosaics on your walls inside your house. Over time, as your walls become covered with lovely glass patterns, you'll constantly be surrounded by reminders that you have worked hard and become a fine marksman. If you follow this wisdom, you will never have to worry about your family's safety or your ability to feed them."

As time went by, both the farmers followed the advice they had been given. They each came across many bottles over the years and they put them all to use, just as instructed.

Farmer Hunter became the best shot in the county. He won many marksman contests and always seemed to have enough meat to feed his own family and sell to others.

One year, a strange illness swept through the county. As a result, both the farmers became ill and, ultimately, lost their vision. Farmer White had accumulated enough money over the years to purchase more milk cows and more bottles. After he could no longer see, he was still able to feel his way to the barn, find his cows and continue to keep his bottles working. Thanks to his wise planning, his family would have safety and food for many years, even after he was gone.

On the other hand, Farmer Hunter could no longer see to hunt game or admire his mosaics. All his bottles had been rendered useless, buried in the walls of his house. He was left with no way to retrieve the bottles for any other uses and no way to feed his family. Farmer Hunter eventually became penniless and lost his farm.

So, What's The Moral of The Story?

Most Americans are following the traditional wisdom that is very much like Farmer Hunter's advice.

Traditional financial advice tells us to take every extra dollar (bottle) and to bury it in the walls of our house by eliminating our mortgage. We are told to increase our safety position by paying into our equity. It's somewhat like being told to put all our eggs (our dollars … our bottles) into one basket (our house).

What's the result of following this traditional financial advice? When a true emergency befalls us, not only would we be unable to retrieve those dollars, but over all those years, they also weren't working for us. They weren't producing tax refund income. They weren't in a safe side account earning a steady, compounding yield. They weren't creating true safety for our family.

Over all those years, those dollars haven't produced nice side profits that could carry us through hardship and possibly give us perpetual income for life.

What are those dollars doing when used to increase our equity position? Absolutely nothing. They are buried away inside our walls earning a zero rate of return. Every dollar paid into our equity builds a larger and larger wall between us and our security.

CHAPTER SIX

WHAT'S A S.A.F.E.T.Y. FUND™ AND HOW CAN IT BE MY PERSONAL FORT KNOX ON STEROIDS?

O.K. So you need a place to put the cash you've liberated from your house's equity using your H.E.R.O. Solution™ plan. This critical cash must be put somewhere safe while it does it's magic. Therefore, let me introduce you to the S.A.F.E.T.Y. Fund™, a *Side Account Faithfully Earning Tax-favored Yields.*

Your S.A.F.E.T.Y. Fund™ requires a tax-favored environment in order to function at top performance over time and provide tax-favored access when you need it for emergencies or for monthly income after retirement. Your critical cash should include the following:

- Extracted equity
- Non-qualified retirement funds
- Major money you wish to grow and protect for long-term wealth

This money should be placed in your S.A.F.E.T.Y. Fund™. Later, in this chapter I'll introduce Real Wealth L.A.W.™, which gives you three simple tests for identifying acceptable places to nurture your S.A.F.E.T.Y. Fund™ cash.

Why Should I Identify And Separate My Critical Cash From My Play Money?

Critical cash is the lifeblood of your wealth. It's crucial to have the ability to identify it, protect it and get it working for you. Those with Real Wealth Vision™ know the bulk of their critical cash is found here:

• Prior tax-free gains earned from the sale of a house or houses.[24]
• Future appreciation gains of current house(s) not-yet-cashed-in.
• All retirement funds.
• Any assets earmarked for long-term wealth and family protection.

When is money AT-RISK?

When you put your cash somewhere and you don't know how much you'll retrieve when you decide to take it back.

These are the largest portions of your wealth and should never be put at risk, always be accessible to see you through life's emergencies and be constantly working earning compounding gains.

---

[24] Gains can be acquired on your personal residence without incurring capital gains taxes. The limit for this is $500,000 for those filing jointly and $250,000 for singles every two years.

On the other hand, it's also important to know which dollars of your wealth get the title of "play money." This is cash you set aside for extras. It's a small percentage of your total income and money that you can afford to spend frivolously. Your "play money" could be lost altogether without any major consequences in your family's financial safety.

We've all heard it said that, "Knowledge is power." Identifying the important components of your wealth and having a plan for its health guarantees you financial success. You've got to systematically recognize and separate these parts of your monthly income. Critical cash is most important and your "play money" is, obviously, your least important. Know which is which.

"O.K.," you say. "I've identified and separated my critical cash. How do I get it out of the unemployment line and put to work?"

Look For A Vehicle That Doesn't Violate Real Wealth L.A.W.™

When the S.A.F.E.T.Y. Fund™ is discussed in the next chapter, you'll be shown several tax-favored vehicles that follow Real Wealth L.A.W.™ These are the best places for your H.E.R.O. Solution™ assets and all your critical cash. If you gain positive tax treatment on the dollars you put into your S.A.F.E.T.Y. Fund™, they will function best. But even without tax benefits, applying Real Wealth L.A.W.™ is still essential for your long-term wealth health.

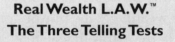

Real Wealth L.A.W.™
The Three Telling Tests

Before a single dime of your critical cash is placed anywhere, those with Real Wealth Vision™ know the vehicle selected must pass the three vital tests of Real Wealth L.A.W.™

The following should always be asked.

If I place my money here, will my assets be:

- **Locked-In?** — In other words, is my cash safe and protected from risk of loss? Will I never lose principal?
- **Accessible?** — Are my funds easy to reach? Can I get to my money quickly and without penalty?
- **Working?** — Does this vehicle keep my assets employed and earning a respectable compounding return?

Any sound, sensible investment vehicle or investment-grade contract should receive YES answers and pass each of these tests.

Positive tax treatment is a powerful plus and can make your choice a winner. But without it, your selection can still be wise and prudent.

No matter your tax situation or tax bracket, your critical cash investments should never violate Real Wealth L.A.W.™ Ask these questions before making any investment decisions and you'll be seeing things using Real Wealth Vision™. You'll move closer to creating real wealth for yourself and your family.

You Can Beef-Up, Bulk-Up, Even Overstuff

Remember, even though your S.A.F.E.T.Y. Fund™ has all the features and benefits of an IRS qualified retirement plan, there's one huge difference. It has no limits to how much cash you can put in it at any time. Those with Real Wealth Vision™ recognize this and direct as much into it as possible. You should always visualize the "big picture" in your mind when you're designing the plan for your life's fortune. If you get a good compounding return in addition to principal protection, ready access, no limits and potential tax advantages, you can actually see the synergy created in the whole picture of your fortune. This process guarantees your wealth success.

Isn't Risk Needed For Reward?
Why Must "Zero Risk" Be So Crucial?

Remember, it's your "critical cash." Its very name implies inherent importance. Real Wealth L.A.W.™ says you must **Lock-In** your principal. Why? It's extremely difficult to recover from principal losses over time. Down years will quickly and systematically wipe out the good years. You really don't want to take that chance with this category of your money.

In the next chapter, you'll see some illustrations of recent stock market years and what devastation was created in the wealth of many families. It actually happened to some of my own personal IRA money after I had followed the advice of a supposed financial advisor. Some people lost almost all of their retirement savings. You'll also see some examples of huge losses experienced by some high-profile people who had placed their critical cash into the equity of their homes. These sad financial moves could easily have been avoided by simply applying the three Real Wealth L.A.W.™ rules. Well, we live and learn.

If you wish, you can gather the "play money" you haven't spent on consumption and depreciating assets and buy some volatile stocks, trade in commodities, seek out IPOs or give junk bonds a try. Those are all fun activities that let you gamble to your heart's content, as long as it's being done with your "play money."

But for your critical cash, you should carefully apply Real Wealth L.A.W.™ any time you select where it will be put to work. It's your future. It's your family's wealth.

If I'm Getting Tax-Favored Growth, How Can I Get To My Critical Cash Without Taxes or Penalties?

Good question! One of the three tests of Real Wealth L.A.W.™ is **A**ccess. You must find a vehicle that allows for access to your money in emergencies. This is where normal IRAs fail the Real Wealth L.A.W.™ tests. You have no way to get to your IRA funds without incurring penalties or paying the taxes you postponed when you funded the account.

This is where the right vehicle for your S.A.F.E.T.Y. Fund™ cash has similarities to some other qualified retirement plans. With 401(k)s and employer-sponsored IRS qualified plans, you can usually borrow against your set-aside funds. That's where the similarity stops.

Your S.A.F.E.T.Y. Fund™ vehicle should let you also have access by way of loans against your funds. This lets you get to your money when absolutely necessary, yet doesn't disturb the long-term compounding growth. Also, loans avoid taxable events, since they are not considered income. The proper vehicle will allow for loans that let you replenish your cash in its sheltered environment once your crisis has passed. You should be able to do all this at your discretion without fear of penalty or taxes.

In the right vehicle, you have the option to make loan payments if and whenever you wish. Actually, repayment should never be required in your lifetime. With 401(k)s and their brothers, you must pay regular set monthly payments on your loans or risk having the loan recategorized as a withdrawal. If you miss your payment schedule, the IRS charges you a hefty 10% penalty and full income taxes on the loan amount. Ouch!

Why Do CDs and Money Markets Not Create Wealth?

Hopefully, you know the answer to this one. No, those with Real Wealth Vision™ don't put their money in low-yielding CDs or money markets.

They apply the tests of Real Wealth L.A.W.™ and select places for their cash that guarantee their principal. They've discovered modern vehicles that give them the required safety but, at the same time, allow for stock market gains.

I know it sounds like a fantasy, but they have found vehicles that offer zero loss of principal, tax-free access and stock market tax-favored gains all in one place. I'll tell you about that find in the next chapter … stay tuned.

> *"There are two big problems with CDs: They have tiny returns, and they can lock up your money for the long haul … Even on a one-year CD, you might be penalized three months worth of interest for early withdrawal."*
> — SmartMoney.com

While CDs or money markets are certainly vehicles that **Lock-In** your principal, their returns over time are dismal. You pay big-time for that safety by selling-out your critical cash's potential income. Yes, they give compound growth, but it's just so much less over time. There are ways to keep your security and get your S.A.F.E.T.Y. Fund™ money truly **Working** for you, per Real Wealth L.A.W.™

What Difference Does Tax-Favored Growth Make?

"What does it matter?" you may be thinking, "Pay taxes now or pay them when I take the money out. What's the difference?"

Well, to some extent your point may be a good one. Historically, advisors have chanted the same mantra, "Defer all taxes. Postpone until you are in a lower tax bracket."

But will you actually be in a lower bracket? Aren't we in the lowest income tax environment America has seen in a long time? Are you going to have more tax deductions after you retire or while you are younger? Do you believe taxes are going up or going down in the future? Is deferring for some yet-to-be-seen better time really a prudent idea?

Maybe your financial planner is hoping you'll be in the lowest tax brackets at retirement. Is that really successful planning? Isn't that planning to fail?

S.A.F.E.T.Y. Fund™ dollars come from two sources of cash — your house's equity that was never taxable and other money on which you paid taxes as you earned it.

It is imperative for maximum future growth to have a tax-favored environment on all compound earnings gained. Incurring payable taxes over the years causes smaller returns and will decimate your compounding results.

This illustration shows how a $100,000 account that grows non-taxed compares to one where taxes are paid over time. The results are dramatically different. After 30 years of earning 8% compounded and paid once annually, the account taxed in a 30% tax bracket grew to only $485,572. The non-taxed account grew to $931,727. That's 92% more!

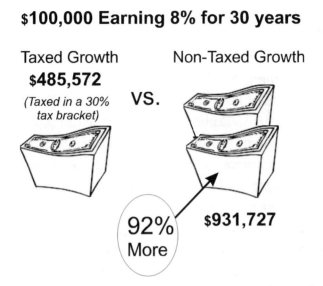

$100,000 Earning 8% for 30 years

Taxed Growth

$485,572

(Taxed in a 30% tax bracket)

VS.

Non-Taxed Growth

92% More

$931,727

An account where taxes are only postponed simply pushes the inevitable debt off until a later time. True, in regular tax-deferred accounts and qualified plans, your assets grow along with your tax liability, but risks also grow over time. As your wealth increases, the potential for losses will also rise due to penalties, higher tax rates and double taxation when your money passes to your heirs.

Don't Postpone Taxes — Eliminate Them Altogether — Legally!

You mustn't forget — it's possible the largest portion of your S.A.F.E.T.Y. Fund™ assets will come from your H.E.R.O. Solution™ plan and will be cash you received as 100% dollars. Taxes never paid — taxes never owed. These are powerful dollars!

I'll show you later on how you can systematically take money out of your tax-deferred retirement accounts to get them repositioned into your S.A.F.E.T.Y. Fund™. Then they can begin churning out tax-favored returns that never have to be taxed in the future.

This will produce retirement income for you that can be as much as 50% more than if you left your money in your deferred accounts. If structured properly, your S.A.F.E.T.Y. Fund™ will function much like a Roth IRA[25] without the restrictions. But it's actually better than a Roth because it allows funding without IRS income limitations or annual dollar caps on contributions.

It will provide tax-favored growth of assets into perpetuity without IRS penalties and rules. It will allow for penalty-free, tax-favored access to cash for emergencies and will also produce monthly tax-favored income at retirement. The IRS can't

> *"A Roth IRA is worth more than a conventional IRA because withdrawals from it are forever tax-free ...*
> — *Forbes*

require you to take it out or tell you when you must take it out. You can leave it untouched and pass it to your heirs because no distributions are required during your lifetime. This is not the case for regular IRAs and 401(k)s. For those non-Roth qualified plans, Uncle Sam wants his taxes whether you are dead or alive.

So, H.E.R.O. Solution™ Cash Inside Our S.A.F.E.T.Y. Fund™ Is Even Better Than A Roth IRA — Wow!

This powerful combination works because it offers you all these benefits:

• Taps volumes of tax-free cash.

---

[25] Roth IRA is an IRS qualified plan that allows you to deposit after-tax dollars that can grow tax-free and will be accessed tax-free. Roth IRAs are allowed only for taxpayers with an adjusted gross income of $100,000 or less.

- No caps on your deposits.
- No limits on income.
- You pay simple interest.
- You earn compound interest.
- Level or decreasing borrowed funds.
- Create profitable arbitrage.
- Principal is safe and locked-in.

You should apply a long-term focus when looking at your H.E.R.O. Solution™ funds. They should parallel the term of any mortgage you have or you'd be getting. Remember, the best ones have longer terms. This means your plan should look at a 30-year time horizon. Even if you are at or beyond retirement age, long-term planning should still be done. Most of us will live many years longer than our parents. We prepare for those bonus years, yet to come.

Time applied to compounding causes the surreal magic of the H.E.R.O. Solution™ in conjunction with the S.A.F.E.T.Y. Fund™ and Real Wealth L.A.W.™

Planning Is Crucial To Success

Why is it so important to structure a S.A.F.E.T.Y. Fund™ properly? Very few financial vehicles pass the test of Real Wealth L.A.W.™ and the added tax-sheltered component adds

> *"So, unless you expect to be in a much lower tax bracket during retirement than you are now, a Roth IRA is a better deal than even a tax-deductible IRA. And it's always a better deal than a nondeductible one"*
> — SmartMoney.com

complexity to the plan. You can easily see why very few financial planners will understand this strategy or know how to put this together for you.

Remember how many people compartmentalize matters? They see an issue, address it individually and move on to the next one, not realizing how they may work together or affect other components. Most advisors are versed in their area of expertise and are limited in their ability to assist in your total plan. Unless your advisor is working with other insightful professionals, they will be like one of the blind men describing the elephant from our earlier story.

A properly structured H.E.R.O. Solution™ working in conjunction with your S.A.F.E.T.Y. Fund™ requires detailed knowledge of tax laws and advanced risk-industry applications, not to mention debt management and monitoring. Believe it or not, there are insightful advisors who can put an effective plan together for you, but they are not your run-of-the-mill financial planner, tax-preparer, CPA or mortgage company.

Why Does Peak Plan Performance Require True Commitment And Systematic Reviews?

We are real people living actual lives. Our personal situations change over time. All these events, along with an unending list of other possible changes could affect the potential success of our wealth plan over time:

- Births of children or grandchildren
- Marriage or divorce
- Employment changes
- Deaths

- Disability or medical events
- Equity growth
- House sale or purchase
- Retirement
- Second home or vacation home purchases

Maybe we find ourselves wandering off the path on our road to wealth. Often our busy lives distract us and take our focus away from our plans. Could be, we just forget why we have our plan in place, what each part of it is designed to do and what it was set up to accomplish in the first place. We just need a personal guide to keep us headed toward our goals.

If you check your entire financial picture with a competent Real Wealth Vision™ advisor annually, you'll always stay on track. At a minimum, you should check-in on it every three to five years. Don't go it alone. Recycling the H.E.R.O. Solution™ every five years instead of just doing it once can actually double or triple your wealth creation. We'll cover that phenomenon in detail in Chapter Thirteen.

Remember My Promise?

A few pages back, I told you I'd discovered where the wealthy grow their separated assets. This vehicle offers zero chance for loss of principal, tax-free access and stock market tax-favored gains all in one place. This secret is about to be revealed to you in the next chapter, so just keep turning pages.

You've really got to see what they've found …

CHAPTER SEVEN

YOUR S.A.F.E.T.Y. FUND™ ASSETS MUST BE PUT TO THE REAL WEALTH L.A.W.™ TESTS

The spectacular wealth achieved over time using the H.E.R.O. Solution™ plan is made possible by the application of two basic, yet different mathematical principles of finance. The extreme success of this method lies in using "other people's money" (OPM) based on **simple interest** and investing this cash acquired, or lending it out, using **compound interest**. With simple interest, the amount charged for borrowing is only calculated on the capital owed in that month. Should another month go by, the amount of interest charged in that month is only calculated on the outstanding loan balance remaining. When you borrow mortgage money, your balance remains the same using an interest-only loan or it declines with an amortized loan.

Why is compound interest such a crucial factor? Compound interest is interest paid on interest. It is exponentially more profitable to receive compound interest, if you are the one lending out the money or, in other words, investing it.

$10,000 Growing at 8% for 30 years

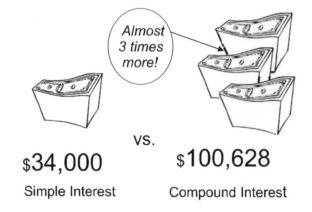

Almost 3 times more!

VS.

$34,000
Simple Interest

$100,628
Compound Interest

Just think of your results if you paid simple interest while earning compound interest?

Real Wealth L.A.W.™ should be applied to your choice every time you make the decision on where to put your critical cash. If each must pass these tests, which investment and savings vehicles out there would **Lock-In** your principal, leave your funds **Accessible** and keep your assets **Working**?

THE POWER OF COMPOUNDING

"The Emperor of China was so excited about the game of chess that he offered the inventor one wish. The inventor replied that he wanted one grain of rice on the first square of the chessboard, two grains on the second square, four on the third and so on through the 64th square. The unwitting emperor immediately agrees to the seemingly modest request. But two to the 64th power is 18 million trillion grains of rice — more than enough to cover the entire surface of the earth. The clever inventor did not gain all the rice in China; he lost his head."

— Recently recounted by George Gilder

Where Can We Put Our S.A.F.E.T.Y. Fund™ Assets?

The following illustration lists most of the potential places we could put our money — aside from burying it in our back yard in a jar. Since we've already extracted the bulk of our assets from inside the walls of our house, we'll eliminate the jar idea.

Ladder of Market Risk

High Risk
Commodities
Options and Futures
Business Ventures
Speculative Stocks
IPO Stocks
Common Stocks
Blue Chip Stocks

Medium Risk
Stock Mutual Funds
Variable Annuities
Variable UL Ins Contracts
Limited Partnerships
Undeveloped Land

Lower Risk
Investment Real Estate
REITs
Mortgage Backed Securities
Corporate Bonds
Municipal Bond Funds

No Risk
Municipal Bonds*
Indexed Annuities
Indexed Insurance Contracts
Fixed Annuities
Fixed Insurance Contracts
Treasury Bills
CDs and Money Markets

SAFETY

*If held to maturity.

Copyright 2006 HERO Solution, Inc.

The above graphic displays the level of risk your principal would face for loss due to market fluctuations. Risks are inevitable and there is no way to eliminate them entirely. The chance exists for municipality or institution insolvency, but federal FDIC insurance and state-mandated insurance guaranty pools or funds are in place for these rare events.

All those choices higher on the ladder than Municipal Bonds do not pass the three Real Wealth L.A.W.™ tests. With the others eliminated, these choices remain:

Pass Real Wealth L.A.W. Tests

- *Municipal Bonds, if held to maturity*
- *Indexed Annuities*
- *Indexed Insurance Contracts*
- *Fixed Annuities*
- *Fixed Insurance Contracts*
- *Treasury Bills*
- *CDs and Money Markets*

Additionally, your S.A.F.E.T.Y. Fund™ requires tax-favored yields, so which vehicles produce a respectable yield that is also tax-favored by the IRS?

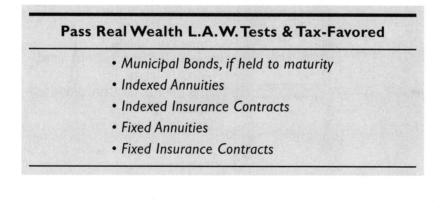

Pass Real Wealth L.A.W. Tests & Tax-Favored

- *Municipal Bonds, if held to maturity*
- *Indexed Annuities*
- *Indexed Insurance Contracts*
- *Fixed Annuities*
- *Fixed Insurance Contracts*

What's the Difference Between Annuities
and Investment-Grade Life Insurance Contracts?

Annuities are simply savings accounts with an insurance company. By virtue of their charter, insurance companies are extremely conservative entities. They are highly regulated and receive ratings for strength and security in much the same manner and by the same evaluating firms that rate banks.[26]

The IRS gives annuities different tax treatment than life insurance. Annuities are taxed Last In-First Out (LIFO). This means the last money going into the annuity account, or the earnings most recently received, are the dollars you are pulling out when you take a withdrawal. Therefore, you must pay taxes on your withdrawals until all your earnings are completely disbursed. Additionally, loans against annuities are not a possibility. While annuities receive tax-favored growth during the time they are held and earning, money withdrawn from the annuity is not tax-favored. Therefore, LIFO leaves annuities lacking in the area of tax treatment on the back end.

Since a properly functioning S.A.F.E.T.Y. Fund™ must receive full tax-favored treatment while it's held and when it's withdrawn, then both the fixed annuity and the equity-index annuity are not acceptable choices for us.

On the other hand, life insurance is given First In-First Out (FIFO) treatment by the IRS. The benefit it offers lies in your ability to withdraw your money initially deposited without tax consequence. When you are ready to receive monthly income from the plan, your own money can be returned to you on demand until depleted.

"But what happens once I've taken back all my money deposited and I need to get to my earnings?" you ask.

---

[26] Rating firms include A.M. Best, Fitch, Moody's and S&P.

Here is where the beauty of a life insurance contract steps onto center stage.

Insurance contracts offer loan features that allow access to your money, but do not require repayment in your lifetime. Because of FIFO tax treatment, you are able to withdraw the cash you put into the contract up front in any fashion you wish. Once that money is depleted, you can begin taking your earnings out of the contract in the form of a loan against the cash value. Zero-wash, or zero-cost, loan features are offered, contractually, which balance the interest you pay on any loans with the interest being earned by your cash account.

You can even set up automatic loan withdrawals so that you receive monthly income from your cash. As long as you take care not to deplete your cash value and the policy remains in force, you will never have to make a payment, never have to repay the loan and never incur any taxes on your gains in your lifetime. When you die, all policy loans are wiped away by the insurance policy. Then, should any proceeds remain, they are paid to the policy beneficiaries.

> *"How many of us can honestly claim that our clients lost no money in the stock market meltdown of 2000 through 2002? Advisors whose clients used EIAs* [equity-indexed-products] were largely protected from those horrifying losses."*
> — Dr. Donald Moine, Morningstar.com

What's The Catch?

You aren't allowed to simply plop unlimited sums of cash into these contracts. While that's what actually happened in the product's infancy, the IRS caught on and changed the rules for depositing into insurance contracts. In order for you to borrow your house's equity and place it into these special vehicles, you must follow some steps to avoid violating IRS rules or causing the creation of a MEC.[27] Not every advisor knows how to put this together properly. More about that in a later chapter.

The IRS dictates how much insurance must come along for the ride in order for you to receive this special tax treatment. Then, good-ol' Uncle Sam also has special instructions for how you put your money into the contract. If your funds for deposit came from your house's equity, there are ways to get this money into your contract and stay within the IRS rules to protect your tax deductions.

Wow! Sounds Too Good To Be True. How Long Have These Insurance Contracts Been Around?

Remember the famous television ad from a little over 20 years ago for brokerage firm E. F. Hutton? In the ad, a group of people sit at a crowded, noisy restaurant, and one guy says to another, "My broker is E. F. Hutton, and he says …" and the whole crowd falls silent, listening. The tag line was: *"When E. F. Hutton talks, people listen."*

The ad conveyed how people desperately want access to an advisor who knows the best strategies. Well, E. F. Hutton was the firm responsible for going to the trillion-dollar, ultra-conservative insurance industry and showing them a whole new way to use the tax benefits offered by the IRS. This concept allowed them to give customers strategies to create and nurture their wealth. In addition, they were provided the risk

---

[27] A Modified Endowment Contract (MEC) does not get the special tax treatment you enjoy in a life insurance contract.

protection inherent to insurance. Thus were born investment-grade, cash-value life insurance contracts.

For many years, those with large assets to invest were acquiring small cash-value insurance policies and placing huge deposits into them. It wasn't uncommon to see hundreds of thousands of dollars being put into a tiny life insurance policy with only a few thousand dollars of face-value. It was a great way to achieve tax-favored growth on big blocks of assets.

The IRS said, "Wait a minute, that's not cash-value life insurance — that's an investment." But as the tax laws were structured at that time, it was proven to be a valid method of funding life insurance contracts. In court, E. F. Hutton won the case.

So, what did the IRS do? They set out to adjust the rules. They created specific guidelines that dictate how much actual insurance must exist in a life insurance contract to keep it from simply being a tax-sheltered investment vehicle. Thus was created the concept of the "insurance corridor," established by the Tax Equity and Fiscal Responsibility Acts of 1982 and 1983 (TEFRA).

That Was Twenty Years Ago ... Now It's The 21st Century ... Has There Been Any Evolution in Insurance?

Well, if we fast-forward just a few years to the early 1990s, I can tell you it was still a challenge for even the largest firms. My spouse and I actually set up a non-qualified retirement plan using an investment-grade life insurance contract with one of the major insurance companies in 1993. Back then, the insurance contract option being presented in this book wasn't available, so we went with a variable universal life insurance contract.

This arrangement was over the head of our regular financial planner. Additionally, it was beyond his supervisor in this major financial firm's local office in the suburbs of Chicago. At that point, they had to bring in a regional specialist from their financial planning division in order to apply the Internal Revenue laws and set up our non-qualified retirement plan using an investment-grade universal life insurance contract.

That was a few years back and I know there are more professionals out there now with the savvy, experience and wherewithal to put these plans together, but they are not easy to find.

Younger ... Smarter ... Better[28]

"It is not that consumers are becoming more risk averse; it's that consumers are becoming more "loss" averse and more educated about investments. Investors are starting to realize that it is difficult to achieve consistent returns above 10% when the average investor in the market achieved only 2.57% from 1984 to 2002."
— Jack Marrion, *Advantage Compendium*

I'll bet you've heard those three adjectives used before on a cable news network or in radio commercials. Descriptive words like these are also very appropriate for the professionals who are astute enough to understand these products. This trilogy of words is perfect to describe the products that have recently appeared in the insurance industry. New choices in

---

[28] Tag line used by the Fox News Network.

investment-grade universal life insurance contracts, as well as annuities, have evolved. After devastating losses in the stock market many experienced due to the tech-wreck of 2000 and the 9-11 terrorist attacks the following year, folks looking for safety have flocked to these products. For those possessing Real Wealth Vision™, these new products have had a great influence on where they now put their critical cash.

Indexed universal life[29] insurance contracts and indexed annuities have been receiving a lot of attention, lately. The real key to appreciating indexed products is in understanding that they are really fixed instruments. Where variable annuities and variable life insurance contracts place the risk for cash-value loss on the policyholder, indexed products leave the risk squarely on the shoulders of the insurance company. Insurance is all about risk protection and these vehicles eliminate most of the risk you face in your quest for asset accumulation.

> *"Most of my investments are in equity index funds."*
> —William F. Sharpe, Nobel Laureate in Economics, 1990

> *"Most of the mutual fund investments I have are index funds, approximately 75%."*
> — Charles Schwab, Guide to Financial Independence

Indexed UL products come with minimum guaranteed interest rates. These yields are contractually promised to the policyholders even when the securities markets or equity indices have losing years. Therein lies the genius of these instruments. Gains in the underlying index to which the performance is linked and

---

[29] Indexed universal life (IUL) insurance contracts are also called equity-index UL, fixed index UL and investment-grade insurance contracts.

interest credited are both "locked-in" and added to the policy's accumulation value in a manner that cannot be lost. So, even in down markets policyholder accounts maintain their values.

> "Most investors, both institutional and individual, will find the best way to own common stocks is through an index fund that charges minimal fees. Those following this path are sure to beat the net results (after fees and expenses) delivered by the great majority of investment professionals."
> — Warren Buffet, Berkshire Hathaway Chairman and legendary billionaire investor

Moreover, indexed UL products offer the best of both worlds, certainty of reasonable interest yield plus securities upside when and if the market gains are available, all without risk of principal loss.

One of the most important rules defining insurance as compared to securities is the role of the insurance company. In order for the fixed product to be classified as insurance, **the company must assume the risk, not the customer.** This is why indexed UL products do not require registration with the SEC[30] and are not deemed a security, unlike variable annuities or variable life contracts.[31]

To be clear, indexed UL and annuity products are fixed insurance products, not securities. These indexed UL, also known as fixed index or equity index, products protect a consumer's principal and lock-in current gains at the end of each period. Then gains achieved cannot be lost to future market downturns.

---

[30] Securities and Exchange Commission
[31] From the "safe harbor rules" enacted by the SEC.

Returns of the insurance contract or annuity are linked to a major index in the equities markets. These vehicles allow the policyholder to participate indirectly in the stock market whenever it is experiencing growth, yet they have a guaranteed floor on the minimum interest rate that is to be credited.

Indices available vary by the insurance company, but indices offered include the S&P 500[®][32], S&P 400, Dow Jones Industrials, NASDAQ and Russell 2000. Cash values can often be divided among several. Over the long term, the broad market reflected in the S&P 500[®] Index has outperformed most managed mutual funds, municipal bonds and corporate bonds. It comprises more than 80% of the U.S. stock market capitalization.

> *"Equity-indexed annuities are a Goldilocks product: not too risky and not too safe. They are long-term investments that safeguard principal, guarantee a minimum rate of return and also offer investors some upside if the stock market does well."*
> — Washington Post

In reality, the money in your insurance cash-value account is not actually invested in the market but is mainly held in conservative bonds, mortgages and fixed vehicles managed by the insurance company. A small portion of the huge pool of assets under management is set aside to purchase index futures, LEAPS[33] and other hedging instruments which will, in turn, provide the added income needed to allow the insurance company to pay the interest equivalent to the stock index performance.

---

[32] S&P[®] and S&P 500[®] are registered trademarks of The McGraw-Hill Companies, Inc.
[33] *Long-term Equity AnticiPation Security* is an option with a long-term expiration.

When the market has a loss or is flat, policy cash values are protected from loss and, over time, will receive a guaranteed interest rate. Most policies guarantee a 1% to 3% minimum rate to be paid. Participation in the market's success during good years is sometimes capped at a ceiling rate. The cap options available will vary by insurance contract product and company offering them.

Interest paid is very often capped on the upper end to compensate the insurance company for the years when they must absorb the losses of the market. Additionally, the interest paid is based on the stock market yield reported, not including stock dividends paid on some of the underlying stocks within the index.

> *"… from the day the New York Stock Exchange opened its doors, through the end of 1997, the average annual rate of return on stocks has been more than 10 percent. [Quoting Jeremy Siegel's book,* Stocks for the Long Run] *Siegel finds that there has never been a 40-year period in American history when the markets have deviated significantly from that long-term trend."*
> — Stephen Moore, Director of Fiscal Policy Studies at the Cato Institute, from the Cato Institute website

But, Isn't There A Cost Involved in Life Insurance?

Of course, the IRS requires the life insurance component to exist in order for this vehicle to receive its special tax treatment. This plan can work with both whole life and universal life products, but because of the market-indexed growth offered by the universal life choice, it's the option with the potential to produce the most future growth.

Universal life insurance consists of term life insurance with a cash value component. The marvelous thing about term life is that its costs have gone down as much as 60% in the last ten years. As mortality rates continue to improve, this trend will probably continue.

There is an expense for this underlying insurance, but if your contract is put together properly and the face value is pushed down of to the absolute minimum allowed by the IRS rules, it most often works out to be about 1% to 1.25% for indexed UL products and less than 1% for fixed insurance products over the life of the contract. This is, on average, actually less than the expense ratios or management fees you must pay with standard mutual funds.

> *"The industry average for mutual fund expense ratios or annual costs is 1.3 percent."*
> — Chicago Tribune, February 26, 2006

TEFRA,[34] DEFRA[35] and TAMRA[36] are pieces of tax legislation that were enacted in the 1980s. These laws dictate how much insurance you're required to hold within the contract to receive special tax treatment and how the cash value can accumulate tax-free within it. Accurate application of these laws is what makes the insurance contract an "investment-grade" vehicle. An advisor must know how to scrutinize your situation, evaluate the total cash you wish to deposit into

---

[34] TEFRA: Tax Equity and Fiscal Responsibility Acts of 1982 and 1983.
[35] DEFRA: Deficit Reduction Act of 1984.
[36] TAMRA: Technical and Miscellaneous Revenue Act of 1988, which made corrections to TEFRA.

your S.A.F.E.T.Y. Fund™ and apply the mathematics within these three IRS rules to determine the face value of the policy you require.

Why Would The Face Value Of The Contract Matter?

This is extremely contrary to conventional thought, but think about this ... the goal you wish to achieve here is the least amount of insurance for the most money paid in.

> Let me repeat this ... You want the least insurance for the most deposited.

I know it sounds backwards, but this method dictated by the IRS actually creates the magic of this vehicle. Universal life insurance is a combination of a term life insurance policy with a cash value account. Your cost of insurance should be cut-to-the-bone when you *push* the face amount of your insurance coverage down. This Real Wealth Vision™ strategy, therefore, allows the maximum amount of dollars you pay into the vehicle to go into your cash value. Then the bulk of your money gets to work earning a compounding return for your S.A.F.E.T.Y. Fund™ growth. This process also slashes the expenses to the bare minimum producing a low net insurance expense. Over the life of the contract, the resulting cost of insurance turns out to be less than most mutual fund expense charges would have been.

Is this whole thing making sense to you? I know the concept is complicated. This is why very few financial professionals, insurance agents or CPAs even know how to explain it to you, much less put a plan together for you. Life insurance

> **What a bonus!** You trade the mutual fund expense charges (you would have paid anyway) for life insurance charges. If you don't need the insurance, then you live a long, long time and are extremely fortunate. If you do need it, your family will be forever grateful you chose to forego the mutual fund investment choice.

provides unique benefits that are unmatched by other financial planning instruments. Although the primary benefit of life insurance is to provide cash upon death, in the final analysis life insurance is for the living. Congratulations! You now know a Real Wealth Vision™ secret!

Let's recap the advantages of our number-one choice for your S.A.F.E.T.Y. Fund™ assets — an investment-grade indexed UL insurance contract. It offers these benefits:

- Guarantee against principal loss.
- Fully accessible funds through zero-cost loans or withdrawals.
- Loans will never require payments or repayment in your lifetime.
- Tax-favored growth is linked to major stock market indices.
- Tax-favored income can be received monthly, if desired.
- Cost of insurance is equivalent to many mutual fund expenses.
- Withdrawals are not mandatory, unlike IRAs and 401(k)s.
- Deposits are not limited, unlike with IRAs and 401(k)s.
- Remaining assets will pass to your heirs tax-free.

It's a no-brainer! It's clearly the best choice for S.A.F.E.T.Y. Fund™ assets. These instruments are gaining popularity and, as more and more companies enter the field, additional alternatives will become available. Competition inevitably creates choice.

How Will I Know What Return I'll Get On My Cash Value?

You must remember this basic fact ... **Cash value within an investment-grade indexed universal life insurance contract is not invested in the stock market.**

Since insurance companies use the returns of an underlying stock market index to calculate the interest you are paid, you receive the benefit of all the market's winning years. Conversely,

> *Forecasting is difficult — especially into the future.*
> — Mark Twain

you are shielded from experiencing the losses in its bad years. Knowing this, wouldn't you suppose it would be important to know the history of long-term stock market returns? Since S&P 500® Index history is public knowledge, it is possible to calculate the gains that could have historically resulted in an indexed UL contract.

Due to regulatory scrutiny, insurance companies are typically quite conservative when projecting expectations for insurance cash value future results. Since the very first indexed universal life policy only appeared on the market in late 1996, a long history of their actual payment performance does not yet exist. Actuaries and statisticians back-tested the models used by insurance companies to calculate the interest a policyholder would have received. These extrapolated results should be a reliable estimation of the earnings the cash value inside an indexed UL policy would have gotten in those years.

Several options are available in the market for indexed UL products. Most are indexed to the S&P 500® but several other market index choices are available. The company calculates your interest to be credited using an annual, monthly or daily average of the underlying index performance and applying a mathematical filter.

One company offers a 17% annual cap with a 1% floor. Others have a 12% cap with a higher floor. Some have no cap at all, use a monthly averaging method and then pay interest equal to 130% or 135% of the annual average for the past 12 months. Most all contracts offer a guaranteed minimum yield to be paid.

In the multitude of life insurance companies out there, I located ONLY SIX (6) that currently offer these new indexed universal life products but ALSO have among the strongest financial strength ratings given by the independent agencies.[37]

These insurance companies performed internal back-tested results using their various crediting methods. The published simulated yields from these six companies are ranged from **7.7%** to **9.6%** annually.

If you talk to any financial planner or stock-broker, he or she will almost always use a 10% return figure when expectations for stock-market returns are discussed. That being the case, let me pose a question.

---

[37] Financial institution rating agencies include A.M. Best, Moody, Fitch and Standard and Poor's.

Which of these choices seems more logical?

1. You place your cash into a vehicle expecting a 10% return while incurring tax liability along the way AND you are risking your cash to loss in the stock-market.
2. You place your cash into a vehicle expecting a 7.7% to 9.6% return that will be accessible without taxation AND your principal is fully protected from stock market loss.

I don't know about you, but my choice would be the second one. Even with optimistic projections for a stock market return of 12% to 13% (as unlikely as that would be, going forward), I would still select the one offering safety of principal protection and accessibility without taxes.

Each state where the insurance company does business, examines their books on a regular basis. Then, for added protection, every state has a guarantee fund designed to protect contract owners if an insurance company were to become insolvent. Based on history, it is extremely unlikely you would ever lose principal or interest because the insurance company failed.

The cost for this insurance is basically absorbed by side-stepping mutual fund management fees and otherwise payable income taxes. Utilizing an indexed universal life contract inside your S.A.F.E.T.Y. Fund™ just seems the most logical and safe.

If you invest in an S&P 500® Index fund through a regular taxable account or even in a tax-postponed account, there would be additional management fees involved according to the way you held the index. You could place your money in an index mutual fund or purchase "spiders" (SPDRs).[38] Mutual

---

[38] SPDRs are an Exchange Traded Fund (ETF) which trades on the American Stock Exchange. SPDRs are a pooled investment representing ownership in a basket of stocks including all the companies of the S&P 500® in weighted percentages.

funds always charge management fees, and fund companies are notorious for confusing expenses.

Let's cover a few points about mutual fund expenses. A recent study was released by the National Bureau of Economic Research, which had been put together by a group of highly acclaimed researchers from Yale, Harvard and the University of Pennsylvania. They found it was nearly impossible to accurately identify what mutual fund fees were just from looking at the prospectus. The fund companies make it hard for anyone to even figure out what they're going to charge.

Excerpts from an interview published in *FORTUNE* Magazine regarding scandals that have been uncovered in the mutual fund industry, what's wrong with the industry and who's to blame:

"This is far and away the most serious and pervasive scandal to hit America's markets in the past century."

"... because of enormous greed. It's an industry that's been changed to a marketing concept; the gathering of assets is all-important because that's where the payoff is. We have seen an industry veer away from fiduciaries toward marketing impresarios."

"I think performance advertising should be banned. The advertising in this [the mutual fund] industry is absolutely outrageous. And they don't really take into account expenses. The numbers are really fudged. I think it's essential that we do more to have the funds use plain English to describe their operations and fees. They use a language that is so arcane it defies comprehension by the average individual."

"The public should know how much of their money is being siphoned off."

— Arthur Levitt, Former Securities and
Exchange Commission chairman

You'll see the prospectus of many companies list innocent-sounding 12b-1 fees. Often, these are taken from your account so the mutual fund company can pay for all of its impressive advertising, brochures, mailings and those unbelievably expensive Super Bowl ads. There are also back-end load fees and outrageous expense ratios with some funds and fund families. You can see why investment fund managers are making a nice living off of your mutual fund money.

In addition to all the accounting unknowns, you'll owe taxes on the earnings received from mutual funds in the form of capital gains and dividend income taxes. If owned in a taxable account, the dividend income would be reportable and you would incur taxes each year. This expense would reduce your reported returns over time. If you held a mutual fund investment in an IRA or 401(k), your earnings would be taxed at your full income tax rate upon withdrawal.

Harvard Study Proves That Traditional Money Managers and Investment Advisors Cause the Loss of Billions in Returns and Fees

"A crisis is looming. Some would say it is already here, based upon the tens of billions of dollars the BCT study found that investors have potentially lost because they worked with financial advisors."
—Dr. Donald Moine, Morningstar.com 07/13/06

"Assessing the Costs and Benefits of Brokers in the Mutual Fund Industry" is a study authored by Daniel B. Bergstresser and Peter Tufano of Harvard Business School, National Bureau of Economic Research, (NBER) and John M.R. Chalmers of the University of Oregon, on January 16, 2006.

Dr. Donald Moine, in his article published in *Morningstar.com*, calls this landmark work the BCT Study and "The Study of the Decade." The project analyzed the cost and performance of more than 4,000 mutual funds, some sold by advisors and others independently selected by investors working on their own. The BCT study found that the mutual fund investments of individuals working on their own significantly outperform the mutual fund selections of investment advisors.

This study, released in 2006, was the most comprehensive one of its type ever performed. It analyzed several trillion dollars worth of transactions occurring between 1996 and 2002. The period studied encompassed both a strong bull market and a strong bear market.

So, how well did investment advisors perform? The study looked at virtually all types of investment advisors who sell mutual funds. Despite all of their training in areas such as modern portfolio theory, diversification, asset allocation, rebalancing, etc., the study found that most advisors deliver poor investment returns. In 2002 alone, investors paid 3.6 billion in front-end loads, 2.8 billion in back-end loads, 8.8 billion in 12b-1 fees and 23.8 billion in management fees and other operational expenses.

The BCT study found the raw returns of equally-weighted equity mutual funds (net of all expenses) were 6.626% for investors working on their own and 2.924% for funds provided by investment advisors.

The conclusion? **Stock market investors who do not use money managers or investment advisors earn billions of dollars more per year and save billions of dollars in fees.**

—Source: Harvard Business School website and
Morningstar.com

Principal Protection in a Down
Stock Market Makes A Gigantic Difference

We are all familiar with what happened to the stock market between 1997 and 2005. The next illustrations show how an indexed UL cash-value account would have fared compared to money invested in several large well-known mutual funds on the market. (All accounts in these graphs start with $100,000 at the end of 1996.)

By December of 2005, the cash value account in an indexed UL account would have grown to $218,179 — **up over 118%!** Comparatively, the closing value of the largest S&P 500 mutual fund on the market produced a return of only 66.17%, which would have left the account-holder a cash balance of only $166,165.

From the ocean of over 6000 mutual funds out there, we selected three very large actively-managed mutual funds to compare. The public has deposited huge amounts of cash and retirement savings into these funds. Maybe results like these could explain why the average investor does so poorly in the market. Don't forget — these funds also charge annual management fees and have other expenses, which would have depressed the illustrated results even more.

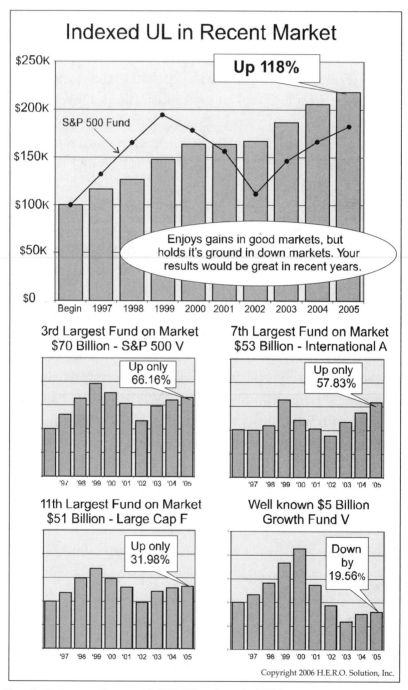

Hypothetical account began with $100,000 at the end of 1996.

The 7th largest mutual fund in the market came in with a final balance of $157,834 (57.83% total return). This fund invests in the international market and boasts $53,068,500,000 in cash under management. Another huge fund was ranked 11th for size and invests in large cap stocks. This fund manages $50,963,500,000 in investor funds. Its return was 31.98% over the period, so those clients ended up with $131,978 in their accounts. Finally, we added a slightly smaller fund that manages over 5 billion dollars in assets. That actively-managed growth fund (V) actually lost money over the nine years and ended up with a cash account of $80,436 for a LOSS of 19.56%.

> This vehicle is the second of the
> **3 Simple Money Secrets**
> Millionaires use.

Critics complain that indexed UL insurance contracts don't receive the full S&P 500® returns over time. They say, that in a raging bull market, you may not realize the same results you'd get if invested in the actual market.

This is true, but do you believe we are to expect long periods of raging bull markets in the future? Will markets be more volatile or even become bear markets? Who can know?

While these last few years were not normal for the market, the first graph, which depicts the indexed product compared to the S&P 500®, demonstrates how you would be protected in a down market relative to being actually "in the market." There are many market environments when this feature can truly be a benefit. In times like the last few years, the security of a guarantee against market loss of your principal proved to be a highly desirable aspect you could take to the bank.

Quite a Comparison to Actively Traded Mutual Funds

The following is a quote from *Myths, Lies and Downright Stupidity*, a book by John Stossel, of ABC's 20/20. Mr. Stossel tells of a conversation with Professor Malkiel from Princeton University regarding the fact that nearly 95% of portfolio managers handling actively traded mutual funds could not do as well as the market in general over the past fifteen years.

John Stossel: *"So the experts are fooling themselves."*

Professor Malkiel: *"Now, I'm not saying that this is a scam. They genuinely believe they can do it. The evidence is, however, that they can't."*

Mr. Stossel, in an appearance on CNBC, said the tiny 5% of funds that did beat the market do not do it consistently. In other words, picking a fund that beat the market last year does not mean it will beat the market in the coming years. The real data proves that active

> *"Over the 15 years ending October 31, 2005, 94.28% of actively managed funds did worse than the S&P."*
> — John Stossel, author and reporter with ABC's 20/20

management of funds with the goal of always beating the market average has proven to be impossible to accomplish over time.

Let's take a look at the figure for the S&P 500® close at year-end from 1968 (103.86 close) to 2005 (1248.29 close). That time frame is probably the working or investing life for many of us in the baby-boom generation.

Zero Market Loss Beats S&P
in Spendable Cash Results!
$100,000 from 1968 to 2005

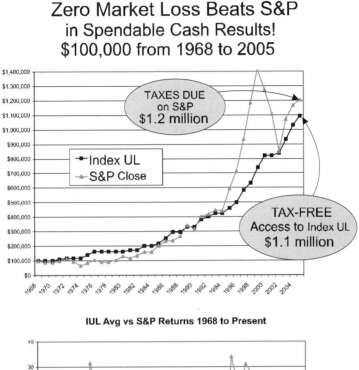

IUL Avg vs S&P Returns 1968 to Present

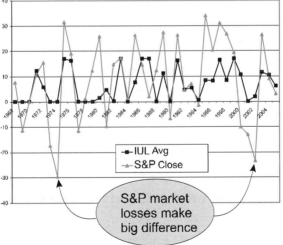

This evaluation gives us over 35 years of market results to review. We compare each year's close with an approximation of what one of the indexed UL products would have done at a single point during that year. Again, the product I've selected to compare provides the index on a monthly average return for the prior year. Gains are received in positive market years and do not go below 0% when the index loses.[39] In other words, each year you move ahead or stay the same and no principal is ever lost due to market downturns.

The first graph is the growing value of a $100,000 account over the 30-year plus time period. The second graph shows the S&P 500 Index and IUL return swings for each year over the period evaluated. It's pretty eye-opening to see how the numbers play out. The market can be highly volatile with extremely wild changes. Downside protection of principal can make a substantial difference, even if you aren't getting the roaring highs of market upturns.

Don't forget — that $1.1 million in the indexed UL insurance contract will be accessible WITHOUT TAXATION via loans against your cash value account, while the $1.2 million will be taxable. Upon withdrawal, you'll lose between 10% to 40% or more, according to how you held the account and your effective income tax bracket at the time you withdraw the funds.

The indexed UL account really holds it's own against the market index in the long term! When the principal receives a no-market-loss guarantee, it performs quite spectacularly by comparison.

Some Insurance Companies Now Offer Diversification Choices Resembling Mutual Fund Families

Most insurance companies offer you the ability to move all or portions of your cash value funds out of the indexed vehicle into a fixed vehicle within the policy, in much the same

---

[39] The indexed UL data plotted was calculated using an "monthly averaging" method from the same month in each year.

fashion as moving from an equity fund into a money market fund within a mutual fund family.

As new products evolve, we are seeing more and more choice for the consumer. Some companies offer as many as nine selections for the cash value portion of your policy. You would be given the option to diversify within the cash value by placing percentages into fixed or stock-market-indexed components. In addition to choices, most companies guarantee a minimum return.

Selections offered, to date, include:

- S&P 500 (annual point-to-point indexing)
- S&P 500 (daily averaging)
- S&P 400 (annual point-to-point indexing)
- S&P 400 (daily averaging)
- Dow Jones Industrials (annual point-to-point indexing)
- NASDAQ 100 (annual point-to-point indexing)
- Russell 2000 (annual point-to-point indexing)
- Russell 2000 (daily averaging)
- Fixed

Please Understand — While I am not an insurance professional, I conducted multiple interviews with insurance specialists as part of my research for this book. I also took a formal insurance class and licensing exam. This was done to verify my research data and the accuracy of its presentation. As a result of my exploration, I now have an insurance license, but I've never sold an insurance policy. The numbers here were not provided by, nor endorsed by, any insurance company and are not a solicitation to sell insurance. This data is the result of back-testing to get a past picture and project what could be expected with the number-one choice for S.A.F.E.T.Y. Fund™ cash.

What About Fixed Universal Life or Whole Life Insurance Contracts?

On average, most insurance companies will provide illustrations using fixed rates that are pretty low compared to those of the fixed index or equity index products. It's not uncommon to see 4.75% to 5.5% listed as fixed returns to expect. The insurance industry is highly regulated and will most always provide very conservative illustrations.

My personal experience with fixed insurance products has been VERY GOOD. One of my own life insurance contracts is a fixed universal life insurance policy acquired in 1994. I have held this fixed policy for over 12 years now and the average return I've received on my cash value has EXCEEDED 8% ANNUALLY. Even in this low interest rate environment! If you seek out a good reputable insurance firm who employs extremely competent money managers, the steady fixed return you receive can be amazing.

Don't forget — as market interest rates rise — the fixed returns received by those in fixed portfolio insurance contracts should also increase.

How About The Municipal Bonds On Our Short List of Choices?

Yes, they were also a viable choice for the S.A.F.E.T.Y. Fund™. What are their advantages and disadvantages?

Bonds are IOUs where you are the lender. In the case of municipals, the borrower — or issuer — is a government-sponsored organization or a state or local government. These entities offer bonds as a way to raise money.

However, you can only get maximum tax benefits when you invest the proceeds of a house sale. If you remove your equity from a home you already own via a mortgage and invest in tax-exempt securities (AKA municipal bonds) the interest on those borrowed funds is not tax-deductible. Individual municipal bonds would actually work for your S.A.F.E.T.Y. Fund™ because most also receive special IRS tax treatment.

Bonds are considered fixed-income investments. When you purchase a bond, you know the amount the issuer promises to pay you and when you are scheduled to receive the payments. The face value can change during the time you own the bond due to market fluctuations and interest rate changes, so your principal is not completely guaranteed over the entire time of ownership.

> "Using tax-subsidized borrowing to invest in tax-exempt bonds is a straight tax arbitrage."
> — Forbes.com, The 2005 Investment Guide

"But wait," you're thinking. "Municipal bonds passed the tests of Real Wealth L.A.W."

Yes, they passed because of one basic fact — when a bond is held to maturity, the face value of the bond is guaranteed to the bondholder. The appeal of bonds is that you are unlikely to lose your money. That's not a concrete guarantee (with the possible exception of U.S. Treasuries) because state and local governments are occasionally unable to repay their debt. Your main risk is the strength or weakness of the municipality issuing the bond. Will that city, county or state become insolvent in the years before bond maturity?

Additionally, many bonds have a call period, in which the municipality could buy the bond back from you. This call period is usually 10 years but can vary. If you are called-out, you will receive the full face value of your bond. Remember, you have also been paid income on the bond over the time you held it.

Since the full tax advantage available with municipal bonds depends on your state of residence, this barrier will restrict your choices.

Income earned from individual municipal bonds is paid to the bondholder semi-annually in the form of a check. Because of the large minimum deposit required to buy additional municipal bonds, reinvestment of these earnings becomes difficult to negotiate effectively. It isn't impossible, but it also isn't easy. This is often why municipal bond funds are easier to hold and navigate. These funds did not make the cut on our "Ladder of Market Risk" because the principal can fluctuate with market changes.

In order to achieve similar yields to those offered with fixed insurance contracts, the managers of municipal bond funds may have to invest in lower rated and riskier municipalities. Often these local city governments could have received ratings of B[40] or less for their financial strength. The lower the strength of the entity issuing the bond — the riskier the investment. There are municipal bond funds currently on the market with 5-year history of returns as high as 9.5% and 10-year returns as high as 7.5%. Some of these bond funds carry a load, or upfront charge, to invest in them.

Costs involved in municipal bond mutual fund investing are similar to the cost of insurance in both the fixed portfolio universal life and the indexed UL insurance contract. There would be expenses in either vehicle, but no bonus life insurance is coming along for the ride with a municipal bond fund. While you can reinvest your earnings in a bond fund, there are management costs involved with fund investing in addition to the possibility of load charges.

---

[40] A.M. Best's rating scale range: A++, A+, A, A–, B++, B+, B, B–, C++, C+, C, C– and D. Their own definition regards any company or entity with a B+ or better to be secure and B or below to be vulnerable.

"What about **Accessibility**?" you ask. "If bonds have to be held to maturity, how am I going to have access to my cash in an emergency?"

Municipal bond funds are highly liquid and, therefore, very accessible. Individual bonds must be acquired through a broker, who almost always offers a margin account with their services. Emergency access to your cash would be available through a simple phone call to your broker.

Finally, municipal bond funds historically pay yields similar to fixed insurance contracts. While these yields are acceptable, on the average, they probably won't compare with the expected yields to be achieved from investment-grade, indexed UL insurance contracts.

> "*[Most investors would] be better off in an **index** fund.*"
> — Peter Lynch, famous stock picker, *Barron's*

All in all, municipal bonds pass the Real Wealth L.A.W.™ tests and provide the tax-favored treatment necessary for your S.A.F.E.T.Y. Fund™, but there are just a few things about them that make them come in at second place in the race for best vehicle available.

One More Word of Warning

Many investment advisors and financial planners will not understand all the benefits of an investment-grade indexed UL insurance contract or even for a whole life insurance contract.

Here are a few of the arguments you are likely to hear from opponents who don't fully understand the concepts and how they work in concert with your H.E.R.O. Solution™ plan:

- *"These insurance products are new and don't have a track record."* On the surface, it appears there is no actual return history to report. But in reality, it's an easy exercise to look back at a long-term history of the underlying index to see what the return would have been through simple back-testing against the index history as far back as records exist. Therefore, a 20-year, 30-year or more histories could easily be and have been created.

- *"You don't get the full stock market index return."* Yes, it is true. The caps in your particular contract may limit the returns you experience, but remember, you have down-side protection in those years where the market produces a negative return and loses principal. Additionally, some crediting methods average the return of the index, which could result in receiving a higher gain than the market index gave. Your return is only calculated on the gains of the stocks in the index and not the dividends paid by some of the underlying companies. The concrete bonus of no principal loss is worth those trade-offs for my cash, but the individual investor must make that decision. The tax-treatment of gains and tax-favored accessibility are additional bonuses you don't get with a stock market investment, even in a tax-postponed retirement account.

- *"You are paying for insurance you don't need."* I addressed this issue a few paragraphs back. The ultimate cost of insurance, if your plan is put together correctly, amounts to no more than the expenses of management fees usually involved in mutual fund investing. At *Business Week Online,* an article recently discussed modern insurance policies compared to those purchased a decade ago. The article stated, *"Universal life policies bought at today's lower rates could produce pleasant upside surprises."* Also, who's to say you're getting insurance you don't need. If the worst were to happen, your family would be happy you were spending that 1%–1.25% on insurance instead of paying mutual fund expense fees.

- *"You'd get a better return invested in a variable insurance product."* It is true that variable universal life and variable whole life insurance contracts would work with this plan, but those contracts are considered securities by the SEC. Your money is actually invested in the market and has no down-side protection from loss. Additionally, the overhead costs are higher in these contracts due, in part, to their stock market activities and SEC expenses. Usually, your cost of insurance, over time, comes in at around 3% annually in a variable policy. All things considered, the yields are pretty much equal in the end. And don't forget the indexed UL contract guarantees your money from loss.
- *"You'd be better off in the stock market through an index fund."* That's according to what you mean by "better off." You could put your money into an actual index mutual fund and reap the benefits of the total market return, but you could also lose a large portion of your principal and not recover for years. If you had deposited cash into an index fund in January of 2000, you would still be trying to regain your cash from those years of losses. Wouldn't that have really produced a zero return for over five years? This real possibility exists anytime you are fully exposed to market risks and can lose your precious cash. What you also lose by being in the market is the tax-favored treatment you get with an insurance contract. If your vehicle isn't shielded from taxation, your 11% market return becomes a 7.4% return in a tax-deferred retirement account after taxes. That same 11% market return becomes between 8–9% in

a taxable account with a combination of capital gains and dividend income taxation. Let's not forget index funds and other mutual funds additionally charge expenses and fees which reduce those yields.

So What Should You Take Away From This Chapter?

You have a multitude of places you can accumulate and grow your life's wealth. Some of them are highly risky and some are extremely safe. Some will be taxed along the way, some are tax-postponed and some avoid taxes altogether. The choices can be confusing and scary.

I don't know about you, but I'd rather just do what the wealthy do. I'd want to lock-in the principal, shield it from loss and take a return that's indexed to the major stock markets but not actually in the market. Especially when my costs work out to be about the same or less than mutual fund management fees and there's a great chance the returns could be about equal in most market environments.

Oh, and let's not forget ... life insurance protection just comes along for the ride. It's almost a no-brainer!

Want to know more of the tactics the wealthy use? How about becoming your own bank? You can use your current equity to begin your personal banking empire. Never again go to a brick-and-mortar bank to borrow money for autos, boats, trips or college tuition. Plan to become the *Bank of Yourself.* Want to know how? Details are in the next chapter ...

CHAPTER EIGHT

BECOME YOUR OWN BANK

Your Personal Unemployment Crisis

Unemployed equity is opportunity lost. It's idle cash lying around doing nothing to increase your wealth. In fact, it's probably dropping in true value due to inflation. How can you solve this personal unemployment crisis? You can become your own bank and hire your house.

In order to achieve full employment of your assets, you must separate your equity and move it into your S.A.F.E.T.Y. Fund™. Turbocharge your wealth and do what banks do to create millions. The tax deductibility you receive on your interest paid lowers your true cost of borrowing. Since liquid markets and competition make mortgage money the cheapest money available, the lower net rate you receive after tax benefits makes this debt extremely inexpensive.

The rate paid can be *the same* as the rate earned, and you will still create successful arbitrage resulting in real wealth for yourself. Actually, your rate paid can be *more* than the rate earned, and you will still come out way ahead. But just imagine if you could create a situation where the rate you earn *exceeds* the rate you pay. The magic this produces will blow you away! We're talking serious wealth creation.

Let's say there's $90,000 of idle equity in your home. It could be from a large down payment or from increased equity over time. Whatever the reason, your cash is just sitting there. Your $300,000 house has a current 15-year mortgage with a balance of $150,000. You decide to implement the H.E.R.O. Solution™ to get $90,000 of your equity working.

Let's start with the worst case. We'll say you pay 8%, but only earn 7%. In other words, your mortgage rate is higher than your earning rate for the entire 30 years.

Earning Rate Lower Than Paying Rate

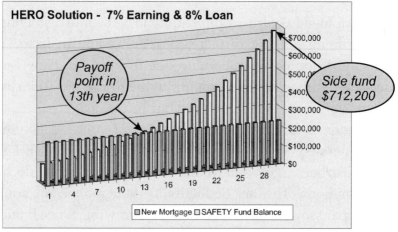

Copyright 2006 HERO Solution, Inc.

At the end of the 360 months, your S.A.F.E.T.Y. Fund™ has a balance of $712,200. After you pay off your mortgage balance, you are left with almost a **half-million dollars**! Yes, you made money paying a higher rate than you earned.

Now, let's look at earning and paying the same rate ... 7.5%:

Earning Rate Same as Paying Rate

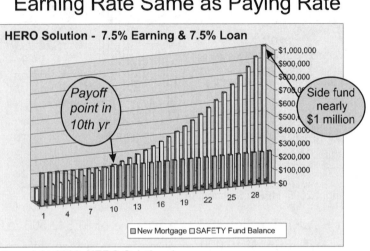

Copyright 2006 HERO Solution, Inc.

If your earning rate and mortgage rate are the SAME, you end up with a S.A.F.E.T.Y. Fund™ balance of **nearly a million dollars.** Should you decide to stop and pay off your mortgage, your remaining cash is **over $750,000**.

Finally, we'll show the most likely scenario. With historical rates back-tested at around 8.5% to 9% in these vehicles, we will still keep the earning rates illustrated as conservative. Let's go with 8% on the earning side and we'll show a borrowing rate of 7%. Your results are astounding ...

Earning Rate Greater Than Paying Rate

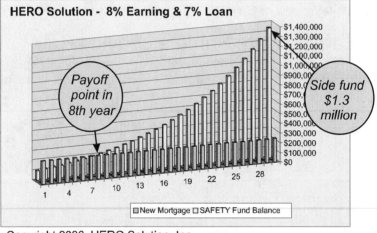

Copyright 2006 HERO Solution, Inc.

Your S.A.F.E.T.Y. Fund™ has a balance of $1,342,500. After paying off your $240,000 mortgage, you are left with $1,100,000 — **over a million dollars!**

You did this with a $90,000 idle equity balance. How amazing!

Why Do Regular Banks Not Want You To Know This?

Look at this from their point of view. Banks love your deposits and they want your cash to stay in their bank. In fact, they spend millions on advertising to lure you into placing your dollars in their banks. They give away all sorts of free stuff and plan gimmicks to get you as a customer. Why?

If you open an account with them, you will likely place more than just your checking account money with them. There's a good chance you will open a savings account, money market account or CD with them, too. You become their source of borrowing. They want your money to create the debt side of their arbitrage[41] plan. Your deposits become their liability or the debt side of their balance sheet. The longer the banks have your cash to invest elsewhere, the more profits they make.

So, what do banks do with your deposit? They lend your money out or "invest" it. They may invest it in other banks or lend it out as auto loans, commercial loans or personal loans. This use of their customer's money (OPM) allows them to make higher returns and keep the differ-ence, or the spread.[42] I've just described arbitrage which, according to Investopedia.com, is *"Also known as a riskless profit."* Arbitrage is the business plan of all banks.

> **Arbitrage** — *Often called "riskless profit." It's simply how banks work.*

Why Do Banks Want You To Believe The Old Way Is The Best Way?

If it's good for the bank, then it must be bad for consumer, right? Guess what ... banks love 15-year mortgages. Yes, those old traditional 15-year, pay-it-off-quicker types of home finance. It's evident because they offer slightly lower rates to lure you to take them. The shorter time they tie up their invested cash, the lower their risk of market change. They know time has a large affect on money, so they want to tie up or lock in their money for shorter terms whenever possible.

---

[41] Buying in one market to make gains on the sale in another.
[42] The spread is the difference between the borrowing rate and the investing rate. It is what determines the level of success in arbitrage.

Banks also love bi-weekly payments. Most banks servicing your mortgage will happily set up a bi-weekly payment plan for free. They want movement of cash toward them whenever possible.

Money received today is worth more to banks than money received tomorrow. That is a basic fact of finance. But isn't it funny? Most borrowers don't know this and the bank certainly isn't going to tell them. The effects of inflation and the shrinking of a dollar over time make banks want to scramble for cash now. They know future dollars will be worth much less.

> "A banker is a fellow who lends you his umbrella when the sun is shining and wants it back the minute it begins to rain."
> — Mark Twain, 1853–1910

Wouldn't it, therefore, make sense to put off paying for your house as long as possible? If you could buy a house for $300,000 today and delay handing over that $300,000 cash until 30 years from now, wouldn't those dollars look like a wool sweater after going through the dryer by then. Think about what a dollar would buy in the mid-1970s and what that same dollar buys today.

Future Dollars, Present Dollars, Past Dollars — Isn't A Dollar Just A Dollar?

The Federal Reserve Bank of Minneapolis has a great calculator on their website called "What Is A Dollar Worth?" which applies the historic CPI[43] to the value of a dollar in any

---

[43] The Consumer Price Index (CPI) is a measure of the average change in prices over time in a market basket of goods and services. It's a practical way to calculate inflation's affect on our spendable cash.

year between 1913 and 2006. It's fun to put in different amounts into their calculator to see what inflation does to the cash over time. I used this tool to compare 1976 dollars to 2006 dollars in the following example.

If you weren't an adult in the 1970s, just pretend you were. Let's say you bought a nice watch in 1976 for $700. We'll not use the brand name, but it was a nice Swiss timepiece. The jeweler said, "Just take it and wear it for 30 years. Come back in 2006 and pay me then." You go back to the store after that time has passed and look in their window. The same watch you got 30 years earlier is now displayed with a price tag of $2500. "Wow, what a fantastic move I made!" you say to yourself. You go inside, proudly hand over the $700 and leave the store with a spring in your step. See what inflation does to purchasing power over time?

How great would it be to be able to buy something for a dollar today and not have to hand that dollar over for 30 years when it is so much less? If inflation stayed at the same rates we have experienced and you got another brand-name Swiss watch from that jeweler today, what do you think the $2500 price tag would change to when you came back in 2036? A whopping $9,000!

Isn't this type of delay exactly what we are doing when we take out a mortgage? Isn't an interest-only loan the purest form of postponing the transfer of the cash until your dollars are mere shadows of their former selves?

Those With Real Wealth Vision™
Think Like Banks — Not Like Borrowers

The financially astute understand the paramount importance of becoming their own bank. They know to utilize all assets at their disposal to maximize the magic of compounding over their lifetimes. Real Wealth Vision™ allows them to see the big picture and always maximize their financial potential.

The wealthy follow all these steps:

First — Don't just work for money; make your money work for you.

Second — Have all your own dollars feverishly compounding for you.

Third — Get other people's money (OPM) employed and compounding for you.

These principles, in concert, will create Real Wealth over time. Arbitrage, which is the third component listed, really boosts your success to the next level. Acquire the most cash you can possibly access at favorable mortgage rates and terms. Borrow present-value[44] dollars and delay the repayment as long as possible. The arbitrage magic reveals true results with this formula.

Why do you suppose banks promote traditional amortizing mortgages? This form of lending causes constant cash flow toward them, not away from them. With a steady stream of incoming cash, their position of safety is increased and incrementally better over time. Remember, a dollar today is worth more than a dollar in the future. Every payment makes the borrower's position weakened.

15-year Mortgage — The Most Expensive Type You Can Get

Well, that statement isn't quite true. Actually a 10-year amortizing mortgage wins the award for the most expensive

---

[44] What a dollar is worth today.

out there. Why do banks reward 15-year mortgages by offering slightly lower rates? Why do they promote bi-weekly payment plans and often offer to set them up automatically for free?

You've got it. Banks want today's dollars, not tomorrow's dollars. Their position of strength grows faster as your loan balance shrinks. Also, if they receive your money back quicker, they can put it to use elsewhere, all over again. While the bank is growing stronger and receiving a slow and steady monthly cash infusion into the their coffers, you are doing away with your own opportunities to invest your valuable dollars elsewhere. Your personal wealth is not being enhanced in this process.

In addition to making you progressively less safe with the passage of time, monthly amortizing moves you away from accessibility to your cash. The portion of your monthly payment going to non-productive equity progressively increases. If your equity payment is becoming bigger and bigger, what is then becoming smaller and smaller? You're right — your tax deduction.

You incrementally slash those wonderful IRS benefits with every month that passes. You purposefully shrink your refund check each and every year. The shorter the amortization time of your mortgage, the faster you cut your tax advantages.

Why Do Those With Real Wealth Vision™ Carry Large 30-year Mortgages?

The financially astute respect the principles of lost opportunity cost and take steps to avoid them. Systematically reducing their mortgage eliminates alternate investment opportunities for their cash, so they know that getting an amortizing and shorter-term mortgage isn't a wealth building activity. Guaranteeing years of a zero return on a present dollar just doesn't make sense.

The astute have better places to put their precious present dollars. Places that enhance their personal wealth. Since they understand the value of tax deduction opportunities, they maximize their IRS benefits each and every year.

The size of the mortgage they select is also important when buying or refinancing their house. Those with Real Wealth Vision™ always maintain the largest sensible mortgage balance possible. Not putting down more cash than necessary when they purchase real estate frees up more cash flow and increases their future tax advantages.

> *Extra principal payments receive a guaranteed zero return on today's valuable present-value dollars. They also create losses of potential future income from tax deductions.*

The same principle applies when considering extra principal payments. They simply would never pay more than the required minimum. To do so would be counterproductive to wealth building. Don't you think there are much better uses for that money?

Why Do Smaller Mortgages With Lower Payments Actually Cost You More?

Of course, a large down payment produces a smaller mortgage. By now I'm sure you see that a lower mortgage balance produces lower tax deductions and fewer tax refunds. Your big equity is sitting idly by earning a zero rate of return and producing huge opportunity costs for you over time. This position also places you farther away from safety, while the bank is enjoying increased security. All things considered, that small mortgage is extremely expensive.

Can you see that a large down payment is probably the worst place you could put any present day cash? Aren't extra principal payments and short-term amortizing loans with increasing principal portions just monthly down payments?

Let me ask you this. Would you wallpaper the hallways in your home with real dollar bills? Picture yourself, every month, systematically cashing your paycheck, going home with handfuls of fresh dollars and gluing them to your walls, one by one, month by month, year by year. How smart would that be? Not a very good use for your hard earned income. Just think of the lost wealth-producing opportunities and the ignored tax deductions over time.

> *The smaller your mortgage — the higher your rate. Lenders make their profit on a percentage basis; so borrowers with bigger loans are usually offered better terms.*

Now think about this. Wouldn't paying cash for a house be the largest down payment you could make? Really — how wise is traditional wisdom?

When Would You Want An Adjustable-Rate Mortgage?

30-year fixed-rate mortgages were designed in the Depression era and were based on Depression-era thinking. In today's world, who keeps the same mortgage or even lives in the same house for 30 years?

Every time you get a loan, you should ask yourself these questions. How long do you plan to keep the mortgage you're getting? How long do you plan to live in your house?

America is a highly mobile society. There's a good chance the mortgage you got when you bought your house will be

> The average person in this country changes residences every 6½ years.
>
> — *National Association of Realtors*

refinanced at least once and maybe several times during the time you live in your house.

Most adjustable-rate mortgages (ARMs) offer lower rates than the prevailing fixed-rate mortgage on any given day. Many initial rate-lock periods are offered for adjustable rate loans. This means you can get competitive agency-backed loans in which your rate is fixed for a period of time that could include three years, five years, seven years and ten years. You can enjoy a rate for that entire initial fixed-rate period which would be lower than the fixed-rate loan that would have been available on the day you locked your rate.

Granted, when you keep the adjustable-rate mortgage beyond those initial fixed years, your loan will convert to a 1-year adjustable-rate loan automatically. But, think about it. Why would you keep it beyond that fixed time? If you planned to re-evaluate your equity position and harvest your cash every three or five years, wouldn't you be getting a new mortgage, anyway? If you planned to live in your home for only the time of the initial fixed period, wouldn't you be getting a new house and a new mortgage by then? So, does it really matter what happens after the initial fixed period? No. You don't care. Your strategic plan is to get a new loan before then.

This type of mortgage product is best for people that plan to move or refinance within the initial time period. What the loan does after you have enjoyed the lower fixed rate your loan product provided should be of no concern to you. All you care about is the great arbitrage you have set up by taking a shorter-term loan product.

Alan Greenspan, former chairman of the Federal Reserve board, in remarks to the Credit Union National Association,[45] stated the following:

> "One way homeowners attempt to manage their payment risk is to use fixed-rate mortgages, which typically allow homeowners to prepay their debt when interest rates fall but do not involve an increase in payments when interest rates rise. Homeowners pay a lot of money for the right to refinance and for the insurance against increasing mortgage payments. Calculations by market analysts of the "option adjusted spread" on mortgages suggest that the **cost of** these benefits conferred by **fixed-rate mortgages** can range from **0.5 percent to 1.2 percent,** *raising homeowners' annual after-tax mortgage payments by several thousand dollars.* Indeed, recent research within the Federal Reserve suggests that many homeowners might have saved tens of thousands of dollars had they held adjustable-rate mortgages rather than fixed-rate mortgages during the past decade ..."
>
> — Alan Greenspan

In other words, fixed-rate mortgages cost the homeowner big time. His calculations say you are paying from half of a percent to over an entire percent more when you get a fixed-rate loan. Even taking into account the tax advantages, the homeowner still pays tens of thousands of dollars more by taking fixed-rate mortgages.

---

[45] At the Credit Union National Association 2004 Governmental Affairs Conference, Washington, D.C., February 23, 2004.

Adjustable-rate mortgages fit the H.E.R.O. Solution™ strategic planning model. Since the recommended plan includes evaluating your position, considering and usually acquiring a new mortgage every three to five years, why would you pay the extra thousands per year to get a fixed-rate loan? Short-term borrowing needs should utilize short-term loans.

> *"... the traditional fixed-rate mortgage may be an expensive method of financing a home."*
> — Alan Greenspan

OK. I'll concede there are probably uses for the 30-year fixed-rate mortgage. If you are going to buy your house, live in it for 30 years, let your idle cash build up earning zero rate of return and never, ever consider moving again, physically or financially, then it may be the right loan for you. Otherwise, you are leaving huge amounts of cash on the table and wasting them again and again every year.

What's The #1 Choice Of Those With Real Wealth Vision™?

Now that you know an adjustable-rate mortgage offers you a lower rate, what if you could go a step farther? Remember, we discussed how you could completely avoid the systematic pay down of your loan balance? What if you were allowed to keep your mortgage balance high over the course of your entire loan? A loan like this could really provide some serious benefits.

As mentioned in Chapter Five, a single variation in your loan could offer you all the following:

- Reduce your monthly payment.
- Keep your tax refund at high levels every year of your loan.
- Stop the systematic, counterproductive pay down of your balance.
- Slow equity build-up inside your house earning a zero return.
- Allow you to borrow a larger loan amount.
- Possibly qualify you for a larger home purchase.

Do you remember what type of loan can do all this? Yes, it's the *interest-only mortgage*.[46] You can get this type of loan in many forms. They come as 30-year fixed ones. You can get 15-year interest-only versions that convert to amortized loans for the last 15 years. Of course, all the fixed-period adjustable rate mortgages, ARMs, come in interest-only versions. The list is almost endless.

If this one type of loan can do all these great things for you, why doesn't everyone use it? It's the old Depression-era thinking again. Everyone wants the good ol' 30-year or 15-year amortized loans. They just don't think it through. Or maybe they don't think at all.

---

[46] As I mentioned earlier, don't confuse "interest-only" mortgages with "Option ARM" mortgages. The interest-only mortgages recommended here have rates fixed for definite periods of time and don't allow negative amortization. Pay Option ARMs can be beneficial to the sophisticated borrower, but should be carefully evaluated with a competent advisor.

Sometimes, you wonder if everyone gets what they always got simply because they always got it. Perhaps they always got it because everyone else always got it. Here we go again following along with all the other lemmings over the cliff. Everyone is doing it, so it must be the prudent thing to do. Right?

Think Before You're Led To Disaster

Doing what everyone else has always done can often lead to some extremely undesirable consequences. How about losing your home completely, along with all that hard-earned equity? I know it sounds unlikely, but you'll be surprised to learn it has happened to the well educated and even some of the famous among us.

If you'd like to learn how to protect your equity and other assets from being snatched away from you, you'll be interested in the stories in the next chapter ...

CHAPTER NINE

HOME INSECURITY

America's passion for homeownership should never be underestimated. Calling it the "American Dream" isn't merely a slogan, but instead a bedrock value. Owning a piece of property — a home of one's own — has been central to our country's values since Plymouth Rock. Our homes are the foundation of our culture. They're where we sleep, where we eat with our family and where we spend time together.

Homes are also central to community life. Remember the image of Tom Sawyer, the classic symbol of Americana, painting the fence and luring his pals to do his work? That proverbial picket fence will always be our home's first impression to the community. It represents our pride and our self-image to the world. We should never take this classic imagery or the passion for homeownership lightly.

When speaking of community, a recent poignant image comes to mind of a small southern coastal city. Shortly after Hurricane Katrina ravaged New Orleans, a second massive storm barreled into the Gulf Coast. It barely missed Galveston and made landfall just north in this little town. Wind damage brought its usual calamity, along with subsequent ripple-effect events of devastation. Many homes were lost.[47]

A reporter appeared with the mayor of that town in a network-news broadcast. She asked, *"So, mayor how are you holding up? Your city is in shambles and we understand you lost your own home in the aftermath. Can you tell us how you feel?"*

"Yes," the mayor replied. *"Our home was completely destroyed. We have nothing left. And, the sad thing was — we had just paid it off!"*

You'll notice he didn't say, "*… and the FORTUNATE thing was — we had just paid it off!"*

No!

He said, "*… and the SAD thing was — we had just paid it off!"*

What Does The Mayor's Regrettable Story Teach Us?

When disaster strikes, would you rather be standing in front of a news camera, like the mayor, telling the world your heartbreaking story or would you, instead, prefer to be proclaiming into the microphone, *"We were certainly blessed. Our home was destroyed, but we had that house mortgaged to the hilt since we bought it. All of our equity was safely separated into a side account. We've got quick access to all the cash we need now to see us through this temporary crisis. I'm really glad we had focused on the big picture and planned for emergencies like this!"*

---

[47] Hurricane Rita caused 10 billion dollars in damage on the U.S. Gulf Coast in September 2005.

Do you think you are safe with big equity in your house? Low mortgage balances and high equity values give you a false sense of security. Although it sounds counterintuitive, the larger your mortgage and the lower your equity position, the safer you will be. It's not the other way around, like most people think. We should re-evaluate the desirability of hefty amounts of cash inside our homes. Traditional wisdom preaches to "eliminate your mortgage and have a paid-off house." When crisis strikes or catastrophe calls, that kind of wisdom could possibly wipe your wealth away in one fell swoop.

Why are we safer with a large mortgage? If all your cash is tied up in a place where you can't get to it, what happens in emergencies? You really don't have control when most of your assets are bricked behind the walls. You have fewer options when you must go through a time-consuming mortgage process to get to your cash. You are vulnerable to market conditions, at risk in crisis and much less safe. If you are experiencing a job loss or temporary disability, getting a new mortgage could be difficult, if not impossible. How safe is that? Who is in control in that situation?

Being house-rich and cash-poor can be a recipe for disaster. This outdated wisdom can leave you in an undesirable position. Most of us just go along doing what we've always done, letting our equity grow and chipping away at that "terrible, big, bad" mortgage. Often, with the rapid appreciation occurring in many areas, we have massive amounts of cash building up that we may never see. It could all be taken away from us in an instant.

Our Senator From Mississippi and Hurricane Katrina

Let's look at a news story involving one of our United States senators. On December 17, 2005, SunHerald.com printed an interview with one of our senators from the State of Mississippi. The reporter said the senator appeared to be frustrated and angry as he spoke. His quote, shown in the box on this page, reveals he had nearly half of his retirement savings stored in his "paid-off" vacation home on the Gulf Coast. The house had been his nest egg for retirement and he lost it to Katrina.

When Hurricane Katrina hit, his beautiful home was destroyed. Initially, I would imagine, he wasn't terribly worried, since he believed his insurance would replace the house. Even if his coverage hadn't been raised to keep up with the increasing costs of new home construction, it would still be enough to rebuild something close to what he had. Then horrors of horrors became reality. His insurance company told him his home was lost to flood waters and not wind. Since his flood insurance was limited, the insurance check would not replace his home.

> *"That was my nest egg. It was about half my net worth. I have a $400,000 loss after the flood insurance. Its appraised value was probably $600,000 to $700,000, but I had been offered more to sell it. That was the first thing I ever had that was paid for. The hurricane certainly complicated my decision across the board. From a personal standpoint, I need a little more income."*
> — Trent Lott, U.S. Senator, SunHerald.com

Half of his nest egg — GONE! His beautiful second home — GONE! But, he had followed traditional wisdom and he probably thought he had a smart plan with a free-and-clear house for his retirement. Was there any way he could have known how insecure he really was?

Expecting The Unexpected

Probably hundreds, maybe thousands, of families lost much of their assets in hurricane disasters in the fall of 2005. Many had insurance coverage, yet received no compensation for their losses. Underinsurance coupled with lack of coverage for specific hazards probably created hundreds of millions of dollars of lost wealth for the victims on the coast.

Why, would you suppose, access to our assets and liquidity in crisis is so important? If those homeowners had removed their equity, had not put down big payments, had not paid off their homes, but, instead, had liberated their wealth, pulled it out as it grew and placed it safely into a compounding accessible side account, their destinies would have been changed forever.

Pretend for a moment that you are a resident of the Gulf Coast and you have just survived that horrific storm. It's the morning after the storm and the day is now dawning. Think about how you feel as you gaze into that sunrise, knowing you have options. Long before the storm hit, you had scooped up your largest asset and protected it from decimation. Your money is now safely tucked away and waiting for you. You can do whatever is best for you and your family.

While others are up against the wall, forced into situations because of limited choices, you are completely free to do as you see fit. You have time, you have choices, you have freedom and, most importantly — you have power. There's no better feeling than knowing you are in total control of your life and your destiny.

What Is Liquidity?

Liquidity is a term you may have heard being bantered about by the talking heads on CNBC or by your own financial advisor. But do you really know what it means?

In the financial world, liquidity means "the ability to access your cash." It's that simple. An example of a liquid account would be a checking account. If you need your cash, you just pop a card into an ATM. You could also write a check. Your money is readily available to you.

There are varying degrees of liquidity. A money market account is readily available by just writing a check on the funds. If you have money in a mutual fund or a stock, even though you must wait three days before your check can actually be cut and sent out to you, it is still categorized by the financial community as a liquid investment. Of course, cash in a jar buried in your back yard is extremely liquid, if you can remember where you buried it. (That safety may also be questionable if your back yard is 10 feet under water.) Pardon the pun …

Stocks and mutual funds don't possess the level of liquidity inherent to immediate cash accounts, like savings, checking and money markets. A bank CD, even though you might have to pay a penalty for early withdrawal, is also categorized as very liquid.

On the other hand, cash inside real estate is considered completely illiquid. Quick access is blocked. In other words, you can't get to it without a lot of time and effort.

Why do those with Real Wealth Vision™ understand the value of liquidity? Because they keep a big-picture view of their total wealth picture, they place a huge significance on accessibility, control and freedom. Protecting their choices, maintaining options and safeguarding their principal are always in the forefront of their planning strategy.

When You Need Your Equity The Most, Why Is It So Hard To Get To It?

When we store our equity inside our house, it is blocked from our reach. The process we must endure to remove any of it can be tedious and time-consuming. Understanding these constraints, applying for a mortgage and waiting for the closing to get our cash is often impractical in times of crisis or immediate need. Additionally, the reason for our cash needs may be a temporary or permanent disability. That's not good. You know banks and lending institutions lend you money based on your ability to repay the loan. If you are unemployed or disabled, your ability to get a loan drops dramatically. It can often be impossible.

> *In reality, a home mortgaged to the hilt provides the greatest safety for the homeowner.*

When you lose your job, your expenses don't stop. In fact, disability can actually increase your expenses due to possible medical costs. Eliminating a mortgage doesn't end property taxes, homeowner's insurance fees, structure maintenance costs and utility bills. Access to your deliberately-built equity disappears when you have no income. This is just when you need your locked-away cash the most.

Having your equity separated, readily accessible and growing in a S.A.F.E.T.Y. Fund™ is a crucial step in the smart planning for your family's security. It could see you through financial storms and actually save you from losing your home in emergencies.

Let me tell you what happened with two Illinois families after the technology sector losses in the stock market back in 2000.

A TECH-WRECK STORY

This story is about some clients of our firm. For sake of privacy, we'll call them George and Mary. They both worked at a large technology company that mainly supported the economy in a small suburb in Illinois. Like many of our clients, we had done multiple mortgages for them over the years. They normally made substantial down payments when they purchased and took out 15-year loans. In recent months, they had taken a hard look at what they were doing and had made some decisions to change a few things.

In 1998, they bought a new home in a suburb near their company, but decided to put down only 20% to avoid mortgage insurance expenses and they took out a 10/1 interest-only ARM loan. These are loans that require only interest to be paid for the first 10 years. They knew they would be moving or refinancing before that time, so they were comfortable with the program.

They took the remaining profits from the sale of their prior house and placed them into a S.A.F.E.T.Y. Fund™ that would grow in a tax-favored environment. Additionally, they took the difference between the 15-year payment they would have made and the new, lower interest-only payment and socked it away into their S.A.F.E.T.Y. Fund™ each month.

They really had no additional monthly expenses, but now they had a fairly large amount of cash reserves readily available.

Shortly thereafter, one of their co-workers was looking for a new house and was referred to us by George and Mary. He worked at the large technology company. His wife worked in a supporting industry. They were in much the same financial situation as George and Mary. Again, for privacy, we'll call this new couple Tony and Cynthia.

Tony was a real company man. He had always contributed the maximum into his company-sponsored 401(k). To achieve the greatest matching benefit, he had placed all his funds into company stock. Over the years it had become a tidy sum.

(continued)

The house they bought was quite similar and in a nearby neighborhood. Tony and Cynthia made a substantial profit from the sale of their current house, so they wanted to make a very large down payment. Also, they insisted on a 15-year mortgage because they truly believed it was smarter, more fiscally conservative and just the right thing to do. Although we explained the virtues of a longer mortgage term, they would hear of nothing else.

Were Tony and Cynthia really more conservative and in a safer position than George and Mary? Let's see how events unfolded.

Then came the tech-stock debacle of 2000. Their company stock plummeted and business fell off dramatically. The entire division was eventually closed which meant massive unemployment. George, Mary and Tony all lost their jobs. Since Cynthia's employer depended on the technology company, she was also laid off. The area was flooded with houses for sale.

Tony and Cynthia tried to find new jobs, but with so many unemployed in their town, it just didn't happen. They used up their small savings and tried to get a home equity loan, but no bank would lend to an unemployed applicant.

He asked the mortgage company if they would consider the bi-weekly payments he had been making as extra payments, so he would be allowed to skip a few months of his monthly amount due. He thought they might let him coast a while since he had paid in advance. Of course, that's not how a lender sees prepayments. His full mortgage payment was due every month, anyway. After trying to keep up with their larger 15-year payments, they gave up and put their house on the market. Sadly, they were going to have to sacrifice the dream home they had fallen in love with less than 2 years before.

They put it up for sale and months passed with no offers. In an attempt to attract a quick buyer, they reduced the price to below what they had paid for it. Still ... no buyers. They were realizing, first hand, the "major industry/small town" effect that is created when large numbers of workers are laid off. There were many homes for sale and very few potential buyers. Nobody was even shopping for a house.

(continued)

As they began to worry about falling behind on their payments, they went to borrow money from their 401(k). No longer an employee of the company, Tony was not allowed to borrow from his company retirement plan. Sadly, most of their retirement investments had been in the company stock, including the company matching.

Now that the market price had plummeted, the retirement account was only a shadow of its former self. They had to liquidate their retirement savings while the stock value was at an all-time low. That's what happens when your choices and freedoms are eliminated.

Then, to add insult to injury, their tiny balance was hit with income taxes plus an additional 10% penalty for early withdrawal. Ouch!

They did fall behind on their payments, but eventually reduced the price and sold their house for just a little more than the remaining balance, which included a negative escrow balance from taxes paid and their back payments missed.

Tony and Cynthia were left with no retirement funds, no house, no jobs and very little cash. Their financial situation had almost been destroyed.

But, what about George and Mary? Remember, they worked at the same company along with Tony. How did they fare?

George and Mary had gotten a great big mortgage on their new place and they had taken all their equity cash (which, by the way, was capital gains tax-free) and socked it away into their S.A.F.E.T.Y. Fund™. They'd also been putting the difference they were saving with the lower interest-only loan into their S.A.F.E.T.Y. Fund™ every month.

Throughout their unemployment, they were comfortably able to make the lower interest-only mortgage payments and they rode out the employment storm by accessing their set-aside cash. After about a year, they both found other jobs and held onto their beautiful home. In retrospect, they were certainly glad they hadn't continued on the path of traditional wisdom.

Whose plan was really wiser in the end?

As I said in a prior chapter, most financial planners, ever sticking with conventional wisdom, would have advised anyone to follow the path taken by Tony and Cynthia. Getting the smallest mortgage possible and a 15-year loan is what the masses believe to be the frugal thing to do. Additionally, that same advisor would have told you to deposit the largest percentage allowed into your 401(k) to get maximum company matching. You saw what that move did for Tony. Knowing how that financial choice decimated his wealth, do you believe following traditional advice was really the wisest move?

Clearly, the less money you have and the less stable your job, the more reason to have a big mortgage with a long amortization time or no amortization at all. But even if you think your employment is secure, events change things. The economy can take sharp turns and leave you in the cold.

After you unexpectedly lose your job, it is just too late to go out and borrow against the cash you have paid into your home. Also, as it accumulates over the years, your property's appreciation dollars are out of your reach. When you need money the most, you may not be able to get it. For the most part, home equity is just illiquid. This is certainly valid evidence that the traditional wisdom and supposed conservative practices of homeownership taught in the past will actually make you more vulnerable and less safe.

But Those Bad Things Only Happen To Other People. Not To Me ...

Sounds strangely similar to the famous last words in a movie.

Financial calamities pop up all the time. Often, they hit the homeowner suddenly and without warning. In the late 1980s,

> *"A bank is a place that will lend you money if you can prove you don't need it."*
> — Bob Hope, 1903–2003

as many as 10 times the current number of home defaults occurred in the "Oil Patch" area of Texas. The market was flooded with homes for sale and more than 15,000 families went into default. It took over 10 years for many to recover and some never did. My personal accountant moved from Texas to the Chicago suburbs to escape that impacted economic area. He owned a home there and was unable to sell it. He finally did find a buyer much later, but only after years of astute property management and making concurrent payments on two properties for quite a while.

Silicon Valley experienced effects in 2000 that were similar to our Illinois tech company problem. I'm sure the unemployed in California during those years could tell many similar and sad stories.

> *"Nearly half of all mortgage foreclosures are due to a disability."*
> — Housing and Home Finance Agency, U.S. Government

Overall, the chance of disability in your working lifetime is pretty high, but your chance of experiencing financial hardships is even greater. Unexpected job loss and budget-busting medical expenses are more likely to hit a family than even temporary physical disability. These events can handicap your ability to get to your equity. Why? You must have a job to get a loan.

Don't Banks Lend Money Based
On The Equity In Your House?

Banks lend on your ability to pay, not on your equity position. If you have a tiny loan balance with a huge home value but don't have a job, you'll most likely be unable to get a mortgage. The main stipulation for loan approval is current employment.

Even your "no-income-verification" and "stated-income" loans require you to have a minimum two-year stable job or documentable history of self-employment at the time your loan is approved and closed. Telephone verifications are done prior to closing your loan to verify the employment status of the applicant. The only time you could acquire a loan without an active job position is when you can prove a multi-year trail of passive income from other sources.

If you've got other true sources of income, you're probably not in a financial predicament that would force you to need a new mortgage. Right? This is usually not the case for those in temporary income crisis.

Even if your home is paid off completely, the bank still lends based on your monthly income. You must prove it is stable and likely to continue. Situations of hardships often damage your ability to get a loan just when you need one the most.

So, Banks Put A Lien On My House,
But I'm Not Borrowing On My House?

Financial institutions lend against your monthly stable income for repayment, but they simply attach your house as collateral to protect them in the event of foreclosure. The value of your property is considered in the loan approval because the banks know a borrower will work harder to make his payments if he's got a large amount of his own cash in the collateral.

If big equity in your house makes the bank's position stronger, what does this mean for you, the borrower? You're smart, you've got that one figured out. You are in a weaker position than the lender when your equity is high.[48]

You can have a beautiful and valuable house with no mortgage balance remaining, but that position alone doesn't guarantee you a loan. This remains true even when your employment predicament is temporary. Strong and long job time, steady income and good credit scores are the strengths that get you a loan. Unemployment doesn't bode well for approval. Often, in situations of job loss, disability or medical issues, credit problems begin to bloom. Recent late payments can devastate your credit scores, which are the pivotal element in the decision to lend you money.

> *"I believe that banking institutions are more dangerous to our liberties than standing armies."*
> *"... [The banks] will deprive the people of all property until their children wake-up homeless on the continent their fathers conquered."*
> —Thomas Jefferson, 1743–1826, *in a letter to the Secretary of the Treasury, Albert Gallatin in 1802*

---

[48] Lenders refer to this as LTV, or your loan-to-value ratio. It's your loan amount divided by the value of your house. A small loan compared to a larger house value, or low LTVs, puts the lender in a stronger position.

"Why should I worry about the chance of disability?"

The number one reason for home foreclosure in America is disability. When this word is mentioned, most of us think of physical disability, but financial disability is also a very real threat. When we lose our job or become unable to work, additional financial liabilities often come along for the ride.

Your ability to keep all your monthly payments current and protect your credit scores become unimportant when you're having difficulty feeding your family and keeping utility companies from disconnecting your gas or electric service. You find yourself thrown back into the very basics: first food, then clothing, then shelter. You remember Maslow's Hierarchy?[49] Getting food and keeping warm often become priorities over paying those pesky monthly payments.

But, here's the problem. The inability to keep up payments places you at risk of foreclosure. Yes, they can come and take away that lovely house, even if your equity position is high. You don't continue your monthly payments, you lose your house — even if you've paid extra payments in the past or made a huge down payment when you bought it.

If you had separated that equity[50] and sheltered it into an accessible, safe side fund, you could tap it to make your payments. Those funds could see you through your rough spots and put your concerns at ease. Think how great it would be to have options if catastrophe were to strike. You would keep control and have power over your life.

---

[49] A theory in psychology, proposed by Abraham Maslow in 1943, which contends that humans meet basic needs in a successively "higher needs" order or hierarchy.
[50] Since Texas laws limit cash-out refinances, one solution would be to sell and buy a new home as your equity grows, always getting the maximum mortgage you can handle. Then, each time, place your proceeds in your S.A.F.E.T.Y. Fund™ to build your wealth. Always check with your tax advisor.

I don't know about you, but I would rather be in that position of power, maintaining control over my life, than the alternative position of helplessness and vulnerability. Wouldn't you?

Speaking Of Vulnerability ... You Could Be Painting A Big Bull's-Eye On Your House

Let's say you go through your whole life dodging the bullet of physical disability or job loss. Maybe you have been a diligent saver and have a large amount of assets set aside to see you through those possibilities. Hooray for you! You've been lucky and you've been a shrewd planner. But, do you really have a smart, secure plan with that low mortgage or paid-off house?

Have you thought about lawsuit liability? Did you know that mortgages are public record? Anyone, including an attorney hired by someone who wants to sue you, can just go down to the courthouse, or even look at the county's website, and see if you have a mortgage. If they did a search on you today, would they find a juicy target or would they come up short?

If you're a potential lawsuit target and are living in a valuable property, the size of your mortgage or lack of a mortgage can make you an attractive, vulnerable and juicy morsel to the circling wolves.

In other words, if you have no mortgage recorded or only a small one showing in the public record, your vulnerability is high. You appear to be a plump source of cash, ready for the taking. On the other hand, if a big mortgage lien is showing against your property, the attorney will be discouraged and advise his client the suit could be fruitless. According to the public record, you aren't a big enough target without a big cash position to pursue.

Your S.A.F.E.T.Y. Fund™ is never public record, yet it's where you've carefully secured all your harvested equity cash. If positioned and established correctly, many attorneys would be unable to discover it and would often be blocked from attaching it.

If you were sued tomorrow, could a predator easily take your largest asset? If you have followed traditional advice, you may be a sitting-target right now.

Are There Other Reasons For Keeping A Large Mortgage?

After the obvious vulnerability vs. strength argument, there are several other reasons for carrying a large loan against your house.

- A low loan or no mortgage at all could reduce your family's eligibility for college grants and loans.
- Risk of neighborhood change, rezoning or economic depreciation may affect your ability to get your equity out in later years.

Many college grant and loan programs list your equity like a cash account. Large equity will hinder your ability to get assistance.

How Can Neighborhood Risks Affect My Ability To Downsize Or Move To Managed-Care In The Future?

Neighborhoods can change. Let's say you have paid off your house and plan to live out your retirement without a mortgage payment. Sounds good, but maybe it isn't always the best long-term strategy.

What if your street is rezoned and that quiet park next door is now a strip mall, causing the value of your house to plummet? What if the blocks all around you slowly begin to suffer economic depreciation? People with the ability to keep up the maintenance of their properties have moved away leaving a neighborhood in disrepair.

Years earlier, you could have liberated the cash value in your home when it was high and put it to work for you. Your S.A.F.E.T.Y. Fund™ would have grown immensely by now. You could easily sell your house, even if the value has dropped. You would have enough to pay off that little deficiency in your mortgage balance from your side funds and, with no trouble, buy another residence anywhere you wish. If you had been smart and planned ahead, you would have recognized, captured and put your money to work when it was real. When the chance to harvest your equity is missed, it becomes a lost opportunity that cannot be retrieved.

What if you now wish to sell your home and buy a smaller one, perhaps in a resort area or managed-care community? If you've invested your retirement into the walls of that house and, over time, your neighborhood has changed and your property value has evaporated, you might not be able to make the move you want. That cash is just gone into thin air. It's lost forever.

Why Is 100% Financed Safer Than Paid-In-Full?

By now, I hope you can see that maximizing your working capital early and often provides you greater opportunity for wealth creation over time. Separating your vital equity is extremely important, whether it originated from cash you paid into your house when you bought it or from pent-up value that has grown due to market appreciation or mortgage pay down. It is absolutely crucial to guarantee your principal is protected in a safe and secure side account.

Your funds should be readily accessible to see you through any potential financial difficulties you could experience due to illness, disability or temporary job loss.

You would also enjoy an added benefit by having a large mortgage recorded against your home. It's just added insurance in our litigious society. Your best pre-emptive move is to keep the largest mortgage possible always recorded to shield your assets.

What Could Stand In The Way Of Your Safety?

Until you have your H.E.R.O. Solution™ in place, your equity removed, your S.A.F.E.T.Y. Fund™ created and your cash protected, time could be your enemy. Today you've got a job and may be perfectly healthy, but that could all change in a flash. The sooner you get your plan secured, the sooner you can have peace of mind.

What if you haven't been much of a saver before now? The wealthy know the tricks that can turbocharge your assets and let you catch up on wealth creation if your balances aren't as large as you want them to be. The next chapter shows how you can catch up and take off toward becoming wealthy.

CHAPTER TEN

H.E.R.O. SOLUTION™ FOR IRA-SAVERS, UNDER-SAVERS AND NON-SAVERS

Maybe you are like the approximately 40 million Baby Boomers barreling down the road-of-life toward retirement who haven't taken the time and trouble to plan for their upcoming largest inevitable liability — their retirement. Like many, you may have not taken the time to even think about it.

But if and when you do think about it, are you engaging in what some psychiatrists call "fantasy thinking"? Are you imagining that you will somehow one day just strike it rich? Your ship will come in? That weekly lottery ticket will finally pay off? If this is the case, are you just hoping the best will somehow magically happen?

OK ... The ad said this all-in-one machine does everything. Where do we click for instructions on what to do with our money? Shouldn't there be a button somewhere?

People, in general, hate to ask for directions when it comes to their personal finances. They may be afraid to find out how much they don't understand. Also, they may find it hard to trust a stranger's advice. Trouble is ... you probably aren't going to tune into the DIY (Do-It-Yourself) Network and suddenly find a weekly program on retirement planning.

This book is a way to get started in the right direction without initially asking for assistance. Eventually — to actually implement your plans — you will need to seek competent professional help, but you can begin to devise these strategies on your own.

Are you bouncing your palm off your forehead about now? OK, so are you coming to a few realizations about your personal planning? If so, are you seeing there may be a solution for your own life's wealth using the ideas presented so far? You may be beginning to grasp what the H.E.R.O. Solution™ could do for you if you've been negligent or deficient in your preparation.

Can you be rescued if you haven't been a very good saver up 'til now? The answer is yes!

Here are a few things a H.E.R.O. Solution™ can do for you:

- **Lets you quickly catch-up on your retirement savings** by creating an immediate, high-balance cash account that will more rapidly churn out some serious tax-advantaged compounded earnings.
- **Allows a lump sum of cash using pre-tax (really no-tax) dollars** in much the same way as a 401(k) or standard IRA payment would be, but without the annual limits on contributions. Ever since the tax law revisions of 1997, your home equity can be accessed without capital gains or income taxes of any kind, within limits.
- **Your earnings grow and compound without being eroded by taxes.** Tax-advantaged growth means your funds earn income and compound over time without being ravaged by capital gains or interest income taxes. A H.E.R.O. Solution™ lets you accumulate much more than you would in a taxable account earning the same return.
- **Increase your monthly cash-to-spend in retirement by up to 50%.** Compared to qualified plans, such as 401(k)s, IRAs, 403(b)s and 457s, a properly structured H.E.R.O. Solution™ can give you many more net dollars every month. Those qualified plans may have grown tax-deferred, but when you are ready for the money, you will pay income taxes on every single dollar you withdraw.

- **Possibly prevent you from outliving your money.** A properly structured H.E.R.O. Solution™ can potentially provide you monthly income into perpetuity. As life expectancies get longer and longer, you are going to desperately need a source of income you can count on. A H.E.R.O. Solution™ can provide for a comfortable life throughout the bonus years you'll most likely experience.

So, Is It Too Late To Become Wealthy?

How bad is our retirement saving record, in general? The average American has a life-savings balance of about $25,000. Many are going through their existence with no savings at all. Of those who work where a company sponsored retirement plan is offered, one in every four is not even signed up for the program.

So, if you haven't saved as you should and you can't turn back the clock, is it just too late to become wealthy? Maybe you just aren't happy with your results so far. If you haven't been diligent in accumulating your life's savings, what can you do now?

It's not too late, especially if you own your home.

There is a way to quickly catch up on your life savings. You can tap a lump sum from your largest asset and, through simple reallocation of your idle equity and your current monthly cash flow, apply the principles of Real Wealth L.A.W.™ to route those dollars into safe, secure, producing vehicles. You must get every asset at your disposal to begin working in concert to grow your life's wealth.

Your current retirement program money or qualified plan may run out of cash before you run out of years. You must have a strategic plan to assure your life's enjoyment for many, many years ahead. You can take a giant leap toward providing a comfortable income until you are age 100, but the plan must include tax-favored income and has to be structured properly in order to provide you with the best results for your success.

> "Your personal finances and your retirement plan are serious business. You can't just read The Wall Street Journal for a few months and expect to suddenly know everything you need to know."
> — Ben Stein

Copyright 2006 HERO Solution, Inc.

So, How Do You Begin?

You seek out a lump sum to deposit that is never-to-be-taxed money. As you have seen in earlier chapters, your home equity is tax-free money for you. Whether it's via a loan, which is never taxable, or through utilization of the 1997 tax laws which now give you access to up to $250,000 for individuals or $500,000 for married couples, you must get those 100% dollars employed.

Earnings that compound and grow without erosion from taxes produce far better results, so tax-favored vehicles must be chosen. As explained in the earlier chapter on *S.A.F.E.T.Y.* and *Real Wealth L.A.W.*, you saw why your best choices include municipal bonds and investment-grade universal life insurance contracts. Both have special tax treatment and can be marvelous tools to grow your wealth.

If you're mainly invested in stocks or stock mutual funds in your IRA, you can create instant diversification to balance your wealth. Most people's two largest assets are in their home's equity and their retirement accounts. The majority of the latter are most likely in stocks, whether in your own company's stock or in the stock market through individual stock purchase or mutual funds of some kind.

You can strive for balance in your total wealth picture by getting your equity to work in a safe but producing vehicle. It can be indexed to the stock market or in a fixed product, but diversification is the key word.

Who Is At Highest Risk To Lose Their Nest Egg?

75% of 401(k) savers have half their retirement account funds invested in their own company's stock. If you are one of them, you may be risking a huge part of your wealth unnecessarily. Your entire life savings could be decimated at any time. You've heard the stories of the employees of Lucent

Technologies, Enron and others. If your company is publicly traded, you have no control over the management or the future of your employer. It's an awfully large bet and probably riskier than some Las Vegas odds.

Many conservative advisors warn that no more than 4% of your entire wealth be invested into any single stock. Some 401(k) plans offer matching ONLY if you will accept it in the form of your company's own stock. If you are receiving stock from your employer, then you should probably hold that portion down to a maximum of 10% of your entire retirement account.[51]

> *"There are two times when a man shouldn't speculate: when he can't afford it, and when he can."*
> — Mark Twain

If you've been a successful saver in your qualified plans, do you know you are about to be clobbered with taxes? There are trillions of dollars in the qualified plans of working America. Since taxes are likely to be higher in the future, we are looking at some huge tax bills to come.

The IRS requires that all your retirement savings be removed and taxed in your lifetime. It's not something you can just leave and pass on to your heirs without taxes. Uncle Sam wants his healthy slice BEFORE you get the remainder.

Using a "stretch" IRA could really give the IRS a cash cow of a long term income. Your heirs could continue to pay taxes on those funds for generations to come! Not to mention the minefield of penalties if they slip up and withdraw too much, too little, too soon or incorrectly. Remember all those strings attached to qualified plans?

---

[51] One conservative advisor who recommends these limits is Bob Brinker, who has a nationally syndicated financial advisory radio show.

Do you believe income taxes will go up or go down in the future? Since we are at historically low rates right now, chances are not good for the lower scenario. Will you, then, likely pay more or less by simply postponing your taxes? Perhaps you are saying to yourself, "I will be in a lower tax bracket after I'm retired." That could be possible if you don't have much of a life's savings. But remember, after you are no longer working, you will most likely have no dependents to deduct, no mortgage interest to deduct and no retirement savings contributions to deduct. Will you REALLY BE IN A LOWER TAX BRACKET?

Additionally, in many cases retirement savings can lose huge portions to taxes and penalties upon your death. Many heirs receive only 28 cents on the dollar of your hard-earned life savings after the dust settles.

Remember, qualified plans do not avoid taxes they only postpone them. They are great methods of forced savings because they use the "out of sight, out of mind" method of automatic investment. But you must always remember that nothing is really gained by simply postponing the taxes due on that income. Yes, they grow more because the untaxed dollars are also growing, but those dollars are growing for Uncle Sam, not for you. They will be owed on the back end but at a time when your deductions will be gone. The odds are quite good that your taxes will be higher in those later years.

How Can You Practice Damage Control On Your Tax-Postponed Accounts?

When you apply deliberate planning to rescue your qualified plans and tax-deferred accounts from future taxation, time is of the essence. You must balance the annual taxes owed on your income with the taxes owed on your retirement funds. If you pay the amounts owed strategically, you can tap your funds early and avoid the potential penalties due, if any.

So, how can you stop the madness and rescue future earnings from tax confiscation? You can begin by halting the funding of non-matched retirement accounts — amounts for which you are simply postponing your taxes for some perceived future benefit. That benefit may never materialize. In fact, there's a good chance you are putting off that tax payment until a time when you will actually be paying a larger percentage of your income.

When I say halt this type of funding, I'm referring to retirement funding where you are not receiving employer matching. Those would be any amounts over and above your employer's limit for their promised deposits into your qualified account. Many plans allow you to put additional amounts into your fund. Never consider that move without investigating other places where those dollars can grow in a tax-favored environment.

Perhaps your S.A.F.E.T.Y. Fund™? Good idea!

Secondly, once you reach age 59½ you should pull your funds out as quickly as possible. Remember, at this time in your life, you can get to those funds avoiding the 10% penalty. But, be methodical about it. Don't pull out so much that you go into the next tax bracket in any single year. Use your mortgage interest deduction, as shown in future chapters, to balance a strategic rollout of those funds. You really should pull them all out and get them working in a tax-favored vehicle.

Yes, you should have a mortgage at this stage in your life, even a really big one. It will be a financial tool for you in getting to your tax-postponed funds. You may need to have that money churning out income for you until you are 100 years old! Planned correctly, you might be able to rescue your current retirement plan dollars paying NO TAXES AT ALL! Wouldn't that be a great plan?

If you are not yet 59½, you can pull out your retirement savings by using a 72t plan to annuitize your cash. This is an IRS plan that allows you to access your money through systematic withdrawals set up by their guidelines. Once you commit to the plan, you must follow through in order to avoid the 10% penalties, but it's a great way to go ahead and get to at least some of your money now. A 72t obligates you to continue with it until you pass age 59½ or for a full 5 years, whichever is a longer time period.

Why Should You Move Your Wealth From A Tax-Postponed To A Tax-Favored Environment And Why Should It Be Done Now?

Long time horizons are emerging for us all after retirement. You should be planning to live to age 100 and beyond. If you can facilitate the strategic rollout of your funds through a deliberate plan, you can gain control sooner, possibly avoid paying taxes at all, through deduction offsets and get your cash working in a protected environment producing income for you that can be accessed free of taxes. No more penalty worries, no more taxes due into perpetuity. Begin pure growth without the strings that are attached to qualified IRS plans.

If you see the marvelous benefits offered and decide the H.E.R.O. Solution™ is the route you wish to take, you should truly commit to it, long term. In order to achieve your goals, you:

- Must have a road map to your financial success.
- Must understand and stick with your plan.
- Can make it easier by setting it up to work automatically.

The automation offered by our modern world makes good plans GREAT. "Out of sight, out of mind" is the system that makes your wealth engine run. Revisiting and adjusting your plan, once it is set into motion, is crucial to your success. Your life changes, so your wealth plan should be revised as your life evolves. Plan to meet back with your enlightened advisor at least every three to five years. Recommit to your plan each time and your wealth success will be guaranteed.

Why Is The H.E.R.O. Solution™
Not Suitable For Everyone?

This plan can work miracles in wealth creation, but the discipline needed to keep your hand out of the "cookie jar" may not be found in everyone. If you can commit to sticking to your plan and avoiding the consumption of your liquid assets, then implentation of the H.E.R.O. Solution™ is what you need.

Additionally, tax situations of individuals may vary. Even if your income level doesn't allow you to take advantage of all the tax benefits offered by the plan, it would still behoove you to keep the largest mortgage possible for liability protection and liquidity. There are other ways to access deductibility of interest on debt through business and investment interest deductions. Your tax advisor would be able to assist and direct you in that area.

You've Got To Stop The Madness

Paying off your mortgage causes you to lose more than just a million dollars. Out of the goodness of your heart you are purposefully over-funding the massive inefficient bureaucracy we call our federal government. You are taking piles of cash each and every year away from your family to let Uncle Sam do with it as he pleases. Want to find out more about this madness and how to stop it? It's revealed in the next chapter.

CHAPTER ELEVEN

SO WE SHOULD JUST DONATE MORE THAN A MONTH OF OUR VALUABLE TIME EVERY YEAR? ARE WE CRAZY?

Why on earth — for what reason could you ever imagine — would someone in their right mind roll out of bed, shower, climb into the car, fight traffic and stagger into work for 25 days — 5 WEEKS — and do their job for FREE?

Doesn't that sound crazy? This is what most financial advisors are telling you to work toward. That's what your parents and grandparents are telling you to strive for. That's what traditional wisdom thinks is wise. Does it really sound like sensible advice to you?

Do You See Why This Traditional Wisdom Is Nuts?

It will take a few paragraphs to explain, but stick with me and follow my logic.

Everyone who has a job also pays taxes on their income. Right? On the average, a little less than one-third goes to pay your state and federal taxes. For simplicity's sake, lets say 31% goes to income tax.

Now lets say you make $75,000, which is a little higher than the median income in the United States. This explanation works for just about anyone in the federal income tax bracket of 25% or more, so if you make more or less, understand this will probably still apply to you. A table follows that will show specifically how much time is at stake for each tax bracket.

So you decide you want to buy a house. With most mortgage underwriting, if your credit is good, you should be able to easily be approved with your mortgage payment being between 28% to 33% of your pre-tax income. In other words, a loan where the total housing payment does not exceed that percentage range of the borrower's total monthly income is considered an excellent risk and would be a desirable loan to sell on the secondary mortgage market. (As an aside — many automated underwriting systems will actually approve loans where this percentage is as high as 50%, but that would be a stretch for most people.)

To make it simple, let's remove taxes and insurance from your total housing costs and take it down the middle. So, for purposes of our discussion, let's say your mortgage payment should be 30% of your total income, which means you have a 30% front ratio. (FYI, the back ratio is the percent of your income that equals your total monthly obligations, including debt payments.)

With a 30% ratio being the number we'll use for your P&I[52] payment, lets do the math:

Your Annual Income:	$75,000	per year *(divide by 12)*
Monthly Income:	$6,250	per month
30% front ratio:	x .30	
Your Approved Payment =	$1,875	per month

Now, the IRS allows you to list and deduct the mortgage interest you pay each year on your Schedule A. This, in turn, is deducted from your income and allows you to receive a tax refund for a percentage of all home mortgage interest you paid.

This is true for mortgages of up to $1,000,000 combined on your primary residence and a second home. On top of that you can deduct up to $100,000 more interest on loans against your equity over and above this amount. Therefore, you should be able to deduct all the interest you pay on mortgage interest up to $1,100,000 per year.

So if you were in a 31% tax bracket, almost one-third of this interest comes back to you in the form of an IRS tax refund every year. That's serious cash!

Since doing amortization calculations can be a little tedious, we'll keep it simple and assume you have an interest-only mortgage. Let's say you are in a combined tax bracket of 31%, so follow along with me:

---

[52] P&I stands for principal and interest, only. This doesn't include hazard insurance or property taxes.

Your mortgage payment:	$1,875	per month x 12
Your annual payment:	$22,500	per year
Your annual deduction:	$22,500	per year
Calculate your refund:	x .31	(31% combined tax bracket)
Your annual tax refund:	$ 6,975	

Are you with me so far? If you paid $22,500 per year in mortgage interest and your total tax bracket is 31 percent (ex. 25% federal and 6% state), you would receive a tax refund check for $6,975 at the end of the year.

Now Lets Look At Your Tax Refund A Different Way

OK, we've established a tax refund of $6,975 annually.

If you work full time for your $75,000 per year income, you probably work 40 hours per week. Right? Then $6,975 would represent what portion of your time? (You'll notice I said your time — NOT your income. OK?)

Let's calculate it:

Your annual income:	$75,000
Divided by your refund:	$75,000/$6,975 = 0.093 (9.3%)
You will be receiving	9.3% of your annual income back

Stay with me. If you work 40 hours per week, then how many hours does that refund represent?

Let's do the math again:

Your hours per week:	40	hours
Times % of your time:	x 9.3%	
Weekly hours refunded:	3.75	hours

Did you understand that? You actually get 3.75 hours of your work refunded back to you for every week you worked that year. That's almost half a day!

Now Here Is The Bottom Line Reality

A smart person, in this tax bracket, who maximizes both time and assets, can get back 3.75 hours — ALMOST HALF A DAY — each week!

You can also look at it as:		16	hours per month
-or-		193	hours per year
-or-		24	days per year
-or-	*nearly*	5	weeks per year

Let me repeat: Nearly 5 weeks per year of your work you're getting back! Literally snatched from the jaws of government inefficiency.

If you follow old-fashioned, traditional wisdom, pay cash or strive to pay off your mortgage in whatever fashion you've devised, you are headed exactly toward this goal! With every payment you make to principal, you are working more and more FOR FREE, out of the goodness and sharing of your own heart. Every payment takes you one step closer to working five or six weeks for free each year. Maybe you want to donate the labor, toil and stress involved in 5 weeks each year for the good of the country.

Number Of Weeks We Work For Free
With A Paid-Off Mortgage — By Tax Bracket

Federal plus State Combined Tax Brackets	Amount of Time You Are Working For Free
25 + 0 = 25%	3 weeks 4 days 4 hours
28 + 0 = 28%	4 weeks 1 day 7 hours
25 + 5 = 30%	4 weeks 3 days 3 hours
25 + 6 = 31%	4 weeks 4 days 2 hours
25 + 8 = 33%	5 weeks 6 hours
28 + 5 = 33%	5 weeks 6 hours
33 + 0 = 33%	5 weeks 6 hours
28 + 6 = 34%	5 weeks 1 day 4 hours
35 + 0 = 35%	5 weeks 2 days 2 hours
28 + 8 = 36%	5 weeks 3 days 1 hour
33 + 5 = 38%	6 weeks
33 + 6 = 39%	6 weeks 6 hours
35 + 5 = 40%	6 weeks 1 day 1 hour
33 + 8 = 41%	6 weeks 2 days
35 + 6 = 41%	6 weeks 2 days
35 + 8 = 43%	6 weeks 3 days 4 hours

If you have a large equity but carry a mortgage balance of less than 80% of your home's value, you are still working for free at some percentage of the weeks shown. If you have a 15-year mortgage, made a big down payment or are utilizing a bi-weekly payment plan, you are also working for free at some percentage of the weeks shown. It's just an unbelievable waste!

I don't know about you, but work is work and charity is charity. I would prefer a situation in which I — not a bunch of guys in ties at our nation's capital — select the recipients who are worthy of my donations.

"You're Doing It Wrong"

In the movie, *Mr. Mom*, Michael Keaton plays a father who loses his job and must stay at home with his kids. He drives his oldest son to school. Upon arriving at the building, he looks at the front entry and, being an engineer, quickly plots out the shortest route to take his son to the door. His logic, had it been applied on paper or in isolation, would have been perfectly successful. In practice, with a multitude of other Mommies driving up, all going the opposite way, it has caused a traffic tie up and his plan just hasn't worked very well.

As he pulls up going the wrong way, the Traffic Mommy taps her fingernail on his driver's side window. He lowers it slowly to see her patronizing smile. She announces loudly so he understands, *"You're doing it wrong!"*

Maybe it's just the way most accountancy schools and certified financial planner (CFP) training classes have always been taught. Possibly it's because the majority of CPAs are advisors to the average and not the more astute. Perhaps it's because every personal finance book on the shelf at *Borders* or *Barnes and Noble* says to do it this way. Could it be because no one can see the solutions because they aren't printed on the inside of the box they are trapped in?

The Masses Out There Are Just "Doing It Wrong"

The wealthy and astute have come to this conclusion. They see things with Real Wealth Vision™, know when to take advantage of all IRS opportunities and never hesitate to seek them out and put them into practice.

It's good for them, but a real shame for all those who keep "doing it wrong." You know, all those who pay cash for real estate, pile equity into their home, make large down payments, pay down mortgage debt, get 15-year amortized loans or make bi-weekly payments.

Hanging Onto Traditional Wisdom Is Just "Doing It Wrong"

Here we are. We're a nation with the lowest savings rate since Depression-era 1938. What are we doing? Taking our money, produced with our precious time, and just giving it away in taxes.

The smartest people, those with Real Wealth Vision™, aren't making this mistake. They maximize all legal, rightfully earned and freely offered deductions offered in the tax code. If you use these tax laws properly, you can arrange to work for over a month for yourself and your family each year, because the money will come right back to you.

Build your wealth with that cash. It's there — waiting for you to take it. Don't just ignore it. Be smart and take off those "Glasses of the Masses." See with Real Wealth Vision™ and see those bucks right in front of your eyes. *Time's a-wastin'.*

While we're talking about snatching our cash from the bureaucratic jaws of inefficiency, wouldn't you like to see how to find additional legal ways to keep more of your hard-earned dough by utilizing your house and your mortgage? Sure, "a penny saved is a penny earned," but how about **thousands saved and thousands earned**? The next chapter shows a plethora of tax advantages that are just waiting for us to utilize.

CHAPTER TWELVE

YOU SHOULD NEVER REFUSE HELP FROM YOUR UNCLE

The mortgage interest deduction has been part of U.S. tax policy since the federal tax code was first enacted in 1913. Uncle Sam's system doesn't "cause" homeownership; it facilitates, it encourages and it assists in ownership. The results? Our nation has achieved a remarkably high percentage of people who own their homes. The tax system supports this by making it more affordable for just about everyone. Our government encourages and rewards us for owning our homes.

Why are we offered home-ownership-related tax deductions? A progressive society promotes ownership in all aspects of life. The secret of personal wealth is found in our freedom to own assets.

> "Everyone deserves a chance to live the American Dream, to build up wealth of their own, and to have assets for retirement that government can never take away."
> —Vice President Richard Cheney, National Summit on Retirement Savings, 2006

The "powers-that-be" understand that homeownership stimulates our economy. Recent evidence of this was demonstrated when a bi-partisan panel was appointed to help create a system recognizing the importance of homeownership and charity to American society.[53] Homeowners generate more income for the federal coffers than the revenues lost by allowing mortgage interest deductions.

Some worry that our legislators may take away the mortgage interest deduction sometime in the future. The MID (mortgage interest deduction) has not been formally attacked since 1966. Considering the fact that homeownership is the backbone of our society and the lobby representing the one-million-strong National Association of REALTORS® is a powerful and influential force, that possibility should remain very slim.

Three sections of the IRS code provide special tax treatment for homeowners. Let's look at each of them.

Tax Benefit Number One — Pay Monthly Mortgage Expenses Using Pre-Tax Whole Dollars

According to IRS Publication 936,[54] interest can be deducted on loans up to $1,000,000 when they are acquisition mortgages secured against your primary residence, your second home or both. Additionally, you can deduct $100,000 more in home equity on top of the million. These maximum figures are halved for single taxpayers or married taxpayers filing separately. Calculations for determining the limits on these deductions are also explained in that IRS publication.

---

[53] White House Office of Management and Budget website, U.S. Treasury page at www.whitehouse.gov, 2006.
[54] IRS Publication 936 is entitled "Home Mortgage Interest Deduction."

If you select an interest-only payment, your entire payment can be paid using before-tax dollars. Regular amortized loans allow for a declining portion to be pre-tax. Additionally, your property taxes are tax-deductible. All in all, if you position yourself correctly, you can arrange for nearly all your monthly housing costs to be handled with pre-tax dollars.

Tax Benefit Number Two — Purchase Costs Can Be Paid With Pre-Tax Whole Dollars

Points paid by a homeowner when acquiring a loan can also be deducted from income. If you closed a purchase-money mortgage transaction in which you paid points[55] to a financial institution in order to receive better terms, you may deduct the full amount of the points on your tax return that year. When refinancing your mortgage, points may also be deducted, but the benefit must be amortized over the life of the loan.

You'll notice I said the life of the loan, not the time you own the house. So, if you refinance or pay off that mortgage in any fashion, you may immediately write off all remaining, not-yet-deducted points in that tax year and begin amortizing the additional points paid in getting the new loan.

Tax Benefit Number Three — Harvest Your Accrued Equity Gains Tax-Free

When selling, the current tax laws allow you to access, tax free, up to $500,000 in profit from the sale of your property

---

[55] Discount points are a percentage of the loan amount. Two points would be equal to 2.0% of the mortgage. Normally, points are paid to acquire better terms and/or a lower interest rate on the note.

used as a principal residence for two of the prior five years. Single taxpayers, or married taxpayers who file separately, are limited to $250,000.

These fruits of your real estate's labor may be harvested as often as every other year. This marvelous wealth tool was made available when the Taxpayer Relief Act of 1997 went into effect. Now your home can be a wealth machine! Tax-free income when you sell your primary home can rocket your wealth to the stratosphere.

> *"The avoidance of taxes is the only intellectual pursuit that carries any reward."*
> — John Maynard Keynes, father of Keynesian economics

"But wait," you say. "I've always been told you had to put all the money you made from the sale of your home into the next one you buy."

Many people mistakenly believe they must reinvest all gains from the prior home in order to avoid having them taxed. Not true. You were always able to buy a new home, get 100% financing each time and invest your gains elsewhere, but previously your new house had to equal or exceed the value of the one sold in order to avoid capital gains tax. Prior to the 1997 Act, you were allowed a one-time exclusion of your gain after age 55 and you were limited to $125,000.

Now, as often as every two years, you may reap your wealth harvest and turbocharge your H.E.R.O. Solution™ by investing you tax-free gain in a S.A.F.E.T.Y. Fund™ each time you sell.

But I've Been Told Not To Pay Points
When I Buy Or Refinance My Mortgage

So, you usually pay your closing costs and zero points. Right? Many advisors will tell you to get a new mortgage in this fashion.

Ah, yes, that traditional wisdom, again. Here's some inside information your advisor may not be telling you or may not even know about. You can negotiate with your mortgage banker to have all your closing costs paid by them — simply pay a slightly higher rate and this is possible at virtually any institution. If your settlement statement shows points charged and no closing costs being listed, you now have paid all your costs with pre-tax money.

Technically, the IRS rule states that points are fees paid to *reduce your rate*. You can negotiate to have your rate slightly higher in exchange for elimination of all closing costs. Then you can renegotiate your rate to a lower position by offering to pay discount points. The results are the same. Most savvy mortgage bankers and brokers know this.

Points do not have to appear as whole percentages, like 1.0 or 2.0 points. You can add up the closing costs you were going to pay. Divide that dollar figure into your loan amount to get a percentage. Then have the mortgage banker charge you that exact percentage in the form of a discount point. (For example: 1.60% or 2.15%) Same out of pocket for you, but now it's paid with pre-tax whole dollars. What a deal!

Remember, as pointed out earlier, you can deduct these points on refinances also, but you must amortize the costs over the "life of the loan." If you adopt the H.E.R.O. Solution™ strategy, you will be planning to refinance every few years. This will enable you to completely deduct the remaining closing costs from your last loan each year in which you pay that loan off with the new refinance.

What If I Want To Harvest My Equity, But I Don't Want To Sell My House?

Loans taken against your home equity are not income, reportable to the IRS. Loans are not ordinary income, earned income, capital gain income, portfolio income or passive income.

People use cash-out refinances for all sorts of needs. What better need could there be than guaranteeing your financial future by digging up the tin can in your back yard and putting that idle cash to work? The IRS has additional rules about where you can put borrowed home equity cash, but that is where a savvy advisor will be able to guide you. There are ways to place your cash into investments that follow all the IRS guidelines and still reap the rewards of tax-favored growth. We talked about these in Chapter Seven.

When you sell, the cash-out loan you acquired earlier will be paid in full with your tax-free capital gains. This is assuming you are realizing an equity profit of $500,000 or less as a married couple under the current tax laws. If your home is appreciating and gaining more than those IRS caps for capital gains elimination, then you need to be selling and moving more often.

If you let more than $500,000 (or $250,000 gains for single taxpayers) accrue inside your house, you may be incurring future capital gains liabilities for all amounts greater than those limits. As stated earlier, you can cash in on those tax-free gains as often as every two years. Because you must have lived in the house as your primary residence for a full two years prior to selling it, your time limits would be 24 months.

After you have harvested your equity and put it to work inside your S.A.F.E.T.Y. Fund™, you may have placed it inside an indexed UL contract. Per the Internal Revenue Code, policy loans from life insurance contracts generally are not subject to income tax, provided the contract is not a modified endowment contract (MEC). This happens when too much premium is paid or your dollars move into your account too quickly, resulting in an over-funded policy. Improperly funding your insurance contract could void its tax advantages so be sure your advisor is very experienced and versed in setting up a properly structured plan meeting all the requirements of the tax code.

How Are IRS Tax Benefits Working As Incentives To Do The Right Thing?

- If you rent an apartment, do you replace the carpet?
- If you rent a tuxedo, do you get it dry cleaned?
- If you rent a car, do you change the oil?

If you don't own it, you really don't care about it. It isn't yours. What incentive would you have to preserve it, care for it or maintain its value? When you own a home, you take pride in your property, causing your neighborhood, in turn, to become a better place to live.

Tax incentives work to reduce or eliminate government dependence. It's better for the government's bottom line to promote ownership of private residences than to subsidize rentals and housing for citizens. Just as it's better to encourage workers who plan for their own financial support in retirement through 401(k)s and IRAs by allowing tax deferral on the money set aside. Similarly, charity from individuals, groups and religious organizations is much more effective in assisting those with needs than government assistance programs.

These practices are encouraged through tax advantages offered by the IRS. It costs less to promote personal ownership, responsibility and charity than to have the government pick up the tab for the alternative.

Warning! This Offer Expires On December 31st

New Year's Eve is always accompanied with familiar sounds. "Auld Lang Syne" playing, voices counting down, glasses clinking and, of course, the loud slamming sound. You know, that deafening noise heard as the annual door shuts on our choice between cash-down-the-drain and a check in the mail. Opportunities taken or opportunities lost? Our chance has left the building and will not return.

Tax deductions offered against income become void if not used in that fiscal year. An opportunity lost is money lost, so planning is crucial. What should you do to maximize your potential benefit?

Those with Real Wealth Vision™ get and keep the biggest mortgage they can afford. This increases their tax refunds due to larger mortgage interest deductions. To the harvested equity dollars they accumulate, they add those refunds and earn more compounded yields on those refund dollars. They understand the present value of today dollars and capture them each year to get them working.

It's Extremely Expensive To Have No Mortgage

Remember the concept of C.O.F.F.E.E.™ from Chapter Two? The costs forfeited by not employing your idle equity can be massive in your lifetime. You suffer additional huge lost opportunity costs when you forfeit income tax refunds each year. Thirdly, the lost opportunity on future earnings of those never-realized tax refunds will hover over your head like a dark cloud.

Millions and millions of people past the age of 65 live under the poverty line, but have paid-off houses. Older Americans are often homeowners who have eliminated their mortgages over decades. By mistakenly relying on Depression-era thinking, they slowly and gradually put themselves in a less safe financial position year by year. Sadly, their home equity often represents nearly their entire life savings and is often their only significant asset.

How Can Mortgage Interest Be A Tool To Increase Your Retirement Income?

Before you retire — yes, I said, *"Before you retire"* — you should acquire the **biggest mortgage possible**. Either the largest allowed for your property's value or the largest one you can afford. It's smartest to get an interest-only payment option. This frees up your cash for investment income and creates a new interest deduction. It can possibly wipe out taxes due on previously tax-deferred retirement income withdrawals. Over time, this cash can create tax-favored monthly income for you — even beyond the age of 100.

The H.E.R.O. Solution™ With The
S.A.F.E.T.Y. Fund™ Will Do This For You

The synergy of these concepts creates a tax-advantaged, non-qualified retirement plan. The tax arbitrage created with this plan is the third secret of millionaires. This combination can also allow you to strategically get to your current qualified plan cash, like 401(k)s, IRAs, 403(b)s and 457s, without tax. If properly structured, many individuals may be able to use these concepts to get to all their retirement fund money free of taxes.

Again, many financial advisors and insurance agents don't know how to structure this type of strategic plan. Perhaps it's compartmentalization, like we talked about in Chapter 5. Most

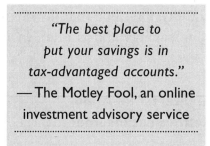

"The best place to put your savings is in tax-advantaged accounts."
— The Motley Fool, an online investment advisory service

just don't realize investment-grade life insurance contracts can be tax-favored, less limiting alternatives to regular qualified plans.[56]

Quite often, the run-of-the-mill advisor has never heard of the TEFRA[57] corridor. This is the IRS-mandated corridor between the death benefit and the cash value that must be maintained for the contract to enjoy its life insurance (versus annuity) tax treatment. The corridor is a percentage of cash value and decreases as one attains a higher age.

---

[56] See IRS Publication 525.
[57] Tax Equity and Fiscal Responsibility Acts of 1982 and 1983.

Likewise, they don't often understand DEFRA[58] and TAMRA[59] tax laws and probably don't know the difference in LIFO and FIFO applications. These are the acronyms for the different tax treatment applied by the IRS to insurance contracts vs. annuities.

It is extremely important to seek out competent advice to put your strategic plan together. You'll need an enlightened advisor or team of professionals to review your financial situation, assist you in preparing your moves, help you implement all components of the total strategy and follow up with you, to regularly encourage you and to keep you on track.

The great part? It's usually free of charge! To your benefit, most often the professionals who are capable of doing this for you do not charge for their services. Because your plan will be based on utilization of mortgages and insurance, those entire industries are usually set up to so that the agencies who service mortgages and the companies who provide insurance coverage compensate your advisor, not you.

It is probably possible to pay a fee-only advisor, but finding one who understands these concepts may be difficult. Ultimately, since fee-only advisors are likely not licensed to sell life insurance or to originate and close mortgage loans, they will need to refer you to professionals in the mortgage banking and insurance industries to complete your plan.

---

[58] Deficit Reduction Act of 1984.
[59] Technical and Miscellaneous Revenue Act of 1988, which made corrections to TEFRA.

IRS Rules Promote The Tax-favored Treatment Of Life Insurance Contracts As Alternative Retirement Programs

Why? It all comes back to ownership. If you take responsibility for support of yourself in your retirement, you are taking control. You are relieving the government of a future responsibility and reducing your government dependence.

This can be achieved through IRAs and employer-sponsored programs, which have strings attached and are usually limited, but you can achieve the same results through properly structured non-qualified retirement plans such as those that can be set up using life insurance contracts. These strategies are only limited by your ability to fund them. What a country!

Do You See How Those With Real Wealth Vision™ Freely Accept All The Help Their Uncle Offers?

The wealthy use every potential tax advantage offered. They

- Harvest their tax-free equity often.
- Keep the largest mortgage they can afford.
- Take the maximum tax deductions possible.
- Reinvest their tax refunds for maximum compounding.
- Pay all loan costs as deductible points.
- Utilize investment-grade life insurance contracts for tax-favored growth, access and transfer to heirs.
- Allow Uncle Sam's tax benefits to easily pay for cost of insurance.

A Caveat Regarding Your Tax Bracket

The only warning I would offer has to do with your federal bracket at which you pay your taxes. This is one of the main reasons why these strategies may not be for everyone. Those who pay their income taxes at the lowest levels — by lowest I mean at the 15% federal bracket or below — may not receive a large enough boost in their results after factoring in the tax deductibility benefit they receive on their mortgage interest deduction. If you are currently paying taxes in the lower brackets, depending on the size of your current mortgage and other deductions, you may find taking the standard deduction is best for your situation.

If your income and housing expense are such that you didn't even take a mortgage interest deduction on your last tax return, you may have to wait until your income and situation has moved you into the 25% federal tax bracket and above for these strategies to provide you with real wealth in your future. Additionally, the alternative minimum tax may affect some taxpayers, so if you currently pay the AMT in your situation, you may not receive the full tax advantages this plan can offer. Many still find the benefits of being secure through liquidity, more protected against liability and receiving a return on your idle cash more than enough reasons to separate their equity, even without the tax advantages.

Your tax advisor can make this determination for you, but be sure your advisor has Real Wealth Vision™ and understands the H.E.R.O. Solution™ strategy. Otherwise, you may receive "Glasses of the Masses" advice taking you back 50 years in its thinking.

Now ... For Some Real Magic!

Want to see how you can **double or triple** your million dollars into **multi-millions**? It really isn't that hard to do. You'll be amazed to discover how the wealthy do it. Once you've seen this plan, you will never be able to go back to the old-fashioned way of handling your house and your mortgage. In the next chapter, I'll part the curtain to expose these advanced strategies. Get ready to see your riches explode — transforming you into a "worry-free multi-millionaire."

CHAPTER THIRTEEN

WANT TO RECYCLE AND EXPLODE INTO MULTI-MILLION DOLLAR RICHES? WHY NOT TAKE THE STAIRS?

No, this isn't a Las Vegas long-shot bet. It's a simple pragmatic plan that takes the wonderful results you receive with the H.E.R.O. Solution™ and transforms it into a stair-step plan. It recycles your equity every five years (or every three years if property values are really climbing in your area) and harvests your cash to get it working.

This is the third of the **3 Simple Money Secrets** Millionaires use. Get off the old-fashioned inefficient financial treadmill and take the stairs to **double or triple your money!**

The following graph illustrates that you could liberate $75,000 in idle equity and create a **million dollar** S.A.F.E.T.Y. Fund™ by implementing the H.E.R.O. Solution™ only once (shown as the darker bar in the second set from the left.)

Alternatively in the same time period, if you were to stair-step the plan by recycling it systematically every 5 years (shown as the lighter shaded bar), your total side fund would become $2,932,790 or nearly **3 MILLION DOLLARS!**

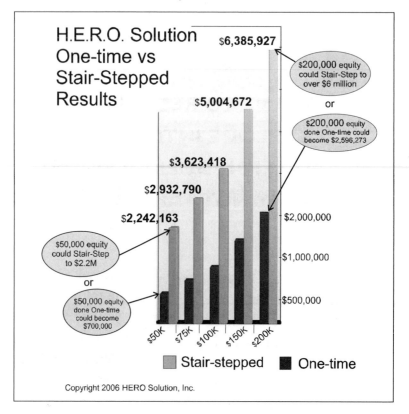

Results after 30 years for a One-Time vs. a Stair-Stepped Plan

The right side of the graph shows the result using $200,000 in idle equity. A one-time H.E.R.O. Solution™ grows to nearly 2.6 million dollars or could stair-step into over **6 MILLION DOLLARS!**

This plan can work at all levels. The following table shows the detail of the numbers appearing in the graphic on page 212. Each line illustrates the results of a one-time application of the H.E.R.O. Solution™ compared to stair-stepping or recycling it every five years.

These numbers assume you'll earn a 7.5% tax-favored yield, acquire an 80% LTV[60] interest-only mortgage with a rate of 7.5% and deposit only your added annual tax refunds.

Initial House Value	Initial Equity	One-Time HERO Solution™	5-yr Stair-Step HERO Solution™
$200,000	$50,000	$700,000	$2,242,163
$250,000	$75,000	$1,016,070	$2,932,790
$300,000	$100,000	$1,422,962	$3,500,532
$400,000	$150,000	$1,964,252	$5,004,672
$500,000	$200,000	$2,596,373	$6,385,927

Results after 30 years for a One-Time vs. a Stair-Stepped plan

Isn't it amazing to see how your wealth could double or even triple? Ending up with accounts like these would also mean your monthly retirement income could increase two- or three-fold, should you choose to withdraw your funds. (Remember — unlike qualified retirement accounts, no one will force you to disburse this money or pay taxes on it.) The cash is available for your needs and could be accessed at any time without tax ramifications.

Here is a year-by-year illustration of one of the examples:

---

[60] 80% LTV means the mortgage taken each time is at 80% of the house value. This practice avoids the expense of mortgage insurance on your loan.

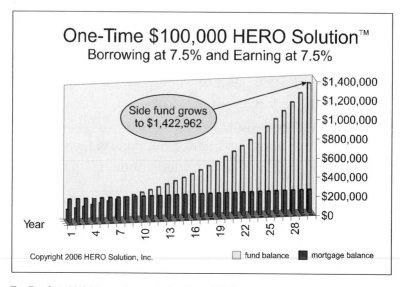

One-Time $100,000 HERO Solution™
Borrowing at 7.5% and Earning at 7.5%

Side fund grows to $1,422,962

$1,400,000
$1,200,000
$1,000,000
$800,000
$600,000
$400,000
$200,000
$0

Year
1 4 7 10 13 16 19 22 25 28

Copyright 2006 HERO Solution, Inc.   ☐ fund balance ■ mortgage balance

Tax Bracket: **32%** House Appreciation Rate: **5%** Earning Rate: **7.5%**
Mortgage Rate: **7.5%** Mortgage before H.E.R.O. Solution™: **$140,000**

This illustration assumes you're a homeowner and have a 15-year 5.75% mortgage with a $140,000 balance. Your house is worth $300,000 and you applied the H.E.R.O. Solution™ to harvest $100,000 in tax-free cash for an initial deposit into your S.A.F.E.T.Y. Fund™. You have decided to deposit the tax savings difference between your 15-year loan payments and your new 30-year interest-only payments into the S.A.F.E.T.Y. Fund™ each year. (Not the entire tax savings of your mortgage payment — only the difference between your original tax refund and the new tax refund you'll be receiving annually.)

One-Time HERO Solution™ - $100K Liberated at 7.5%					
$300K House Apprec at 5%	By Age	Mortgage Balance	After Tax Payment	At Year	SAFETY Fund™ Cash Value
$380,000	40	$240,000	$1,020	5	$165,438
$488,000	45	$240,000	$1,020	10	$264,763
$625,000	50	$240,000	$1,020	15	$414,742
$800,000	55	$240,000	$1,020	20	$635,583
$1,015,000	60	$240,000	$1,020	25	$956,531
$1,300,000	65	$240,000	$1,020	30	$1,422,962

Your side account earns 7.5%, which is the same as your borrowing rate. Now, fast-forward to your retirement age, 65, and you decide to pay off your mortgage with funds from your side account. You'll have well over a million dollars remaining in your S.A.F.E.T.Y. Fund™. If you continue to earn a rate of 7.5%, your fund will produce **$7393 per month** of spendable cash at that time.

Pretty great results. Wouldn't you say?

Home values in many areas of the country have been soaring the last few years. Leaving that idle equity just languishing inside your house would be a real shame. Especially, when just a few steps taken every few years could give you amazing results like this!

If Once Is Great, Why Stop There?

If the H.E.R.O. Solution™ creates such a wonderful arbitrage for your life's wealth by doing it just once, why would you only do it once? Once is good, but more could be better. Right? You can "leapfrog" your way to wealth in a fashion you might only have dreamed about before. These results aren't a little better; *they're a lot better!*

Your house keeps appreciating over the years, so you decide to recycle or stair-step the H.E.R.O. Solution™ every five years. (If your house is in a rapidly appreciating geographic area, it would be wise to evaluate refinancing or selling as often as every three years.)

Let's look at a year-by-year graph of the stair-stepped plan for the same homeowner shown in the previous graph:

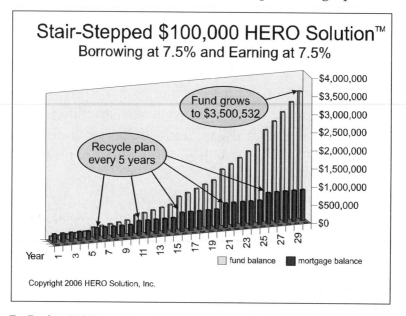

Tax Bracket: **32%** House Appreciation Rate: **5%** Earning Rate: **7.5%**
Mortgage Rate: **7.5%** Mortgage before H.E.R.O. Solution™: **$140,000**

Wow! The nest egg more than doubled to over 3.5 million dollars by applying this laddering or stair-step technique to your H.E.R.O. Solution™.

Stair-Stepped HERO Solution™ Every 5 Years at 7.5%					
$300K House Apprec at 5%	By Age	Mortgage Balance	After Tax Payment	At Year	SAFETY Fund™ Cash Value
$380,000	40	$240,000	$1,020	5	$165,438
$488,000	45	$306,300	$1,300	10	$367,315
$625,000	50	$390,900	$1,660	15	$702,380
$800,000	55	$520,000	$2,225	20	$1,280,911
$1,015,000	60	$668,600	$2,840	25	$2,163,108
$1,300,000	65	$850,000	$3,625	30	$3,500,532

Equity grows year over year. Smart homeowners use these opportunities to create stair-steps to greater wealth. Remember, they never consume this cash. It must be earmarked as critical cash and placed in a vehicle that passes the three components of Real Wealth L.A.W.™

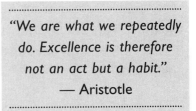

"We are what we repeatedly do. Excellence is therefore not an act but a habit."
— Aristotle

To maximize tax advantages, you should also consider recycling the plan every time you have an income increase. Having the maximum mortgage you can afford allows for the most in benefits for your tax refunds and for your S.A.F.E.T.Y. Fund™ growth.

Why Get Your Cash Out? Safety And Bubbles ...

Safety is a very important reason to keep a big mortgage. You lock in your gains, shield them inside your financial pocket and put that cash to work.

"But what if my house's value goes down?" you ask.

If you had lived in one of the few roller-coaster property markets of our country back in the 1980s that experienced real estate bubbles, you would have been ecstatic if you had pulled out your gained equity while prices were high, especially if you had placed your cash in a secure side fund. Then your equity would not have simply evaporated into thin air in a sluggish real estate market. You would have had huge amounts of cash generating returns for you. You'd have had choices, you'd have had cash for living expenses, you could've waited out the storm and you wouldn't have been forced to sell at deflated prices. Cash gives you choice. Cash increases your freedom.

Remember October 19, 1987, known as "Black Monday?" The stock market lost 22% of its value in one day. This was truly a "crash."

No real estate market has dropped 22% in one day, one week, or even one month. In fact, the real estate "crash" of the late 1980s took several years before it hit the bottom in most markets.

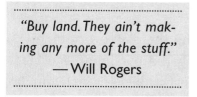

"Buy land. They ain't making any more of the stuff."
— Will Rogers

There have only been a few markets where real estate value actually declined for a time. In the 1980s, markets like Houston, Hartford and Los Angeles lost as much as 21% of average property values from the top of their respective markets, but each one came back within a few years.

For example, according to CNN Money Online, Los Angeles had an average home value of $214,800 in 1989 following a five-year, 77% jump. Back in 1984, homes had sold for an average of $121,400. After the "real estate bubble" struck, which took 7 years to play out, home values were pushed back to $172,900 on average. While this may have been tough for those who bought at the top of the market, the actual bottom-line appreciation was 42.4% over the entire period. This was still nearly a 4% per year gain at the absolute bottom.

Supply and demand works differently in the housing market than in the stock market. Right now, demand outruns supply in some hot real estate pockets like Southern California, San Francisco and Washington, DC. But, people are starting to realize that even if they sell for top dollar, they will have to pay top dollar to stay in the same area, so why bother to cash in?

This phenomenon is causing a restricted supply and even HIGHER prices. In other words, the price increases aren't necessarily due to "irrational" demand but rather more due to limited supply.

Why Should You Liberate Every Dime Of Equity You Can Sensibly Harvest?

Removing and shielding your equity helps you maintain a maximum defensive position. If the public record always shows a large mortgage against your property, lawyers sniffing for targets will more likely pass you by. Maximum compound growth works on the largest account balances. Remember, idle dollars are worthless and home equity is just that: idle dollars.

All our illustrations use cash-out to 80%, because it avoids the added cost of mortgage insurance. It also covers you in the event of local real estate market declines, however unlikely or temporary.

If you really wanted to maximize your leverage, you could get an additional home equity loan and tap your equity up to 100%. As the homeowner, you must decide what makes you most comfortable and weigh it against your potential gains.

Those with Real Wealth Vision™ separate their critical cash regularly and often to get it working. They don't want to lose opportunities that are presented. Taking advantage of the maximum in tax benefits each and every year is crucial for boosting their wealth. It would actually be a misuse of their assets if they didn't do this. Careless waste slows you down on the road to real wealth.

> *Mortgage insurance (MI) must be paid whenever your first mortgage balance exceeds 80% of the house's value. It's best to keep your loan close to, but not more than, 80% to avoid this cost. MI is not a tax-deductible expense.*

Now you are ready to retire and want to move to a warmer climate or maybe you don't want such a big house anymore.

Ouch! How Can You Downsize From A 1.3 Million Dollar Dollar House Without Capital Gains Taxes?

You decide you want to downsize or possibly buy separate summer and winter homes. Uh-oh. You have a capital gains problem with your house. Actually, this problem would have existed in any case if tax laws remain as they currently are and you had stayed in the same house for 30 years, even if you had kept that original 15-year loan and paid it off long ago.

Now, if you sell your 1.3 million dollar house, you could have a whopping $500,000 in capital gains income that will be taxed. Remember, the limit on tax-free equity access when you sell your home is $500,000 every two years for a married couple. Your profit will be over $1,000,000 after you pay off your initial loan. Every dollar over half a million will be taxed, if you are a couple, and anything over $250,000, if you are single.

But you say, "There's no way to avoid those capital gains taxes. I'll just have to bite-the-bullet and pay them. Right?"

Want The Purest Tax Benefit? Buy A New House

Well, there could be a better way — and one that avoids capital gains at the end. For the purest and maximum tax benefit, you could have simply sold your house and purchased a new one every time your equity accumulated up to the capital gains limits for tax-free treatment. Each time, you should have gotten a new 80% mortgage or even gone with 100% financing using a first and second mortgage combination. This would have created maximum acquisition indebtedness and put you in the best possible position for future tax deductibility.

Had you done this a few times over the years, you would have also eliminated future capital gains problems associated with holding onto a single home over long periods. It's very easy to exceed the $500,000 tax-free gains limit for married couples when you keep a house for 30 years. If you are single, it's even easier to exceed the $250,000 limit. It could slip up on you and put you in a tax bind.

Cashing in on your equity and harvesting it tax-free as it grows avoids the pain you'll feel if you want to down size. The alternative is to face writing a huge check to the IRS and who wants to do that?

Homes Have Been Bursting With Growing Equity!

What do you think property appreciation rates have been historically? Well, average home prices in this country rose by almost 11% in 2004, up from 7% in 2002 and 2003. Between 1978 and 2003, the nationwide House Price Index (HPI)[61] grew an average of 5% per year.

Is there a possibility for a real estate bubble? The FDIC[62] examined the historical pattern of home price booms and busts for U.S. metropolitan areas from 1978 through 2003.

One conclusion of this study was that a housing boom does not necessarily lead to a housing bust. In fact, boom was found to lead to bust in only 17% of all cases prior to 1998. Moreover, when busts occurred they were typically preceded by significant distress in the local economy.[63]

If there is a real estate bubble, how could you be affected? In 2005 the Federal Reserve chairman said he believed any real estate bubbles that might occur would only be regional.

Don't forget, ready access to your wealth allows you to weather most financial storms.

Eliminate Real Estate Bubble Worries And Lock In Your Gains

If you live where a bubble experience might occur, there should be no cause for worry because you have guaranteed and locked-in your gains by employing the H.E.R.O. Solution™. Now, you just wait it out. Your cash is accessible and working for you even if your house has temporarily stopped appreciating. Liquidity offers choices. Liquidity offers options. Liquidity offers peace of mind.

---

[61] House Price Index (HPI) is published by the Office of Federal Housing Enterprise Oversight (OFHEO).
[62] Federal Deposit Insurance Corporation.
[63] FDIC February 2005, *FYI* report.

Your safety of principle has been guaranteed. Truthfully, if your equity is NOT harvested, you have set yourself up for potential disaster. If most of your assets are tied up in the equity of your home, even if you have a lower mortgage balance, you could be less safe. If your local economy experiences problems, you lose your job or a local industry fails, your income situation could be impacted. With no income, you must continue to pay mortgage payments, utilities, food and living expenses — sometimes for extended periods.

Remember, without an income it is extremely hard to get a home equity loan or refinance your house to get to your equity. Where will you get the cash to make it through difficult times? It's pretty easy to lose your home to foreclosure or by a forced sale, even if your mortgage balance is lower.

Turn Your Windfalls Into Cyclones

Your home equity is money that is never to be taxed. So in essence, as long as the real estate market is appreciating in your area, you pretty much have a huge source of tax-free income to tap as your home value grows.

Those with Real Wealth Vision™ know to cash-in on their equity as it starts bursting at the seams. They buy a new home and never roll their equity cash into the new house. Why would they do such a silly thing?

That is tax-free cash! They get it working in a tax-favored environment to grow their wealth. Each time they sell their residence, they purchase a higher valued home and parlay their equity into their S.A.F.E.T.Y. Fund™. Making a big down payment is just counterproductive to wealth creation.

When viewing the wealth files of thousands of financially successful people, one dramatic reality popped out of the numbers. No matter their income level, they all consistently directed a large portion of that income to their housing. This component, on average, consisted of between 33% to 40% of their pre-tax dollars.

As your income grows, you should continue to acquire larger properties and larger accompanying mortgages. Actually, you should get the largest mortgage you can comfortably afford. You keep putting your equity aside to increase your wealth and maximize your tax benefits.

Those With Real Wealth Vision™ Always

- Get largest primary residence they can comfortably afford.
- Get the largest second home they can comfortably afford.
- Never put down more than 20%.
- Go for 100% financing when prudent and possible.
- Always keep 80%–100% LTV mortgages over the life of owning.
- Lump sum their tax-free equity profits into their S.A.F.E.T.Y. Fund™.
- Create two growing assets each time: a house plus a side account.
- Use interest-only loans to maximize tax deductions.
- Always pay closing costs as points for tax deductibility.
- Capitalize on all their real estate windfalls.

Many also utilize a second home. With two properties growing in the rich real estate markets we've been experiencing, the net-worth of these folks will just continue to skyrocket. On top of this, a larger S.A.F.E.T.Y. Fund™ creates greater lifetime wealth as it compounds.

What Does "Glasses of the Masses" Wisdom Tell You?

Those who see things through the "Glasses of the Masses" tell you to dig a hole and bury your tax-free equity cash in your new back yard. In other words, put down all your real estate earnings and get the smallest mortgage in order to "save" money on interest. I hope you know by this point in your reading how that kind of thinking is a big financial mistake.

The masses mistakenly believe you must reinvest all your earnings to avoid capital gains taxes. That is outdated thinking, since the Taxpayer Relief Act of 1997.

Most folks continue to follow old wisdom. There's a general misunderstanding of capital gains tax laws as they relate to your real estate.

When You Buy A Retirement Or Vacation Home, Should You Ever Pay Cash?

The answer is, of course: ABSOLUTELY NOT!

Reroute all your idle cash earmarked for that purchase into your S.A.F.E.T.Y. Fund™ to accumulate tax-favored growth and generate tax-favored income for you. Always put the minimum down when you purchase your real estate. Create arbitrage with all the other cash. Your vacation or retirement residence appreciates. Your cash is shielded and put safely away while it compounds for your wealth. It is still available for any emergencies that may arise.

Had it been put down on that house or used for paying cash for the real estate, it would be very hard to access. Remember Doris Fox, age 74, from page 32, who said paying cash for her home was the biggest mistake she ever made? When she needed her money, it cost over $12,000 and three months to get her HECM[64] reverse mortgage and those loans have a monthly adjustable rate. Not quite the best terms ...

Why Should I Go For 100% Financing Whenever Possible?

There are several ways to achieve 100% financing on your primary and secondary residence. Often, depending on your credit score and personal finances, it is quite easy to get these types of loans. The market provides more and more choice as time goes by.

It's usually least expensive to get a regular 80% first mortgage and 20% second lien financing, such as a home equity loan or a fixed second mortgage. If you only put 5% down and get a single loan for the remaining 95%, you will pay costly mortgage insurance. This expense is usually not tax-deductible; so evaluate all your choices before selecting this option.

103% loans are readily available which finance all your loan costs, in addition to the entire purchase price. Veterans are able to get 100% financing and conventional 103% loans are available for just about anyone with a decent credit score. Mortgage insurance will be required for these loans and it is at the most expensive levels.

FYI: At the end of 2006, Congress passed a one-year law to make mortgage insurance tax deductible for some homeowners. There are income limitations and your purchase or refinance loan would need to close in the year 2007 in order to receive the benefit. Congress will need to renew this law to make it apply to 2008 and beyond.

---

[64] FHA sponsored Home Equity Conversion Mortgage, the most popular reverse mortgage on the market. FHA sets the rates and fees.

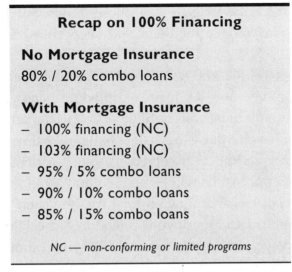

Remember, 100% financing, in whatever form, provides maximum tax-deductibility freedom in the future because it allows you to establish the most in acquisition indebtedness. Your future allowable tax-deductions will be based on the loan you acquired when you bought, plus up to $100,000 in home equity loans. Under current tax laws, this IRS rule applies to any combination of your primary residence and your second home for loan amounts up to $1,000,000.

Let Me Reiterate — This Solution Offers Extreme Safety, But It Is Not For Everyone

Maximizing the H.E.R.O. Solution™ takes a real commitment. You can truly "set-it and forget-it," but you mustn't forget why you have that S.A.F.E.T.Y. Fund™. Stick with your plan to achieve the marvelous results it can offer.

You must never, never, never consume your removed equity on depreciating assets, vacations, boats, jet skis, electronic toys, etc. It's not wrong to have those things, but you must use your play money for them and keep your critical cash separated.

This is why the H.E.R.O. Solution™ strategy may not be suitable for everyone. If you are tempted to spend your liberated equity, you must wait until your financial maturity level has grown beyond those urges. Just remember, time is money when compounding is involved. If you postpone creating your plan, your results will be severely impacted.

So *get a move on* and put your Real Wealth Vision™ plan into place. Go ahead and mark your calendar to check in on your plan and recycle it every few years. Then you'll simply "stair-step" your way to multi-million dollar riches!

You are on the way to being rich and secure for the rest of your life, but your Uncle Sam may be waiting ahead at the *tollbooth to retirement* with his hand held out. He's eager to get his cut of those tax-postponed retirement account funds in your 401(k)s, IRAs, 457s or 403(b)s you've been accumulating all your working years.

How can you avoid forking over huge chunks of your wealth to him? There is a way to slash the toll charge. The next chapter gives you amazing Real Wealth Vision™ strategies used by the wealthy to keep more of their cash at home for a rich and secure retirement. Want to know how? Details ahead!

CHAPTER FOURTEEN

BEWARE! YOU'RE DESTINED TO BE THE VICTIM OF THE NATION'S BIGGEST BULLY!

Though you probably already know it, I hope you understand this fact:

When you place your money into retirement accounts, you don't avoid taxes — you only postpone them.

What is the second largest asset most people have? Since your residence combined with the equity in it are likely to be the resting place of your biggest asset, your *retirement accounts* are likely to fall in line as the next largest chunk.

Planning for retirement is possibly the most daunting, yet the most important financial concern facing folks in these times. Age or economic standing has no bearing. This issue should be an equal worry for just about everyone.

While most of America is under-performing in the area of life savings, many of us have excelled in the accumulation of assets in our qualified plans. In fact, some balances have reached the stratosphere and the prospect of huge tax bills, possible penalties and likely estate taxes may be looming in the future for many retirees.

Saving too much of your golden-years assets inside standard qualified retirement plans, such as 401(k)s, 403(b)s, 457s or IRAs, can expose you to significant risk. All these plans are heavily regulated and subject to changes in legislation that affect the minimum distribution rules, taxation of distributions, spousal rights, etc.

ARE RETIREMENT PLANS SUCH A GOOD IDEA FOR YOUR HEIRS?

Think about this — If, upon your death, you leave your spouse a $400,000 stock portfolio, it will be received at its full value on the day of your death. There will be no income tax due when he or she receives it.

Likewise, if you leave your daughter a $200,000 vacation home, she will owe no income tax because it will also be received at the stepped-up basis.

But wait a minute! If you leave your son your $200,000 IRA, he will owe full income taxes on it,* just as would have been due if you had taken the distributions yourself. Then, for some people, there could be estate taxes due, additionally.

Ouch!

* As tax laws currently stand.

The distributions from these plans are extremely complicated to maneuver and generally taxed at high ordinary income tax rates. This creates a predicament if you're expecting to be in a higher income tax bracket during retirement or are concerned about having to pay taxes on your Social Security income.

The IRS Wants All Your Funds Withdrawn Even If You Aren't Going To Spend Them. Need You Ask Why?

The basic rule is that you must begin withdrawing funds **and incurring taxes on them** no later than April 1 of the year AFTER you turn 70½. This rule exists so that retirement funds will be distributed and taxes paid, **whether or not you spend the funds,** before you die. If you pass away before all the money is withdrawn, your heirs must pay the income taxes you deferred, plus full income taxes on every dime of your gains.

SAY THIS OUT LOUD:

"I will be paying back much, much more in taxes when I access my retirement funds than I ever avoided upfront."

As you sock money away into your retirement accounts, you have been blindly and mistakenly enjoying the benefit of tax-postponed growth. I say "blindly and mistakenly" because approximately one-third of those fat, juicy accounts hold cash that isn't even your money. Guess whom you're actually saving for ...

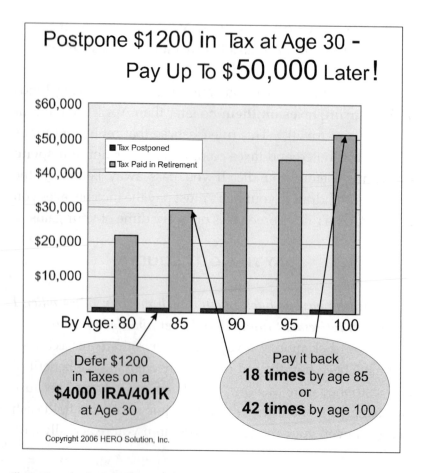

Illustration of a single $4,000 tax-deferred retirement account deposit at the age of 30. Assumes 30% combined marginal tax bracket and a 7.5% rate of earnings on the funds.

In our example, you're in the 25% federal and 5% state marginal tax brackets and you deferred $1,200 on the $4,000 deposit. The tax dollars you didn't pay that year still belong to Uncle Sam, but they will simply ride along beside your own $2,800 and grow with it over the years. You are no more than a caretaker for the IRS's cash.

You look at your statement every year and mistakenly think to yourself, "Wow, my retirement account is really getting plump." If you receive a 7.5% return on the total account (including the $1,200 you are babysitting) that single deposit will grow to the tidy sum of $65,170 by age 65. Let's say you begin withdrawing your earnings each year after you retire. That account will earn about $4880 annually, so taxes due on your distribution will be $1466 each year.

You avoided the $1,200 tax payment when you put the money into your IRA at age 30, but you'll pay $1,466 every single year you withdraw your funds in retirement. You will pay back that originally deferred tax **18 times over** by age 80 — and as much as **42 times over** if you make it to age 100! Required minimum distributions after age 70½ could change this figure slightly, but you get the picture.

Whose retirement were you planning, anyway?

> *"Why don't Americans save? ... The brief answer is: Why should we? The tax code punishes us for thrift. The double and triple layers of taxation on saving imbedded in our income tax system claims up to 90 percent of the rewards from saving and investing."*
> — Stephen Moor,
> Director of Fiscal Policy
> Studies at the Cato Institute

Of course, taking personal responsibility for our own support and well-being in our senior years by amassing a nest egg for our future is a noble endeavor, but is reaching this goal through IRS-sponsored qualified plans really the best way to create our life's fortune? We are unknowingly creating an annuity for Uncle Sam's wealth, rather than for ourselves. This could be especially true if we're extremely successful in building our qualified plans and die before we can enjoy all the fruits of our labors. (Remember, any remaining taxes due on deferred accounts must be paid by our heirs.)

This discussion, in no way, should be taken as an argument against saving for your retirement. The intent is only to make you question whether deferred qualified plans are really the best way to design the wealth accumulation plans for your life.

Here Are A Few Of The Strings Attached To Qualified Retirement Plans

- Did you know … the IRS wants you to pay taxes on **every dime** of your retirement money and its earnings before you die?
- Did you know … **traps** in this complicated tax code section could **cost you** and your family big time, before and after you die?
- Did you know … retirement and pension distributions are **taxed as ordinary income** and not lower capital gains tax rates?
- Did you know … your heirs can receive your regular investments, insurance proceeds and real estate without being taxed, but they **must pay** the IRS at **their ordinary income tax rates** on your retirement plan money you leave to them?
- Did you know … investment losses in your retirement account **are not allowed as deductions** on your income tax returns?
- Did you know … once you hit 70½, retirement account distributions are **mandatory**, even if you don't need them?
- Did you know … if you take the money out incorrectly after 70½, the **penalty is 50% plus taxes**?
- Did you know … the tax code is very strict about required **minimum** distributions (RMD) from your qualified plan?

- Did you know ... if you or your heirs fail to take out the required minimum in any year after you reach 70½ the **penalty** is based on what **should have been withdrawn?**
- Did you know ... the IRS switches your 401(k)-loan to a distribution and **charges you taxes plus penalties** if you make your required payments incorrectly?
- Did you know ... the tech-wreck, which began in March of 2000, decimated many IRA accounts and those **losses cannot be deducted** against present income or future investment earnings?
- Did you know ... Roth IRA investment losses **can never be deducted** against your income or earnings, even though taxes were already paid on those dollars?

If You Plan To Be In A Lower Bracket, Then What Kind Of Retirement Are You Or Your Advisor Planning? Sounds Like You're Planning To Fail!

The mantra from all financial advisors has classically been, *"Put the most possible into your retirement fund, because you will postpone your taxes until a time when you are in a lower tax bracket."*

Will you really be in a lower tax bracket at retirement? You may be simply delaying your taxes owed until they will be even more.

Granted, if you deposit into your company sponsored plan and receive matching of 50 cents on the dollar or more, it behooves you to take advantage of

> *"But taxes will eat up so much of our retirement funds. Not that we will need it all, but we were hoping to get more value out of our life savings."*
> — Jerry, retiree, Lexington, KY

that offer. In essence, your employer will be donating enough to pay your future income taxes when you withdraw your funds. The employer's 50 cents going in with your own dollar makes their portion represent one-third of your total deposit. When you withdraw those funds, the employer contribution remains to be one-third of your cash out. Therefore, it's just about enough to pay your income taxes on the back end.

Any match less than 50% may not be worth it. Also, funding your plan with additional dollars, over and above the amount they will match is just like a regular IRA. You will only be delaying the inevitable for no future benefit.

If you need the forced-savings aspect of payroll-deducted retirement funding in order to successfully amass your fortune, there are alternate ways to create this type of system for yourself inside your own bank account. Automatic transfer or deductions are often available at no cost to you.

Once You Are In A Qualified Plan, You Must Take Your Steps Very Carefully

Tax rules and regulations governing withdrawals from qualified plans and IRAs are extremely complex. Without careful planning, the tax burden on retirement plan assets can be devastating. The "double whammy" of income and estate taxes on a qualified plan can result in as little as 33%[65] of your remaining undistributed retirement money passing on to your heirs.

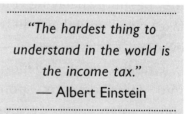

> "The hardest thing to understand in the world is the income tax."
> — Albert Einstein

---

[65] Assumes a 45% estate tax and a 40% combined federal and state income tax bracket.

Sadly, your deferred retirement plan earnings will be taxed as ordinary income, which are the highest income tax rates. Had money grown in a taxable account, most of your earnings would have incurred interest, dividend and capital gains taxes when received. The problem with taxable accounts is the "pay as you go" system. If you must pay the taxes as the money is earned, your compounded return is seriously impacted and your results are much less stellar.

When your beneficiaries receive assets from your estate, they generally get them income tax free because of the stepped-up basis applied to inherited assets. Unfortunately, this general rule doesn't apply to your retirement plan cash. Whoever gets that money will still eventually owe full income taxes on it. They don't even get the benefit of lower capital gains rates.

Can You Safely Navigate Through The Multitude Of Landmines In The IRA Distribution Terrain Ahead?

If you do it wrong, huge penalties may await you amounting to upwards of 50% plus the tax? This flaw in our tax code penalizes those who don't do strategic planning.

Let me reiterate. If you, your bereaved

WILL HISTORY REPEAT ITSELF?

FACT: A 1986 tax law levied a 15% "excess accumulation tax," also known as the "Success Tax," on retirement plans. Many heirs to large retirement accounts found themselves owing the IRS even more money than the balance of the account they had inherited. The law was later repealed.

loved-ones, your beneficiaries or your heirs, fail to take out the full amount required within the appropriate time period, a tax penalty will take 50% of what should have been withdrawn but wasn't. Additionally, income taxes will be due on top of that massive monetary punishment.

The IRS Penalties And Taxes Don't End When You Die

The rules as to how fast your beneficiaries or heirs must withdraw funds from your IRA account and **pay the income tax** differ, depending on the beneficiary you select. If your heirs don't follow the complicated steps correctly, they could also be subject to penalties.

The IRA distribution rules, after age 70½, are calculated by taking the life expectancy of your beneficiary that is less than 10 years younger than you. Only where your designated beneficiary is a spouse more than 10 years younger than you is his or her actual life expectancy used to figure the withdrawal period during your lifetime.

There's no early withdrawal penalty on what your heir withdraws after your death, even if the heir is under age 59½. But if your spouse is your heir and rolls over your retirement account to his or her IRA in hopes of delaying the taxes owed, a withdrawal from the funds while the spouse remains under 59½, is subject to penalties.

Your spouse can roll over from your retirement account (IRA or other) to his or her IRA, but no other heir can roll over from your account.

A Roth IRA allows for roll over to the beneficiary's account, but there are also special rules governing this process.

If you die before April 1 after the year you reach age 70½ having named no beneficiary or having named an estate or a charity as beneficiary; all funds must be distributed, and income taxes paid, within five to six years of your death. Heirs don't get the option of using their own life expectancy.

Did You Know Your Retirement Account Could Almost Vanish Legally Through Tax Confiscation?

What good is it to earn a great return for years if the IRS just takes most of it in the end? It's extremely disheartening to see money a parent or grandparent has sacrificed to save just wiped away by taxes. Imagine how your own children or grandchildren will feel if they experience this horror with your retirement accounts once you're gone.

With residential real estate currently growing at unprecedented rates, you may find the combination of your home's value and your other assets actually creating huge unexpected tax problems for your heirs.

A large taxpayer retirement account, in combination with extreme house values in many areas, highly increases the chance your estate will be cut down by the federal estate tax on top of the federal income tax. Granted, the estate tax is scheduled to

Estimates are that estate and income taxes could eat up as much as 70% to 75% of retirement assets under certain circumstances.

be slowly phased out, but the laws are currently set to have it return in the future. We don't really know who will be in charge when that time comes. Who's to say what tomorrow will bring for the tax code?

The law currently has specific rules about how fast the money must be taken out of the plan after your death. These rules push most inherited estates into higher tax brackets for the beneficiaries. This system also provides the IRS with more confiscated taxes in the end.

Distribution of IRAs after your death is based on the actual life span or life expectancy of your beneficiary. Taxes could be spread out and become a huge cash cow for good old Uncle Sam.

So, How Do You Safely Navigate These IRS Traps?

Those with Real Wealth Vision™ know to steer around the pitfalls associated with most IRS qualified plans. They wish to protect the bulk of their wealth and pass it on to their heirs. With this in mind, they always maximize their participation in any 401(k) employer-sponsored plans available to receive the matching provided. Having someone else pay your taxes is the same as not incurring taxes. This is a no-brainer for wealth success. But, that's where they stop with the qualified plan path.

A Roth IRA is a second possibility for those who qualify, but those plans also have strings attached. The caps and limits in the rules eliminate the Roth IRA choice for many people. Besides, these IRAs are for those who only have a few thousand to put away each year.

If you really wanted to sock away a large sum and watch it grow with tax-favored glee, you would have to go via a different vehicle. So, what is the alternative? A properly structured non-qualified plan will remove deposit caps, ignore income ceilings and utilize investment-grade life insurance to allow for **tax-favored growth, tax-favored access** and **tax-favored transfer to heirs**. It's the perfect solution!

Ed Slott, CPA, IRA expert and author of *The Retirement Savings Time Bomb and How To Defuse It*, states in his book, *"The single best, most cost-effective yet amazingly underutilized strategy for protecting retirement account balances, especially large ones, from being decimated by the highest levels of combined taxation is buying life insurance ..."*

Life insurance has long been recognized as the best solution for counteracting the devastation wrought by taxes. Not only is it great for protecting fortunes that exceed the threshold for estate taxes, but it can be utilized for just about anyone who wished to enhance their wealth situation.

How do those with Real Wealth Vision™ follow IRS guidelines and utilize life insurance as protection against taxation and a tool for wealth building?

Here are just a few of the tax-advantaged H.E.R.O. Solution™ ways someone with Real Wealth Vision™ can create a non-qualified plan for a better result:

- They tap their home's equity for a **tax-free** initial S.A.F.E.T.Y. Fund™ deposit.
- S.A.F.E.T.Y. Fund™ assets are placed in investment-grade life insurance contracts.
- They simply swap mutual fund fees they would have paid for the minimal cost of their insurance.
- Their assets grow **tax-favored**, indexed to market returns, but not in the market.
- Their assets are shielded and protected from principal loss and downside risk by being in a non-variable instrument.[66]
- Funds are easily accessible via **income tax-free** loans or withdrawal of cash deposited.
- Accumulated assets then transfer to their heirs **income tax-free** upon death.

---

[66] Remember, in years when the market has a loss, these instruments lose no principal. There is a minimum guaranteed rate with each individual product. Cost of insurance and company expenses will be incurred each year, but if invested in regular accounts, mutual fund management fees would also be charged in years when the market loses. These costs are a part of financial reality.

Have You Checked The Expiration Date
On Your Current Retirement Account?

Two of the legs of your old three-legged stool for income in your golden years have gotten really wobbly in the 21st Century. It's probably going to be completely up to you to provide a comfortable income until you reach age 100 or beyond. Will your current plan do the job or will you outlive your money?

The wealthy have discovered how to expand their monthly retirement income by 50% from funds they already have and then stretch that monthly income to last into perpetuity. Want to see the secrets of this phenomenon? The next chapter provides the details ...

CHAPTER FIFTEEN

YOU'D BETTER CHECK THE "EXPIRATION DATE" ON YOUR RETIREMENT ACCOUNT

Risks are everywhere in our world. You've probably heard of many of them: market risk, safety risk, health risk, hazard risk, economic risk and credit risk. The list could go on and on. These are all dangers we might need to genuinely be concerned about. But now there's a brand spanking new one to add to the list.

So what's the latest big peril in the 21st Century? How about **Longevity Risk**? It's defined as the potential hazard that you'll live too long. "So, how could that be a risk?" you say. "Sounds like a good thing."

We are improving our healthcare and our lifestyles. We're eating healthier, exercising, finding cures for disease, practicing stress management and making massive strides in quality of life. So how could living too long be a problem? You would think it would be a great thing, a wonderful thing.

Yes, everyone wants to live beyond age 100, stay active and enjoy life. But this fabulous possibility could, in turn, create a serious problem you may not have considered.

What happens if you run out of money? There's a huge likelihood that you may outlive your assets. Wow! What would you do then?

LET'S FAST-FORWARD TO YOUR FUTURE

Picture these two dramatically different scenes when you are 78 years old:

Possibility 1: You are in a charming familiar restaurant with soft music playing. The fireplace is dancing nearby and the fresh flowers on the table add splashes of color to the evening. A waiter is assisting with the menu selections: a nice cut of steak or the "catch of the day." You contemplate the options and make your decision. It's the toughest choice you face at his point in your life.

Possibility 2: You are in a tiny kitchen sitting by the stove. It's been a long time since your oven was used for roasting or baking. Now you mainly need it for warmth. Since there isn't much choice in your pantry, dinner is the same just about every night. You crouch at the tiny table and ask yourself, "Which will it be tonight? Should I use a fork this time or just my fingers?" It's definitely not the toughest decision you face at this point in your life. You contemplate the question and make your choice. You pick up your meal and begin to nibble at your entrée — **cat food on a cracker, again!**

Sound scary? That's the very real threat in **Longevity Risk**!

Which scene will ultimately be played out in your life? Your present planning will determine this for you. You can't depend on the government to rescue you. The sheer numbers of future takers versus pool of working depositors make the Social Security safety net look threadbare at best. Your fate most likely will be completely yours to determine.

If we are going to reap the rewards of longer and longer lives, we must face this risk head on and guarantee comfort for our futures.

> *"Americans' greatest fear is running out of money in retirement."*
> — USA Today survey

Are We Going To Be Able To Support Ourselves As We Age?

In 2006, over half of all Americans aged 45 to 54 currently have less than $50,000 in their accumulated savings. How much SHOULD they have in place right now in order to live in their upcoming retirement? At this point, a little over $600,000 would produce the income they'll require. Additionally, about half of younger working adults, aged 20 to 30, see no reason to save their money right now and aren't doing it.

> *"By 2030, retirees will have $45 billion less in retirement income than they will need for basic living expenses like food and housing, according to the Employee Benefits Research Institute."*
> — Chicago Tribune

Currently the U.S.-born 65 million-member baby boom generation has swollen to 84 million due to immigration. This group now makes up approximately half of the entire work force of this country. Before we know it, we'll be in the year 2030 and the youngest of this group will have reached age 65. That's 84-million people at retirement age or older!

A 1998 AARP survey found that about 85% of the baby boomers think they'll need more money in retirement than their parents needed in order to live comfortably. Will the money be there? If our only reliance for support is Social

Security, how will the government be able to provide a safety net for the huge number of retirees who aren't prepared? The answer? It may not be able to ...

> "When the boomers retire, as soon as they use up their savings, which will take the average family a few years more or less, they will have to cut their life styles in a more dramatic way than any age group in America has done since The Great Depression. The whole glorious dream of living on the golf course, of having a cabin and a boat on the lake, of traveling, of helping out the grandkids ... well, it was just some people talking. The reality will be having to sell the family house, living under conditions of extreme stringency, waking up at four a.m. in fear, cutting pills in half, and bitter memories of what might have been."
> — Ben Stein, noted author, economist, actor and comedian, Yahoo Finance, March 6, 2006

In the not too distant future, we may be living beyond 100 years of age. Advancements in medical technology and healthier lifestyles could result in additional dramatic improvements to our life spans. If we are going to live for more years and we're also going to need more money in those years, where will we get the dollars?

Our parents were always taught to depend on a **"three-legged stool"** for their total retirement income:

Leg #1:   Social Security
Leg #2:   Company Pension
Leg #3:   Personal Savings

But in the 21st Century, two of those legs have become quite wobbly. In fact, they may just give way and collapse before long.

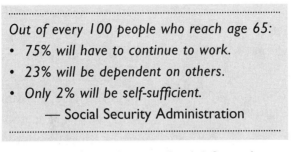

Out of every 100 people who reach age 65:
- 75% will have to continue to work.
- 23% will be dependent on others.
- Only 2% will be self-sufficient.
  — Social Security Administration

Leg Number One — Social Security

The questionability of the current Social Security system is a topic for another book entirely, so we'll skip that discussion in this one. Who knows if America's broken plan will provide any of us with much of anything? Dependence on Social Security income for sustenance in your golden years could result in either disappointment or belt-tightening.

In the summer of 2005, Alan Greenspan[67] warned, while Social Security traditionally provided workers with around 40% of their pre-retirement income, that was **unlikely to continue,** leaving them even more dependent on savings and pensions.[68]

"Today, Social Security, Medicare and Medicaid account for 40 percent of the entire federal budget — but they are growing faster than the economy — and are putting more and more pressure on the federal budget. In 10 years' time, these programs will account for 50 percent — and by 2030, spending for Social Security, Medicare and Medicaid alone — just those three programs — will be almost 60 percent of the entire federal budget."
— Remarks from the 2006 Saver Summit, Washington, D.C.

---

[67] Alan Greenspan was the Chairman of the Federal Reserve Board in 2005.
[68] *New York Times Online,* July 22, 2005.

> *"I've got all the money I'll ever need — if I die by four o'clock."*
> — Henny Youngman, comedian, 1906–1998

If you want to roll the dice and keep depending on that kind of security for your future livelihood, then keep dreaming. Otherwise, I would recommend you grab your list of sources for retirement cash and cross off Leg Number One … *Social Security.*

Leg Number Two — Company Pension … Disappearing From The Landscape?

Imagine this scenario:

"Your company had promised you a fixed sum per month from your pension, and you had a plan to meet your expenses in old age with that money. Now imagine that after years of hearing these promises from your employer — and with no warning at all, just days before you retire — you see your pension cut drastically, maybe even cut in half. You have little remaining earnings capacity, and the money you thought you could count on is suddenly reduced to a fraction of what you'd expected. You'd be pretty mad about it, and worried, too."

These are words from the White House's remarks presented at the 2006 National Summit on Retirement Saving.[69] This scenario is *also* what actually happened to **my own father** when he retired a little over 10 years ago. Sadly, the pension problem has only gotten worse since then.

Traditional pensions supplied by the employer are simply being phased out in today's world. Mr. Greenspan spoke on a

---

[69] Official Whitehouse website: www.whitehouse.gov, 2006.

different occasion regarding the topic of personal savings in an address to the Bureau of Economic Analysis in 2004. He purposefully excluded pension assets in his total U.S. savings figure because, according to his statement, *"... companies are regularly abandoning their pension obligations."* He questioned the validity of including pension funds in our total savings picture.

According to the executive director of the federal Pension Benefit Guaranty Corp (PBGC), more and more pension programs are now only legacy plans, closed to new employees and no longer accumulating benefits for workers within them. PBGC is an insurance fund designed to step in when a company pension plan becomes insolvent. The maximum annual benefit guaranteed by PBGC is only $12,870 per worker for multi-employer plans.

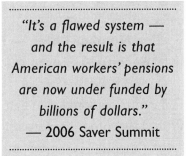

"It's a flawed system — and the result is that American workers' pensions are now under funded by billions of dollars."
— 2006 Saver Summit

So, let's say you've been planning for a monthly pension income of $6000, but before you retire, the plan defaults. PBGC insurance would step in to provide you monthly retirement income, but it could be as little as $1075 per month. That would be more than an 80% cut in your benefits!

The Center on Federal Financial Institutions estimates PBGC will collapse in 2020 or 2021 and a rescue would cost 78 billion to 100 billion dollars[70]. Could this issue become another taxpayer bailout crisis like the Savings and Loan debacle of the early 1990s?

---

[70] *Rocky Mountain News:* December 29, 2004.

Standard and Poor's[71] reports that the vast majority of the assets in S&P 500® pension funds are in only 22 of its 500 companies.[72] That's a tiny minority.

Many say the traditional three-legged stool may have to become a single solid stump with no legs at all, supported entirely by personal savings. The majority of us were never offered a company pension plan, but those who are depending on them better be sure their employer is financially strong and is prepared to provide the bucks when the time comes.

O.K. So on our list, cross off Leg Number Two ... *Company Pension.*

Leg Number Three — Personal Savings — It Better Become A Stump Wide Enough To Support You!

Is your personal nest egg alone enough to take care of you? Will it become depleted too soon? Have you considered future income tax rates might be higher and take a larger chunk when you withdraw your money? Are you aware of just how big the tax burden will be on retirement withdrawals in the future? How much will inflation increase the cost of your future basic expenses?

Remember the **Rule of 72**? It easily projects how long it takes for your savings to double by dividing your compound rate of return into the number 72. Say you are getting a rate of return of 8%. 72 divided by 8 yields an answer of 9. So, your money would double in about 9 years.

---

[71] "Standard and Poor's" and "S&P 500" are trademarks of The McGraw-Hill Companies, Inc.
[72] *New York Times:* July 22, 2005.

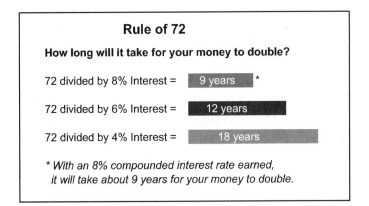

This same principal can be applied to expenses. Want to see how? What do you think inflation rates will be as we move forward in time? You know a gallon of milk was much cheaper 15 years ago. Price changes happen so gradually over time, we often don't even notice them.

Most recently, in early 2006, inflation was almost touching 4% but it had exceeded 11% in the 1970s. For the sake of this discussion, let's say the historical average is around 5%. This illustration shows how the **Rule of 72** can be used in your planning:

"RULE OF 72" APPLIED TO FUTURE COST OF LIVING

Your living costs today* =	$2,500 per month
72 divided by 5 = 14.4 (We'll round to 15)	Doubles every 15 years
Cost of living in 15 years =	$5,000 per month
Cost of living in 30 years =	$10,000 per month

*Dollars you spend monthly on milk, bread, gas, etc.

Will Your Retirement Account Expire? Will You Run Out Of Cash Before You Run Out Of Years?

Let's say you've reached retirement age and wish to begin withdrawing an income. To make our illustration simple, we'll say you and your spouse, at this time in the future, need $75,000 per year to live comfortably.

You've accumulated a nest egg of $1,000,000 and you are receiving an earnings rate of 7.5%. That means you're getting $75,000 in earnings on your account. If your money is in a regular IRA and you need that $75,000 for living expenses, you will need to withdraw a higher amount and pay the taxes due in order to net your required after-tax cash to live.

How Much Do You Need To Withdraw In Order To Net $75,000 Per Year?

In a 33% tax bracket — you'll need to withdraw $112,000 annually.

In a 30% tax bracket — you'll need to withdraw $107,150 annually.

In a 25% tax bracket — you'll need to withdraw $100,000 annually.

If your account is earning 7.5% and you withdraw and pay taxes, how long will your million dollar account last? Let's not forget — more and more people are living until the age of 100 and beyond. Will your funds provide what you need?

At what age will you simply run out of money? The following table shows how long your cash will last. You'll have money until age 81, if you are in a 33% tax bracket. If you're in a 30% bracket, you'll make it another year to 82. At a 25% bracket, you will make it until age 84. Then, what will you do for income from age 85 until age 100? You could have retired with a million dollars and still have a serious problem.

How long will $1 million last
if you need $75,000 net income annually?

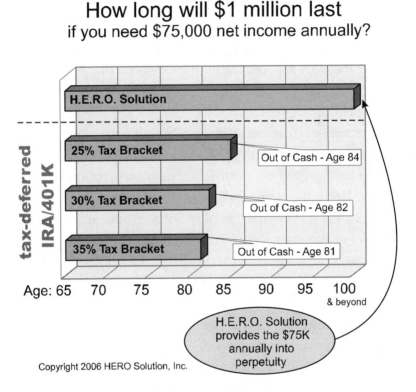

H.E.R.O. Solution

25% Tax Bracket — Out of Cash - Age 84

30% Tax Bracket — Out of Cash - Age 82

35% Tax Bracket — Out of Cash - Age 81

tax-deferred IRA/401K

Age: 65 70 75 80 85 90 95 100 & beyond

H.E.R.O. Solution provides the $75K annually into perpetuity

Copyright 2006 HERO Solution, Inc.

Wouldn't You Prefer An Income That Keeps Flowing? And Flowing? And Flowing?

Somewhat like a pink, wind-up toy you may have seen somewhere? Well, that toy was going — not flowing — but, you get the picture.

How can you make your retirement income last into perpetuity or beyond age 100, whether its $75,000 or whatever your personal figure comes out to be? You must create a nest egg growing in a tax-favored environment that will produce a large enough monthly cash flow without needing to tap into your principal.

In other words, your money must generate enough dollars for your monthly income through its own earnings. If you can make this happen, your income-producing money machine can keep churning out tax-favored income as long as you need it.

Your best bet to achieve this goal is to gather every dime of tax-free cash you can get your hands on and get it working for you in a tax-favored environment. The more avoidance of taxation up front, the more cash is working for you.

You can begin on the first of those critical steps, tax-free cash, today through the H.E.R.O. Solution™. The other two, tax-favored growth and access, are facilitated with the S.A.F.E.T.Y. Fund™. The magic of this synergy is your best possible chance for success.

Instead of outliving your money (as just illustrated by using a regular IRA), you could have had your retirement cash growing in a S.A.F.E.T.Y. Fund™ utilizing the H.E.R.O. Solution™. Then your $1,000,000 would be accessible without tax hits.

How does this impact your results? You can receive your $75,000 annually without ever touching your million dollars! It just keeps going, churning out your annual needs and you may never need to withdraw your principal.

How Is The H.E.R.O. Solution™ Superior To IRAs For Your Retirement Dollar?

Let's bring our focus back to the present. If you are currently putting cash into an IRA, whether it's a tax-postponed regular IRA or an after-tax Roth IRA, there is a better way to make those dollars become cash machines in the future. As just illustrated, for long-term retirement income planning, the H.E.R.O. Solution™ can provide as much as **50% greater income** in retirement!

When you're saving for retirement using IRAs, your choices are usually only a Roth plan or a regular one. What if a third alternative could allow you to take that same pre-tax money you are placing in the regular IRA but provide you the tax-favored growth and access offered by the Roth IRA? This super-combination could result in a boost to your monthly spendable retirement income that could be as large as 50%! It's like an IRA, but without the limits on your income or the annual ceilings on your deposit amounts. How great is that?

The H.E.R.O. Solution™ allows you to back into retirement income by taking idle, non-working equity in your home and transforming it into a tool for your wealth.

"Why are you laughing? Congress just raised taxes again!"

"I'm on a great big FIXED income ... It's FIXED not to owe income taxes!"

Copyright 2006 HERO Solution, Inc.

Here's how it would work. You borrow your home's equity and put that tax-free cash to work in a side account, which is, of course, your S.A.F.E.T.Y. Fund™. You take those same dollars per month you were putting into your IRA, but instead you use them to pay the tax-deductible monthly payment on your borrowed equity. Your monthly costs are the same. You are receiving tax-favored treatment for your monthly dollars just like a regular IRA, but your side account has a large chunk of cash working in a tax-favored environment creating your retirement wealth.

This example uses a H.E.R.O. Solution™ equity figure of $114,000 borrowed at an interest-only rate of 7%. The illustration uses a conservative earnings rate of 7.5% for all accounts. A 30% income tax bracket is assumed. You'll receive $6,000 monthly with your H.E.R.O. Solution™ plan compared to only $3957 per month with both types of IRA. This level of monthly contribution was chosen because it is the current maximum allowed for IRAs: $4000 for each spouse for a total of $8000 per year.

Take a look …

H.E.R.O. Solution™ Compared to IRA Deposits

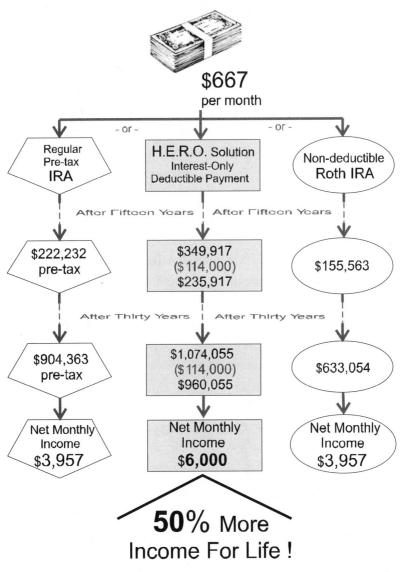

$667
per month

- or -   - or -

| Regular Pre-tax IRA | H.E.R.O. Solution Interest-Only Deductible Payment | Non-deductible Roth IRA |

After Fifteen Years | After Fifteen Years

| $222,232 pre-tax | $349,917 ($114,000) $235,917 | $155,563 |

After Thirty Years | After Thirty Years

| $904,363 pre-tax | $1,074,055 ($114,000) $960,055 | $633,054 |

| Net Monthly Income $3,957 | Net Monthly Income **$6,000** | Net Monthly Income $3,957 |

50% More Income For Life !

Assumptions: 30% tax bracket, 7.5% earnings on all accounts and 7% interest-only $114,000 mortgage (shown bracketed above.)

After 15 years, your H.E.R.O. Solution™ is over $13,000 ahead of your not-yet-taxed regular IRA account after deducting the $114,000 mortgage owed (the amounts shown in brackets). This does not account for the accrued taxes due on your regular IRA. It's about $80,000 ahead of your Roth IRA in that same time period.

Move down to the 30th year of your plan, you've paid back your mortgage and you're ready to access your monthly cash. If you've gone with the H.E.R.O. Solution™, your account has approximately $960,000 that can work to earn you a tax-free monthly income. If you had paid the taxes on your $667 per month and put your money into a Roth IRA, you would only have about $633,000 to produce your retirement income.

Would you rather receive a tax-free check for $6000 or $4000 ($3957) each month? It's $2000 more — or 50%! You spent the same dollars in your working years. You got the same tax-deductible treatment for those dollars (the IRA was deducted on page one of your 1040, while the H.E.R.O. Solution™ was deducted on Schedule A under mortgage interest). Same dollars spent, but a huge difference in your results.

Your S.A.F.E.T.Y. Fund™ Can Be A Fantastic Tool

- S.A.F.E.T.Y. Fund™ allows tax-favored growth.
- S.A.F.E.T.Y. Fund™ allows tax-favored withdrawals.
- S.A.F.E.T.Y. Fund™ provides for income into perpetuity.

As soon as feasibly possible, you must transform any taxable nest-egg accounts you have into a S.A.F.E.T.Y. Fund™ to set up the money machine that will produce monthly tax favored income forever. Investment-grade life insurance contracts allow for tax-favored accumulation. Money paid into the cash value of a contract may be withdrawn without tax ramifications, and loans against the cash value of a life insurance contract are not taxable. Now you have every piece in place.

Life insurance contracts allow for systematic monthly withdrawals or on-demand access to your cash after a number of years through return of your amounts deposited or policy loans. These loans are not due and payable until the death of the insured and are paid from the life insurance proceeds. So, in your lifetime, payments will never be due.

Care should be taken to assure the insurance contract remains in force during your lifetime to avoid causing a retroactive taxing event. Several companies provide special riders that guarantee the policy will remain in force to protect its tax-favored status. If the policy is not lapsed or cancelled, the non-qualified plan remains viable until the death of the insured.

If you utilize your H.E.R.O. Solution™ and acquire an investment-grade life insurance contract to hold your S.A.F.E.T.Y. Fund™, you must be sure to ask your advisor about the no-lapse rider. If the company you select does not offer this type of rider, you must be diligent to meet with your enlightened advisor periodically for a review and check-up of your plan. Annual meetings are best, but you must stay abreast of your H.E.R.O. Solution™ and S.A.F.E.T.Y. Fund™ to keep it healthy over time.

Will My Current Retirement Plan Last?
How Much Will It Cost To Live In The Future?

The following table shows the effects of inflation on your household income needs into the future. Say you're a married couple making a joint income of $85,000. Let's estimate that, after state and local taxes, you are left with an after tax income of $4000 to pay for your expenses each month. You can find your current age on the left. Then, go across to find a future age, then follow down the table to see how much you'll need, at that age, to keep the same lifestyle you have today.

How Much Will It Cost To Live In The Future?
$4000 Per Month After Tax Today

	With A 3.0% Inflation Rate, What Will $4,000 Per Month Today Be In The Future?						
Age Today	When You Reach Age:						
	65	70	75	80	85	90	95	100
25	$13,048	$15,126	$17,536	$20,329	$23,566	$27,320	$31,671	$36,716
30	$11,255	$13,048	$15,126	$17,536	$20,329	$23,566	$27,320	$31,671
35	$9,709	$11,255	$13,048	$15,126	$17,536	$20,329	$23,566	$27,320
40	$8,375	$9,709	$11,255	$13,048	$15,126	$17,536	$20,329	$23,566
45	$7,224	$8,375	$9,709	$11,255	$13,048	$15,126	$17,536	$20,329
50	$6,232	$7,224	$8,375	$9,709	$11,255	$13,048	$15,126	$17,536
55	$5,376	$6,232	$7,224	$8,375	$9,709	$11,255	$13,048	$15,126
60	$4,637	$5,376	$6,232	$7,224	$8,375	$9,709	$11,255	$13,048
65	$4,000	$4,637	$5,376	$6,232	$7,224	$8,375	$9,709	$11,255

	With A 4.0% Inflation Rate, What Will $4,000 Per Month Be In The Future?						
Age Today	When You Reach Age:						
	65	70	75	80	85	90	95	100
25	$19,204	$23,365	$28,427	$34,585	$42,079	$51,195	$62,286	$75,781
30	$15,784	$19,204	$23,365	$28,427	$34,585	$42,079	$51,195	$62,286
35	$12,974	$15,784	$19,204	$23,365	$28,427	$34,585	$42,079	$51,195
40	$10,663	$12,974	$15,784	$19,204	$23,365	$28,427	$34,585	$42,079
45	$8,764	$10,663	$12,974	$15,784	$19,204	$23,365	$28,427	$34,585
50	$7,204	$8,764	$10,663	$12,974	$15,784	$19,204	$23,365	$28,427
55	$5,921	$7,204	$8,764	$10,663	$12,974	$15,784	$19,204	$23,365
60	$4,867	$5,921	$7,204	$8,764	$10,663	$12,974	$15,784	$19,204
65	$4,000	$4,867	$5,921	$7,204	$8,764	$10,663	$12,974	$15,784

	With A 5.0% Inflation Rate, What Will $4,000 Per Month Be In The Future?						
Age Today	When You Reach Age:						
	65	70	75	80	85	90	95	100
25	$28,160	$35,940	$45,870	$58,543	$74,717	$95,360	$121,706	$155,331
30	$22,064	$28,160	$35,940	$45,870	$58,543	$74,717	$95,360	$121,706
35	$17,288	$22,064	$28,160	$35,940	$45,870	$58,543	$74,717	$95,360
40	$13,545	$17,288	$22,064	$28,160	$35,940	$45,870	$58,543	$74,717
45	$10,613	$13,545	$17,288	$22,064	$28,160	$35,940	$45,870	$58,543
50	$8,316	$10,613	$13,545	$17,288	$22,064	$28,160	$35,940	$45,870
55	$6,516	$8,316	$10,613	$13,545	$17,288	$22,064	$28,160	$35,940
60	$5,105	$6,516	$8,316	$10,613	$13,545	$17,288	$22,064	$28,160
65	$4,000	$5,105	$6,516	$8,316	$10,613	$13,545	$17,288	$22,064

The top table illustrates the effect of an inflation rate of 3%, the second at 4% and the bottom shows at 5%. In other words, if you spend $4000 per month to live, then it will cost you this much in the future to buy the same bread, gasoline, electricity and clothes you're buying currently.

Bottom line? We had better keep our future needs in mind constantly, no matter our age. Obviously, the younger you are the longer you'll have to prepare for your future, but the more you'll need once the future arrives. Let's all cross our fingers and hope that inflation remains at the low numbers going forward.

Your Best Bet For Being Prepared?
The H.E.R.O. Solution™

If you can make a pledge to create your life's wealth — if you will commit to not consume your equity, but instead protect it — then, you are ready for this type of financial plan.

For those who currently carry credit card or other consumable debt, you should consider postponing implementation of this plan until you can gain control of your expenditures. Your advisor may be able to assist in repositioning that type of debt to free up monthly cash for you. This cash and your current equity could then be rerouted into your personal solution to create your Real Wealth Vision™ plan.

Do You Currently Have
Tax-Deferred Retirement Accounts?[73]

If you do, want to hear how you can
- Increase the monthly retirement income they produce for you?
- Drastically cut the taxes you'll owe when you tap that cash?
- Stretch the income to keep it producing to age 100 and beyond?

If you'd like to see an *amazing* plan for turbocharging your current qualified plan accounts and slashing the taxes due by 85%–100%, the secrets are uncovered in the next chapter.

---

[73] The term "retirement account" refers to any type of qualified plan where taxes have been postponed, like a 401(k), regular IRA, 403(b) or 457 plan.

CHAPTER SIXTEEN

TURN YOUR HOUSE INTO AN AMAZING RETIREMENT MACHINE™

Just Because You Stop Punching the Clock, Does Your House Have To?

Would you like to get to the cash in your current 401(k)s, IRAs, 403(b)s, TSAs or 457 plans (you know, those accounts that still have taxes due) — **owing almost no income taxes**? Would you like to **boost your retirement income by 50%?** Would you like to leverage some of your otherwise-idle equity and capitalize on your tax-deductible mortgage interest to neutralize the taxes on your retirement income?

Well, you're reading the right book!

If you are not yet near retirement age, you can incorporate this into your ongoing planning. If you've already reached that age (in other words, you are between 59½ and 70½ years old), then pay special attention to what I'm about to reveal to you.

Because whenever that day arrives for you (you know — the day when you want to switch the cash-flow valve on your retirement accounts to "output"), you'll be able to access much, if not all, of that cash with very little or no taxes due.

Want to see how this works?

H.E.R.O. Solution™ Retirement
Roll-Out Plan — Age 59½ to 70½

Remember how we talked about the importance of getting tax-free upfront cash for deposit into your S.A.F.E.T.Y. Fund™ and how the whole dollars, rather than the partial dollars, really could boost your returns? The H.E.R.O. Solution™ Retirement Roll-Out Plan partners with Uncle Sam to provide you a net-zero tax consequence for much of your retirement income. Ultimately, if you do owe any taxes on these funds, they'll only be a fraction of what would have otherwise been payable had you not implemented this plan.

"O.K. This is some kind of trick, right?" you're thinking.

Nope. But it's a little difficult to explain.

Look at the total retirement account value you wish to access. For this example, we'll say you've got $250,000 in your qualified plan and you've reached 59½ years of age. That means you have 10 years or so in which to remove your money at your discretion without penalty before the IRS dictates the amount you must withdraw per the Required Minimum Distribution (RMD) rules and when it must be distributed.

Now, let's say you have a fair amount of equity inside your house, and this equity exceeds the balance of your retirement fund. You take out an interest-only mortgage that gives you cash-out equal to the amount of your retirement account. (In our example we'll use $250,000.) Take those tax-free dollars and put them into your S.A.F.E.T.Y. Fund™ so that they may begin working in a tax-favored environment for future income.

O.K. You have taken the same amount of cash from your left pocket (a $250,000 mortgage equal to your retirement account) and placed it into your right pocket (a $250,000 deposit into your S.A.F.E.T.Y. Fund™). To make all calculations easy, we are illustrating all accounts with an 8% earnings rate and a mortgage rate of 8%. Your results can be even better with a lower rate or a better return, so let's just look at the concept for now.

"But, how am I going to pay for that mortgage?" you say. "All my retirement account money is still in my *taxes-due* deferred account."

Yes, but keep following along and you'll see ...

... Here's Where The Tax Magic Begins To Work!

Every month, withdraw an amount equal to your mortgage payment from your retirement account. That's right — take a distribution. You can do it monthly or annually in anticipation of the payments you'll have due that next year. In our example, the mortgage has an 8% interest-only payment of $1667, so from your deferred account, you withdraw either $1667 each month or $20,000 once a year to pay for the upcoming payments.

"But, won't I have to pay taxes on those withdrawals?" you ask.

That's the beauty. You report your IRA, 401(k) or whatever-qualified plan distributions on the front of your Form 1040 as income, but you deduct an amount exactly equal to that on your Schedule A under mortgage interest deductions. So,

$20,000 will be listed as a retirement account distribution, but $20,000 will also be listed on Schedule A under mortgage interest deductions.

So, what is your bottom line? That's right. It's zero. They cancel each other out.

You have just, effectively, taken the exact amount of your taxable retirement fund's balance and put it to work in your side account earning income that will ultimately be accessible without taxation. Your mortgage loan payment (which is the entire amount if you have an interest-only loan) will be withdrawn from your qualified plan's earnings each year. This, effectively, leaves your plan account balance the same over the approximately ten-year period.

Here's how the plan looks between age 59½ and 70½:

H.E.R.O. Solution™ Retirement Roll-Out Plan Age 591/2 to 701/2						
Age	SAFETY Fund	Annual Income	Portion From IRA	Taxes Due	Retirement Account	Mortgage Balance
60	$250,000				$250,000	$250,000
61	$270,750	$0	$20,000	$0	$250,000	$250,000
62	$293,222	$0	$20,000	$0	$250,000	$250,000
63	$317,559	$0	$20,000	$0	$250,000	$250,000
64	$343,917	$0	$20,000	$0	$250,000	$250,000
65	$372,461	$0	$20,000	$0	$250,000	$250,000
66	$403,376	$0	$20,000	$0	$250,000	$250,000
67	$436,856	$0	$20,000	$0	$250,000	$250,000
68	$473,114	$0	$20,000	$0	$250,000	$250,000
69	$512,383	$0	$20,000	$0	$250,000	$250,000
70	$554,910	$0	$20,000	$0	$250,000	$250,000

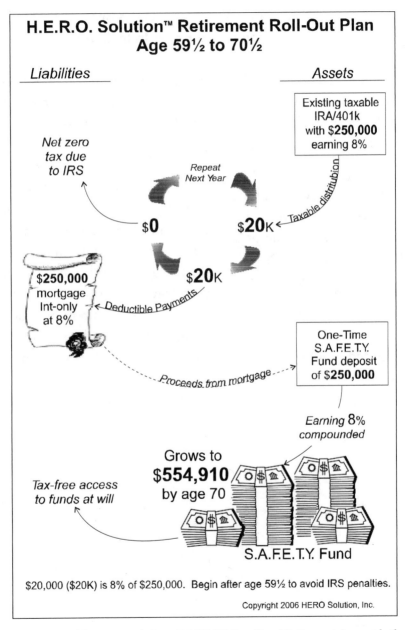

H.E.R.O. Solution™ Retirement Roll-Out Plan
Age 59½ to 70½

Liabilities   _Assets_

Existing taxable
IRA/401k
with **$250,000**
earning 8%

Net zero
tax due
to IRS

Repeat
Next Year

Taxable distribution

$0 $20K

$250,000
mortgage
Int-only
at 8%

$20K

Deductible Payments

One-Time
S.A.F.E.T.Y.
Fund deposit
of **$250,000**

Proceeds from mortgage

Earning 8%
compounded

Grows to
$554,910
by age 70

Tax-free access
to funds at will

S.A.F.E.T.Y. Fund

$20,000 ($20K) is 8% of $250,000. Begin after age 59½ to avoid IRS penalties.

Mortgage is an 8% interest-only loan. S.A.F.E.T.Y. Fund™ and Retirement Account both are illustrated as earning an 8% compounded yield.

Don't Want To Make A Decision?
Can't Decide or Commit? Indecisive?

Here's the alternative: Just leave the money in the qualified plan until you are **forced** to remove it; then face the **pain** at the highest level of taxation as **ordinary income** — not even at slightly less-painful capital gains rates.

> "When you have to make a choice and don't make it, that is in itself a choice."
> — William James,
> American philosopher

You say you don't really need your money from your qualified plan, so you leave it there until the IRS requires that you begin to take it out per the RMD rules.[74] You must begin withdrawing those funds and paying the taxes after you reach an age of 70½. Your account continues to grow at an 8% compounded yield over the ten years and your balance becomes $554,910.

---

[74] IRS required minimum distribution (RMD) — the minimum amount that must be withdrawn in a particular year is the total value of all IRA accounts divided by the number of years the IRA owner is predicted to live, per IRS life expectancy tables.

	Regular Retirement Qualified Plan			
	Waiting for IRS Forced Distributions			
Age	Retirement Account	Annual Income	Portion From IRA	Taxes Due
60	$250,000			
61	$270,750			
62	$293,222	*"I don't really need*		
63	$317,559	*this money now, so*		
64	$343,917	*I'll just let it grow until*		
65	$372,461	*I have to take it out."*		
66	$403,376	**- Retiree**		
67	$436,856			
68	$473,114			
69	$512,383			
70	$554,910			

If you do nothing, you end up with the same balance the H.E.R.O. Solution™ Retirement Roll-Out Plan has in the S.A.F.E.T.Y. Fund™ at the end of the same period, but you'll owe a whopping tax bill as you distribute your funds. If you utilize the Roll-Out Plan, you get access to that entire $554,910 without taxation!

H.E.R.O. Solution™ Retirement Roll-Out Plan — Age 70½ and Beyond

OK. Now you're 70½. 10 years have passed and your S.A.F.E.T.Y. Fund™ has more than doubled to $554,910. The IRS requires that you begin to take distributions from your $250,000 qualified plan. (Lucky for you, the retirement fund has remained at $250,000 instead of $554,910.)

In our example, at age 70½, the IRS annual required minimum distribution (RMD) is $14,700[75] so you continue to distribute the annual $20,000 in earnings from your $250,000 remaining qualified-fund balance. You'll report this cash distribution, but the $20,000 in mortgage interest you pay for that year is deductible for most.

If you had NOT used the H.E.R.O. Solution™ Retirement Roll-Out Plan and had simply left your money growing in the taxable account, your RMD, or forced withdrawal, on the $554,910 balance would be around $32,650 per year — incurring at least $5,000 annually in taxes and netting you **only $27,650 per year**.

With the H.E.R.O. Solution™ strategy, you can choose to begin receiving an annual spendable income of **$44,392 per year** into perpetuity and pay NO INCOME TAXES on it. But you could just leave the money to continue to grow. It's your choice.

This Strategy Just Leaves Other Plans In The Dust

Now, let's suppose you've decided you'll need $50,000 spendable cash each year. So you begin withdrawing that amount from your S.A.F.E.T.Y. Fund™.

---

[75] IRS 2005 Life Expectancy Table states the life expectancy for a 70 year-old is 17 years. $250,000/17 = $14,705. This RMD amount can vary according to the age of your beneficiary.

Both these retirement accounts in the following example began with a $250,000 qualified plan balance at age 60, but the outcomes are extremely and dramatically different! The H.E.R.O. Solution™ Retirement Roll-Out Plan provides a **$50,000 annual spendable income** that continues until **age 100**. That's spendable income AFTER paying the mortgage payment on the outstanding balance.

	H.E.R.O. Solution™ Retirement Roll-Out	IRS Qualified Plan Distribution
Beginning Assets:	$250,000	$250,000
Rate of Return Used:	8%	8%
(in our example)		
Annual Spendable Income:	$50,000	$50,000
Money Lasts to Age:	Age 100	Age 82
Total Income Received:	$1,500,000	$558,968
Total Taxes Paid:	$13,740	$238,880

The H.E.R.O. Solution™ Retirement Roll-Out Plan keeps flowing … and flowing … and flowing …

If you follow the "Glasses of the Masses" way, your monthly income could run out by age 82. But with a little forethought and planning, your account could churn out $50,000 every year between age 71 and 100.

Since it's highly possible you'll live to be that ripe old age, which of those plans would you rather have?

H.E.R.O. Solution Retirement Roll-Out Plan					
$50,000 Spendable Annually					
Age	SAFETY Fund	Annual Income	Portion From IRA	Taxes Due	IRA Account	Mortgage Balance
70	$554,910	$0	$20,000	$0	$250,000	$250,000
71	$550,967	($50,000)	$20,000	$0	$250,000	$250,000
72	$546,697	($50,000)	$20,000	$0	$250,000	$250,000
73	$542,073	($50,000)	$20,000	$0	$250,000	$250,000
74	$537,065	($50,000)	$20,000	$0	$250,000	$250,000
75	$531,641	($50,000)	$20,000	$0	$250,000	$250,000
76	$525,767	($50,000)	$20,000	$0	$250,000	$250,000
77	$519,967	($50,000)	$20,661	($99)	$249,339	$250,000
78	$514,715	($50,000)	$21,872	($281)	$247,414	$250,000
79	$509,909	($50,000)	$22,909	($436)	$244,298	$250,000
80	$505,590	($50,000)	$23,951	($593)	$239,891	$250,000
81	$501,575	($50,000)	$24,731	($710)	$234,351	$250,000
82	$498,095	($50,000)	$25,753	($863)	$227,347	$250,000
83	$494,907	($50,000)	$26,436	($965)	$219,098	$250,000
84	$491,976	($50,000)	$27,049	($1,057)	$209,577	$250,000
85	$489,249	($50,000)	$27,576	($1,136)	$198,767	$250,000
86	$486,653	($50,000)	$27,995	($1,199)	$186,674	$250,000
87	$483,727	($50,000)	$27,862	($1,179)	$173,746	$250,000
88	$480,318	($50,000)	$27,579	($1,137)	$160,066	$250,000
89	$476,245	($50,000)	$27,130	($1,070)	$145,741	$250,000
90	$471,297	($50,000)	$26,499	($975)	$130,902	$250,000
91	$464,813	($50,000)	$25,174	($776)	$116,200	$250,000
92	$456,550	($50,000)	$23,715	($557)	$101,781	$250,000
93	$447,563	($50,000)	$23,671	($551)	$86,252	$250,000
94	$435,593	($50,000)	$21,038	($156)	$72,115	$250,000
95	$420,725	($50,000)	$18,978	$0	$58,906	$250,000
96	$402,009	($50,000)	$16,364	$0	$47,254	$250,000
97	$379,275	($50,000)	$13,899	$0	$37,136	$250,000
98	$352,735	($50,000)	$11,980	$0	$28,126	$250,000
99	$321,711	($50,000)	$9,700	$0	$20,677	$250,000
100	$286,072	($50,000)	$7,659	$0	$14,672	$250,000
	Totals:	$1,500,000		$13,740		

WOW! One and a half million dollars in retirement income PLUS only $13,740 due in income taxes for it![76]

In comparison, what would you receive by sticking with your regular qualified plan distributions? Take a look.

---

[76] This table uses the IRS Life Expectancy Chart published for 2005 to calculate the required minimum distribution (RMD) at each age past 71. Taxes due were listed when the RMD exceeded the $20,000 mortgage interest deduction.

Qualified Plan Taxable Distributions
$50,000 Spendable Annually

Age	Retirement Account	Annual Income	Withdrawn From IRA	Taxes Due
70	$554,910	$0	$0	$0
71	$522,160	($50,000)	$71,429	($21,429)
72	$486,790	($50,000)	$71,429	($21,429)
73	$448,590	($50,000)	$71,429	($21,429)
74	$407,335	($50,000)	$71,429	($21,429)
75	$362,779	($50,000)	$71,429	($21,429)
76	$314,658	($50,000)	$71,429	($21,429)
77	$262,688	($50,000)	$71,429	($21,429)
78	$206,560	($50,000)	$71,429	($21,429)
79	$145,942	($50,000)	$71,429	($21,429)
80	$80,474	($50,000)	$71,429	($21,429)
81	$9,769	($50,000)	$71,429	($21,429)
82	$0	($7,386)	$10,551	($3,165)
83	$0	$0	$0	$0
99	$0	$0	$0	$0
100	$0	$0	$0	$0
Totals:		$557,386		$238,880

Out of money at Age 82

Huge taxes paid

The cash from your plan has pretty much evaporated after age 82. Once the regular qualified plan cash is distributed, your income stops. **You've just outlived your money!**

The total of spendable retirement income ultimately provided by your $250,000 account (it's value at age 60) was $557,386, and you had to pay over $238,880 in income taxes to get that cash.

In comparison, your H.E.R.O. Solution™ Retirement Roll-Out Plan provided an annual $50,000 income until age 100. Your total retirement cash received was $1,500,000, and you only paid $13,740 in taxes along the way.

This strategy could almost triple your retirement income. Additionally, had you elected to stay with the regular taxable

IRS distribution plan, you would have paid over **1600% more in taxes** than you would have owed using this plan.

Of course, if you have more equity in your home and a larger taxable retirement account, you can even improve on these numbers. The only limit is the equity you have available in your residence and your second home, if you have one.

H.E.R.O. Solution™ Retirement Roll-Out Plan can do this for you:

- Helps you to not outlive your money.
- Doubles or even triples your retirement income over time.
- Places more monthly spendable cash in your hands.
- Lets you pull out your current qualified plan money with the little or no taxation.
- Provides many additional years of monthly income.
- Employs an asset most people just ignore: the idle equity in your house.

What About The Mortgage Balance? It's Still There!

"Wait, I'll be 100 years old with a $250,000 mortgage balance," you say.

Yes, but your home is probably worth over $2 million, 40 years later. You could pay off that balance with the remaining funds in your S.A.F.E.T.Y. Fund™ or leave the house to your heirs, along with the mortgage balance. You could also tap your equity for more cash or acquire a reverse mortgage at any time during your retirement years, should you decide to adjust your income strategy.

Why Should You Always Get the Biggest Mortgage Possible BEFORE You Retire?

Mortgage lending is based on the applicant's income, not on your house. You will get much better terms while you are still gainfully employed. It's just good planning to go ahead, while you're still working, and secure your equity, remove it and utilize the tax deductions a mortgage can offer. It's a crucial component to your overall financial plan and the success of your wealth creation.

Go ahead. Partner with Uncle Sam to allow for tax-free access to your retirement funds. Tap your house's equity with a cash-out refinance or get a new mortgage if your home is paid off. Be sure to get this critical cash working in your S.A.F.E.T.Y. Fund™ immediately. You saw, in our example what can be done for you through age 100 by maximizing the cash you possess at age 59½.

Oh, by the way, don't forget interest-only mortgages work best. You get the maximum tax deduction and you don't erode your mortgage balance. If you pay it down, you'll just have to go out and get another one. Why plan to do that if you don't have to?

The sooner you begin, the better your results.

Remember Those "Glasses of the Masses" Financial Planners Spinning The Tales of Lower Tax Brackets In Retirement?

How can you be in a lower tax bracket after retirement if all your deductions are gone? Financial planners tell you to eliminate the mortgage interest deduction and pay off your mortgage before you retire so you will "save money." What a joke!

A Lower Tax Bracket In Retirement?
Quite a Feat, Without Deductions:
- *No dependents to deduct*
- *No 401(k) deposits to deduct*
- *No Mortgage Interest (usually)*

It is best to do just the opposite — get the biggest mortgage you can swing and never pay if off! Those individuals and financial advisors with Real Wealth Vision™ will attest to this fact. You'll find a multitude of ways to rearrange your finances to allow you to afford the monthly payment. The benefit a mortgage brings far outweighs any reasons you could find for eliminating it.

The H.E.R.O. Solution™ Retirement
Roll-Out Plan Is A Roll-Out ... NOT A Roll-Over

This is a permanent repositioning of your cash and not merely a rollover into another qualified account to continue to postpone your taxes. The cash you liberate begins to create future earnings that are tax-favored forever.

Remember, with this plan you have:

- No required withdrawals or distributions.
- No IRS penalties.
- Tax-favored growth and wealth creation.
- Complete freedom to access your cash.
- Account passes to your heirs without taxes.

Earlier, we talked about Uncle Sam getting his taxes due on all the money left inside your retirement accounts. **The**

IRS will tax your qualified plan money even after you die!
Yes, your heirs will owe income taxes on all those funds if
they inherit the accounts. Wouldn't it be best to utilize this
plan, get a mortgage, systematically get that cash out and
taxed at minimum levels? **Or maybe even without taxes?**
Rescue it and put it in a tax-favored vehicle so it may continue to grow without the threat of future taxation.

If you do it right, the taxes that would have been due on
much of your retirement funds are forgiven through a wash
against mortgage interest deductions. After that money is liberated, your heirs will never have taxes due.

Those with Real Wealth Vision™ Keep
Their Mortgage Working Forever

Why retire your mortgage just because you retired? If you
can keep more accessible cash in your S.A.F.E.T.Y. Fund™, you
should do what is necessary to get it there. You also maximize
the benefits of the tax code. The rules are published for all of
us, we should discover how they can potentially help us and
use them when possible.

With longevity improvements in our society, there is a
potential for creating arbitrage for 40 years or more even
after retirement. We should continue to be our own banks
from age 65 to 105 or even 125. It just takes vision, planning
and execution.

CHAPTER SEVENTEEN

TRAVEL DOWN THE ROAD OF LIFE WITH REAL WEALTH VISION™

If you're funding your wealth using after-tax dollars, you're moving along with a flat tire on one wheel. If your money is growing in a vehicle that will give you only tax-handicapped or tax-challenged income for your livelihood, then your wealth plan has another flat tire.

It's funny how we can all step through the motions. We can practice do-it-yourself financial planning or meet with an advisor. We can set up retirement accounts and can go through some measure of wealth pre-

> Why are most people thumping down the road of life with two nearly-flat tires and a foggy windshield?

paredness. But the average person will most likely never have more than two good tires out of the four that are possible.

The four wheels of your wealth vehicle are 1) tax-free upfront cash, 2) tax-favored growth, 3) tax-favored access at withdrawal and 4) tax-free transfer to heirs. Most of those viewing their world through the "Glasses of the Masses" will only achieve two of these in their financial planning.

Those possessing Real Wealth Vision™ have discovered ways to have all their wheels speeding along the road of life sporting fully inflated radials.

Why do most folks travel down the road of life with their Uncle hitched to the bumper? Not only is he making their ride bumpy and tough, but also their good-ol'-Uncle is getting bigger and heavier every year. Yes, Uncle Sam is coming along for the ride and fully expects to be there when their ride is over. He'll be holding out his hand waiting for a very large chunk of cash. The farther down the road they ride, the larger and plumper Uncle Sam grows.

Sadly, if they don't take steps to extricate themselves from him, he'll be with them draining away assets until all their cash is virtually gone. The retirement vehicle for those wearing the "Glasses of the Masses" is not operating very efficiently as it travels the road of life.

Most folks have their Uncle hitched to the bumper, and he is getting bigger and heavier every year.

"Glasses of the Masses" Retirement Vehicle

Wheel #1:   **Pre-tax dollars for initial deposits** into regular IRA, 401(k) or other retirement accounts.

Wheel #2:   **Tax-favored growth** for earnings on those dollars.

Wheel #3:   **Tax-favored access — NO —** you'll pay taxes
(flat)   on income gains at higher earned-income tax rates.

Wheel #4:   **Pass to heirs tax-free — NO —** must pay taxes
(flat)   at higher earned-income tax rates on all retirement account money inherited.

Those with Real Wealth Vision™ know the secrets that allow them to navigate the financial map of life, taking the straightest and most-illuminated route. They understand the methods and inside maneuvers that create maximum accumulation of wealth, using tax regulations appropriately and to their best benefit.

Real Wealth Vision™ Retirement Vehicle

4 Fully-Inflated New Radials

Wheel #1:   **Never taxed dollars for initial deposits —** Initial cash from never-to-be-taxed source allowing a maximum turbo-boost for each dollar.

Wheel #2:   **Tax-favored growth —** Working environments for your dollars that allow for growth without taxation.

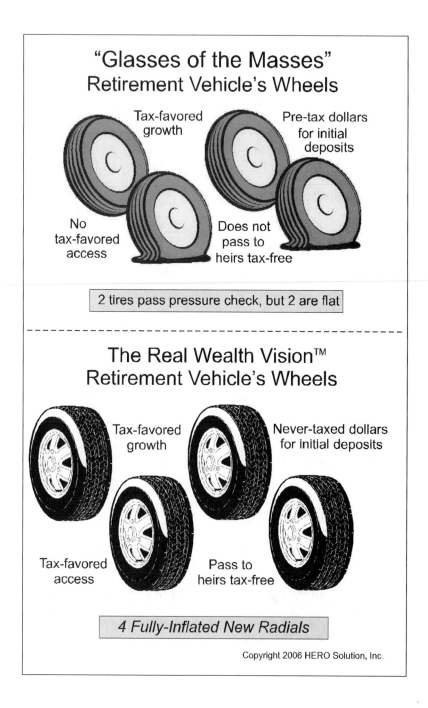

"Glasses of the Masses"
Retirement Vehicle's Wheels

Tax-favored growth

Pre-tax dollars for initial deposits

No tax-favored access

Does not pass to heirs tax-free

2 tires pass pressure check, but 2 are flat

The Real Wealth Vision™
Retirement Vehicle's Wheels

Tax-favored growth

Never-taxed dollars for initial deposits

Tax-favored access

Pass to heirs tax-free

4 Fully-Inflated New Radials

Copyright 2006 HERO Solution, Inc.

Wheel #3: **Tax-favored access** — Uses strategies to withdraw spendable cash without taxes at your discretion.

Wheel #4: **Pass to heirs tax-free** — If put together properly, any wealth remaining can pass on to your heirs without a dime of income taxes due.

Copyright 2006 HERO Solution, Inc.

Will You Accept The Challenge
To Get Rolling On Four Sleek New Radials?

Check in with a qualified advisor possessing Real Wealth Vision™ periodically. Keep your plan on track. Ensure your path is clear, unrestricted, illuminated. Be sure your aerodynamic vehicle has four fully inflated radials and you are unfettered. In other words, you aren't pulling along future tax burdens to ravage your riches.

Take a look at the map illustration that follows. The top path represents the route taken by those who follow the outdated plan of people who wear the "Glasses of the Masses." Their Uncle Sam is coming along for the ride on their winding and, sometimes, treacherous or unsafe route to their retirement.

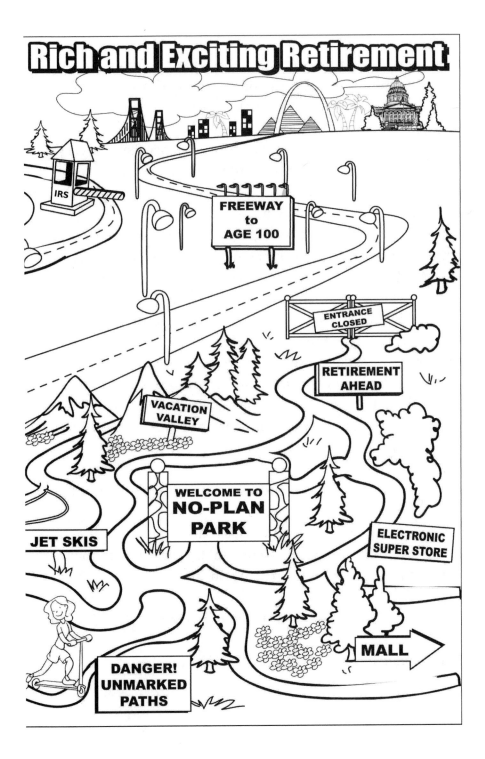

The bottom path shows those sad individuals who proceed through life with no plan at all. Often, they are vulnerable to influence from our rampant consumer-based society. Many simply find it depressing to think about a time when they'll be old, their careers will be at an end and their good health may be a thing of the past. Some people just feel it's very scary to plan for retirement — hard to face up to. So, they just never get around to having a plan at all. Their unfortunate future is a complete unknown.

Finally, the middle superhighway is straight, wide, unobstructed and lined with bright streetlights. The illumination comes from regular meetings with a H.E.R.O. Solution™ advisor to stay on track with your H.E.R.O. Solution™ plan and keep your S.A.F.E.T.Y. Fund™ operating at peak performance. If this is the route you've selected, you can look forward to a rich and exciting retirement filled with choices and rewarding experiences. You'll enjoy peace of mind — knowing that if you're one of the many among us who lives to be age 100, you'll do it with financial peace, security and dignity.

Conclusion

I hope you now possess Real Wealth Vision™ yourself and know the 3 simple money secrets millionaires use to make you rich and secure for the rest of your life.

Just Do What Millionaires Do!

1. They keep all idle tax-free equity in their real estate working.

2. They place all critical cash in secure and accessible vehicles for total safety.
3. And they maximize every advantage offered for tax-favored growth and tax-free accessibility to explode retirement income as much as 50%!

Good things come in threes. We are fortunate to live in a time with unprecedented financial benefits. The 21st Century has served up three recent opportunities that have converged to create a synergy that can propel the H.E.R.O. Solution™ to work explosively:

1. Access to up to $500,000 in tax-free equity cash every two years for married couples and $250,000 for individuals.
2. New mainstream loan programs that allow us to get larger loans, greater tax deductions and lower payments.
3. Vehicles for our critical cash that participate in the growth of major stock market indices in good years, but are protected from losing principal in bad years.

From this moment on, you'll have the ability to clearly see and understand these round-world concepts but you'll still be completely surrounded by people who only see a flat world. (You know, the ones wearing the Coke-bottle-thick "Glasses of the Masses.")

This quandary may be difficult for you. Until you're able to explain these new insights to others, I can guarantee you'll be up against some real resistance. Old beliefs are very ingrained. Financial planners, CPAs, relatives and friends, believing they are right, will continue to cling to the traditional ways of thinking.

> *"To change one's life:*
> *Start immediately."*
> — William James,
> American philosopher

Your best strategy will be to seek out enlightened advisors who also have Real Wealth Vision™. They'll understand the H.E.R.O. Solution™, know how to set up a S.A.F.E.T.Y. Fund™ and be privy to the intricacies of implementing your properly structured personal H.E.R.O. Solution™ strategic plan. Their support will possibly prove to be a real "shot out of the cannon" to propel you ahead down the path to wealth and security for the rest of your life.

To begin to establish your personal financial wealth goals, try not to "beat yourself up" about your present situation. That was the past — what's done is done — you can't change that. Now you must discard the outdated advice others provided before and begin to use your newly acquired Real Wealth Vision™. Can you just imagine what your present financial situation could potentially become? The thought of it can be exciting and even mind-boggling.

Remember the real power of time we talked about in Chapter Two, C.O.F.F.E.E. Crisis™? Now, all that stands in your way is the clock and the calendar.

If you're ready to begin, don't put it off to analyze, evaluate or procrastinate. You may have a great job today. You may have your good health today. But, that could all change tomorrow.

Therefore, YOU MUST ACT NOW:

• While you can get a new mortgage.
• While you are insurable.

- While you're clear on your goals.
- While you have a good time horizon.

You never know what tomorrow may bring to block your success. So, air-up your radials and "peel-off" TODAY down that broad, beautiful road of life toward being truly rich and secure for the rest of your life.

The following section is entitled *Epilogue* because it really isn't another chapter, at all. Here, you'll be introduced to three couples selected for an imaginary reality television show we call *Home Free*.

The three participant couples' experiences will demonstrate how each of them begins with the same income, family size and housing expenses, yet, ends up with a totally different wealth outcome than the others.

One of the participants will reveal basic Real Wealth Vision™ principles in action. Which couple will it be? Who'll become a millionaire and who'll be left penniless? The principles they demonstrate should illuminate the path for you like switching on runway lights. You may discover traits, notions and habits they possess that are much like your own.

As the show begins, each of the participating couples will start at exactly the same place. They will each be given an equal opportunity to become millionaires. They'll be provided with the tools and the time to create real wealth for themselves. Without question, if they follow the show's plan as prescribed, they will all end up with riches. But what goes wrong?

HOME FREE — OUR NEW REALITY TV SERIES

This new long-term reality show will be a behavioral experiment that hopes to shed some light on actual applications of the H.E.R.O. Solution™ and how its proper use will change peoples' lives. Will the contestants apply it correctly? Will they make changes? Will their weaknesses blow it? Let's watch and see.

What Will Our Show Be Like?

In 1998, there was a fairly popular movie released called *The Truman Show*, starring Jim Carrey, in which the main character lives a perfect little life in a perfect little town. Seaside, the small planned Florida community where it was filmed, has actually become quite famous because of the movie. There is an interesting twist within the story. Unbeknownst to Truman, he is living inside a 24-hour-a-day comedy-melodrama being broadcast on live television, in which he is the star.

With the idea or concept that long-term broadcasting can become the ultimate reality show, let's create yet one more possibility for the world's entertainment consideration — *Home Free*.

The producers of our new show will find three couples as contestants or participants. Those three will be allowed to select a house in which to live and raise their families. Unlike the shows where they knock down an old house and build a new one in its place for a deserving family each week, these participants are followed as they select the house of their choosing and as they ultimately experience their lives in the new homes they've selected.

Their day-to-day events, both mundane and exciting, are to be captured on live TV for the next three decades. The new program will document human behavior as it appears over the 30 years of average families, culminating with a big finale once the 360 months have elapsed. These families are allowed to live in their new homes absolutely free of charge.

What's The One Simple Rule?

Following is the only stipulation on the contestants for the time they live in the home provided:

The One Simple *Home-Free* Rule: To live in the house for free, the contestants must make a monthly deposit into a personal side account equal in value to what the mortgage payment on that home would have initially been.

Therefore, for the period in which they reside in the house, these couples will have no mortgage to pay. In exchange for receiving access weekly to the lives of these contestants for

30 years, the producers of the show, in essence, allow the families to live in the house they have selected without payments. Other than having cameras documenting their lives to be aired to the world, the monthly amount set aside is really the only prescribed condition.

The participants are made to understand the goal of the show is to test how families can hold up under constant public exposure. The entertainment factor in documenting people for such long time is a social experiment. They aren't advised of the ultimate twist of the show.

Isn't This Like Some Other Reality Shows We've Seen?

Yes, it's like what happened in *The Bachelor*, where women compete for a man they are told is a millionaire. At the end of the season, they surprisingly find the man is flat broke. The contestants are not made aware of this final twist during the competition. Unknowingly, the women battle it out until the bachelor narrows down the group and decides to marry just one of them.

After the selection is finalized, the winning woman is told *The Bachelor* is penniless. Although she hasn't been made aware a cash prize is at stake, she may still agree to marry the guy for "true love." If she follows through and decides to take him anyway, she is surprised with a reward of one million dollars. If she decides not to marry him after discovering the poverty truth, the bachelor is presented with the cool million. You get the picture. The twist at the end is entertaining for the audience and an unexpected surprise to the participants.

Well, back to our own reality show, where three sets of cameras have begun to roll and will keep documenting for 360 months. You will now be introduced to each of the three teams and be able to follow their progress in the story boxes that begin on this page. Their experiences will reveal how three different couples take the same assets and situations and come out with completely different results. Let's start by getting to know them.

FAMILY ONE — ZEKE AND LIZ

Liz had been late for her monthly color touch-up with Renee, her stylist. She felt so bad for making her wait that she gave her an extra twenty on top of her usual tip. As Liz left the parking lot of the salon, a billboard caught her eye. To avoid causing an accident as she craned to read the details, she quickly pulled over and reached for her Palm Pilot on the seat. She mumbled to herself, "Every time my nails are wet … "

Though it was tricky, the information was captured. She would check out their web address at home.

Later that evening …

"Beep. Beep. Beep." The screech startled her from a mesmerized state. The glare of the computer screen was the only light in the bedroom where Liz sat. With her heart in her throat, it took her several seconds before she was able to realize what was going on.

"Oh, no. The lasagna!" she yelled out loud. "What time is it?" The smoke detector was telling her dinner was going to be pizza again.

"Poor Zeke! He was really looking forward to a home-cooked dinner for once," she thought. Her mother's lovingly prepared dish was now burned beyond recognition.

After opening the oven and tossing the blackened blob into the sink, she climbed up on a kitchen chair to take the battery out of the alarm. Back at the computer, she opened her favorites folder and then clicked on the list of pizza delivery sites she used so often. "Let's see. I'll do the large special. One click and I'm done. Now, back to that site," she said.

She just had to read every word. The chance of being part of a new reality series was so appealing to her.

(continued)

The glistening newly-washed SUV pulled into the driveway. Zeke caught a glimpse of the pizza guy hopping out of his little clunker car at the curb. He punched the opener button to stop the garage door halfway down. As the door began to rise again, the familiar face raced up the drive. "Hi, Mr. Kantwayt!" he called to Zeke. "Looks like you guys really love this week's special deal. It's the third one I've delivered here this week."

Squeezing between the row of neatly arranged power tools hanging on the garage wall and the riding lawnmower, Zeke managed to step onto the drive.

"Let's see, that's twenty for the special and a five for you." He said to the smiling kid.

"Gee, thanks, Mr. Kantwayt. Enjoy!" He ran back to the street and the car sped away streaming the sound of Aerosmith into the night air.

Zeke entered the front door and was greeted by the odor of burned pasta. It made his nose quickly wrinkle up. "Hey, Liz! Pizza's here!" he called.

As they gobbled down the thick-crusted slices of their dinner, Liz explained the upcoming opportunity for a chance to try-out for the reality show. Zeke beamed as he thought about the possibility of actually becoming nationally recognized television stars. Living in a new house for nothing sounded too good to be true.

He agreed to take a day off work and go to the auditions later that week. The rest is history. They were exactly what the show's producers were looking for and were chosen to be the first contestants.

Liz and Zeke Kantwayt, became "Family One" of the *Home Free* reality show, and selected their $300,000 house in a medium-size suburb in Virginia. Their son, Chad, age 2, and daughter, Erica, in kindergarten, shared their new digs.

Their dramatic reactions to being selected made for some great footage that aired in the initial episodes. Liz, having been a professional hairdresser and makeup consultant at an upscale salon, had a great camera presence. Zeke, always the clothes hog, made sure to dress to the max whenever the filming was going on. "You can't make a second first impression on America," he kept telling Liz.

(continued)

When they realized they were going to be in front of the world every week, they called in a decorator and bought all new furnishings. With no house payment to make, they felt they could easily afford those great no-interest financing deals now and would catch up the missed deposits later.

Of course, they were aware of the rule about putting the mortgage payment equivalent into the side fund, but they knew there'd be plenty of time for that in later months. After all, they'll have three decades do it. With the feeling of complete financial freedom, the upcoming years should be quite interesting for the Kantwayts and for all of America.

FAMILY TWO — MATT AND JULIA

Matt saw the advertisement in the lifestyle section of the local Dallas paper. "Wow! A chance to live in a house for free," he said out loud. He and Julia had been making it on his income alone since the kids had come along, but it hadn't been easy. This just sounded unbelievable. "There has to be some kind of catch," he said to himself as he read the ad again.

Julia looked at the paper after Matt plopped it into her lap. "Well, it sounds like a wonderful opportunity ... but a future filled with the constant intrusion of the cameras and filming crews? There could be some real negatives," she said. "But, then again, I don't suppose we could sleep at night if we don't take a shot at it." After pondering a moment, she resolved, "Oh ... Let's give it a try!"

Since Ben and Amy had arrived, Julia had put her career on hold to be a stay-at-home Mom. As they sat in the waiting room at the audition, Julia's mind wandered back to a fall day on campus before they were married. It was a day she'd always remember ...

Julia sat on the tiny little bench outside the biology building. "Sit here next to me, Matt," she said with a shy smile, as she patted the bench next to her.

The leaves were starting to fall and were blowing around their feet whenever a gust came along. The air had a crispness that Julia
(continued)

can still feel to this day. She could smell the smoke from a bonfire that was just being started. Homecoming rituals were underway. In the distance she could hear the rhythmic thuds of bass drums echoing from the band's practice field.

Julia looked in Matt's eyes and squeezed his hand. She took a deep breath and began, "Since we're getting married now, I've really been thinking of our lives and our future." Without a blink, she continued, "We've got to talk about a few things."

He swallowed hard, knowing she was expecting to hear certain replies. Though he wanted to get it right, he wasn't prepared for these questions. Not yet. The conversation had gotten so honest, so quickly. Julia was the most important thing in his life. He couldn't let just anything stumble out of his lips, so he sat silently. "No words were better than the wrong ones," he thought.

Seemingly, unconcerned about the moment of silence, she went on, "The most important things in our lives should be our children and providing a stable and happy environment in our home." She looked at him again. "Don't you agree?"

Matt gazed back at her serious face. She was so beautiful, with her auburn hair lightly blowing in the breeze. If he knew anything at that moment, he knew he always wanted to be this close to her. He simply nodded and smiled.

"Do you know why we've got to talk about these things now?" she asked, squeezing his hand even more tightly. "I want us to be on the same page ... to want similar things. We've got to be sure we are a true team in everything."

Julia looked up into the trees. She crossed her arms and then closed her eyes, saying, "I can still remember the sugar and spice aroma of Mom's fresh baked oatmeal cookies. The scent wrapped itself around me like a fuzzy blanket when I stepped in my front door. Mom was always there waiting for me and my sister. Just about every day."

Then she stood up and began to pace. "The minute we got off the school bus, we could usually see her standing inside, by the front window, waiting for us to tell her about our day. She was involved in our lives in just about every way." Julia was using her

(continued)

hands animatedly now as she walked, the way she always did when making a point.

Matt could feel the conviction in Julia's voice. She was passionate about this. He could tell there was no question in her mind about what path they should take. His thoughts were rushing.

He finally broke his silence, "Jules, before today, if anyone had asked me what I thought about families and kids, I'd have said, 'What do I know? I'm just a boy in college.'" He stood up, wrapped his arms around her and continued, "Though I've probably never said it, I would hope you know I feel the same. I have special memories of my mother and being a kid, too."

"So, what do you think?" Julia asked. "We'll be down to one income during those years. You know it's not going to be easy. I mean financially."

"Truth is," he went on, "You amaze me. You're bright. Top of your class. Highly competitive."

Julia turned her head, blushing.

Matt put his hand on her chin and turned her face to his. As he looked into her eyes, he told her what he really thought, "Here you are with the potential to have anything ... be anything. And you'd put it all on hold for me and our kids ... for our family."

Grinning, Matt said, "Besides, it will be a good career strategy for me. With you out of the way, my path to the top will be cleared of all worthy adversaries." Giving her a swat on the behind, he took off running.

"You'd better look out, mister!" she said as she jumped back, shocked. Then she chased after him with the leaves shuffling under her feet ...

"Five minutes!" the producer's assistant called out.

The voice startled Julia and brought her back to reality.

"Well, Matt, this is it," she said, squeezing his hand. "Let's cross our fingers."

On that Tuesday at four o'clock, Matt and Julia Best became "Family Two" of the *Home Free* reality series.

FAMILY THREE — TOM AND SAMANTHA

Tom put his key into the door lock of his green Dodge minivan. No, it didn't have electric locks or windows, but it had served him well since he bought it as a dealer demonstrator eight years earlier. His friends had laughed at him for buying it, but in his mind it was the perfect vehicle. After saving up all the cash he had earned from his part-time jobs held during college, he had just enough to buy it. He intended on helping his dad's business by making deliveries on the weekends after beginning his full-time job.

When he found this van on that Saturday afternoon, Tom had said to himself, "It's just what I need. Dependable, lots of room and just the right price."

It had been a good vehicle and still had lots of working years left in it. The clock on the dash was broken, so he looked at his reliable Timex. "Fifteen after five. Great, I can still catch that funny guy on Z105," he had said to himself. "I can never remember his name, but he's always good for a laugh on the way home." He switched on the radio and began to turn the dial. As he watched the road and tuned in his station, he listened for the familiar voice of the radio personality that kept him in stitches.

"Ah!" He had found his favorite radio guy.

Today he was interviewing the producer of a new reality show in pre-production. The show, to be called *Home Free*, was seeking families in the area who would be willing to live in a great house for free.

What would the value of the house be?" the radio host asked.

"Around $300,000."

Tom sucked in some air and whistled. Any other type of television program would have held no attraction for him. Fame just wasn't something he wished or wanted.

Tom said to the radio, "I wouldn't make a fool of myself for many things — but for a house? I'd be a fool in front of a million people it in a New York minute!"

Tom and Samantha Cash had both been born and raised in Milwaukee. Tom's strong work ethic and midwestern value system had been instilled in him by his parents from a very early age. He began working after-school jobs at 16. He stuck with that practice

(continued)

all through college until receiving his business degree from Marquette University.

These his father had taught him: the importance of teamwork, to believe a man's word is his bond and how one should value integrity, honesty, mutual respect and self-respect. Although he received several job offers, Tom became a planning manager with a local manufacturing company.

He had selected the position because of the solid benefits package offered by the company. From day one, Tom contributed the maximum allowed into the company savings plan, even though it only matched the first few thousand with company stock.

After the kids came along and his wife Samantha had stopped working, he had to cut back on the contributions into his plan. Samantha, a CPA by career, hadn't worked full-time since the kids were born. She had kept her contact with the working world by assisting the local hospital foundation with their accounting work eight hours a week.

When Tom walked in the door, he closed his eyes and took in the wonderful aromas of baking bread and pot roast. Alex, the three-year old came running to him. "Daddy! Daddy!" He jumped and hugged Tom's leg.

Tom looked down at his little guy. He grabbed and tossed him up in the air. Then he gave him a huge hug, declaring with just enough volume to be heard in the kitchen, "Hi, son. Do you smell that wonderful dinner? What did we ever do to deserve the best Mommy in the whole wide world?"

Samantha called from the kitchen, "You're right on time, Tom. Bread's hot. You two wash up."

At the table, Tom told Samantha all about the opportunity for the free house and the show. Being able to see his excitement by Tom's animated expressions, she just couldn't say no. She agreed to give it a shot and they immediately made plans to go to the auditions.

A perfect match for their final team, the producers asked them to join the reality series as "Family Three" of the *Home Free* show. They found their $300,000 house in a Milwaukee suburb, moved in and began their lives in front of the cameras.

Fast-Forward In Time — The 15-Year Mark

Home Free is now in it's fifteenth year. While the three families have been opening up their lives to the world for a decade and a half, its time to check back in to see how they've done with their individual quests.

Family Number One

Zeke and Liz. Well, what can we say about Zeke and Liz? They are so caught up in living for the day that they just haven't gotten around to looking ahead. The show producers have let them proceed without receiving any reprimands. After all, the show is a behavioral experiment.

They've made a few deposits into their side account, but things just keep coming up. You know — vacations, furniture, new gadgets, clothes and summer camps. Their side account is pretty puny, but they keep telling themselves they'll catch it up once the kids are out of college. Their plan is to just put it off until it is easier to do.

After 180 months, they have made only 20 payments into their side account and its balance has only reached $37,008. Knowing they aren't doing as they promised the show's producers, they just try to put it out of their mind for now. But, once the kids are gone …

Family Number Two

Matt and Julia took their challenge very seriously. Every month their check was electronically sent from their checking account to their side fund, just as most people systematically send their mortgage payment in. Nothing emerged that proved to be extremely dramatic in this couple's story. They furnished their home, paid for their vehicles and clothes for their kids. Tuition was difficult to scrape up, but they had planned for its need and borrowed for some of those expenses. They were able to make it through the raising of their two kids without getting off track along the way. They might be considered quite boring or average in the show producer's minds.

Their side account has a hefty $556,448 in it and they see the value of having their house for free. They certainly wish to stay on track with the show's plan.

Family Number Three

Tom and Samantha have gone along through the years putting the side money away just as instructed. They've done well and their two children have been thriving. After the first 15 years have passed, they look at their situation and pat themselves on the backs. Well, Tom did finally sell that green Dodge van. Some things just don't last forever.

They've been diligent with the systematic plan and their side account balance has also accumulated into the tidy sum of $556,448. They have negotiated with the show's producers to opt-out of the plan and buy their home outright for the original price plus interest. Their side account has amassed enough to pay for their home's original value ($300,000) and pay the full interest on that balance for the entire 15 years ($315,000), after they reduce it by the tax refund benefits on the interest they would have deducted ($103,950), which the producers agreed to credit to them. They've settled on a buy-out amount of $511,050. Which leaves them with a remaining side account of $45,398.

Oh, by the way, their house is now worth about $625,000.

Since they treasure the traditional wisdom they've received over the years, they believe owing a home free-and-clear and being debt-free is the best way to live their lives.

They believe they have made a fantastic deal. They paid a 30-year payment equivalent for only 15 years. This non-traditional system allowed them to have enough to pay off their house at the half-way point, eliminate the need to make any further payments and they are left with a valuable house and a nice $45,000 nest egg to boot! They feel it's time to "take the money and run"!

With no required monthly investment to make, they decided they can now better afford to pay for costly braces and private high school tuition. Their children have been quite academically successful and both are planning to attend Ivy-League universities. They know expensive college tuition will be inevitable and they wish to be "smart" and pay cash as they go.

Fast-Forward In Time — The 30-Year Mark

The children have all grown up and left home. The family finances are not so stretched. The three couples spent the last 10 years living in the houses as empty nesters, so let's see who won the *Home Free* challenge.

Family One — Third Place

Zeke and Liz have gotten so comfortable with finding other uses for their monthly investment check that they just never have found enough discipline to send it in. After the entire time, a total of 54 payments were made into their side account and their balance is now $110,730.

Home Free Family One - Zeke & Liz

House Value	$300,000
Required Monthly Deposit = 7% Mtg Pmt	**$1,750**
Phantom Mortgage	$300,000
Ending Age:	60
Beginning Age:	30
Investment Earning Rate:	7.000 %

Deposits They Actually Made	Earning at %	Thru Year	Side Account Balance
6 of 60	7.00	5	$10,653
13 of 120	7.00	10	$23,562
20 of 180	7.00	15	$37,008
27 of 240	7.00	20	$51,012
31 of 300	7.00	25	$59,275
54 of 360	7.00	30	$110,700
Less Phantom Original Mortgage:			($300,000)
Less 7% Int for 30yrs:			($630,000)
Get back 30 Phantom Tax Refunds:			$207,900
Not enough cash to stay for free:			**($611,400)**

If they want to keep the $1.3 million house, they owe the show producers >>   **$611,400**

They could move out now and rent - or -
pay this mortgage payment until age 90:   **$4,044** *< Ouch!*

This couple put off their monthly deposits, fully intending to catch them up when they had extra money. They spent the exact number of dollars as couples two & three, but never systematically deposited per plan.

Balance of Investment Account:	**$0**

Time to face the music. The show's producers call them in and give them the bad news. While their house is now worth almost 1.3 million dollars, their side account isn't enough to pay back the original $300,000 price. The interest for the 30 years at 7% has tallied up to $630,000. The producers will give them credit for the income tax refunds they would have received over those years, and that brings their interest owed down to $422,100, but they still don't have the cash to keep the house.

Looks like the producers will be keeping Zeke and Liz's $1.3 million house unless they get a mortgage for $611,400 to keep it. Not only do they not have a nest egg, but they will have to pay a mortgage payment of over $4000 per month until they are 90 years old or give up their lovely home and rent somewhere in retirement.

Well, Zeke and Liz come in at last place.

Family Three — Second Place

Tom and Samantha, although they opted-out and bought their home outright 15 years ago, remained in the running. They thought their plan was good and they would probably still come out ahead of the other two because paying cash is just smart.

Well, if you look at their results, you will see how they now stand. They did proceed with paying for tuition, braces and a wedding with cash. After all, "Cash is king," Tom always said.

They have a remaining side account of $55,398 and a free-and-clear house worth 1.3 million dollars. Looks good, but it wasn't enough to beat Matt and Julia.

Oh well, second place.

Home Free Family Three - Tom & Samantha

House Value		$300,000	
Required Monthly Deposit = 7% Mtg Pmt		**$1,750**	
Phantom Mortgage		$300,000	
Ending Age:		60	
Beginning Age:		30	
Investment Earning Rate:		7.000	%

Deposits They Actually Made	Earning at %	Thru Year	**Investment Acct Balance**
60 of 60	7.00	5	**$125,286**
120 of 120	7.00	10	**$303,627**
180 of 180	7.00	15	**$556,448**

*** After 15 years, they decide to Opt-Out ***

Payback of Phantom Mortgage:	**($300,000)**
Payback 7% Int for 15yrs:	**($315,000)**
Get Back 15 Lost Tax Refunds:	**$103,950**
House Free & Clear plus Cash of:	**$45,398**

Thru Years:	Expenses paid in cash:	
20	HS tuition,braces, etc	($93,000)
25	College Tuition	($124,000)
30	Tuition, wedding	($88,000)
180 x $1750 pmts re-allocated to expenses		$315,000

Remaining Cash at 30-yr point: | **$55,398**

They own their paid-off house worth
$1,300,000, *but only have $55K in reserves.*

This couple thought it was best to take the $45K they could get
after 15 years had passed. They wished to free-up monthly cash
to pay for upcoming high school & college tuition and wedding
expenses, believing it was wisest to pay cash and avoid debt.

Family Two — The *Home Free* Winners!

Matt and Julia made it all the way through without wavering.
How did they do it? Matt said, "It was easy, thanks to out-of-
sight-out-of-mind automatic payments from our checking
into our side account. We never missed the cash and we never
missed a payment into our fund."

Home Free Family Two - Matt & Julia			
House Value		$300,000	
Required Monthly Deposit = 7% Mtg Pmt		**$1,750**	
Phantom Mortgage		$300,000	
Ending Age:		60	
Beginning Age:		30	
Investment Earning Rate:		7.000 %	
Deposits They Actually Made	**Earning at %**	**Thru Year**	**Investment Acct Balance**
60 of 60	7.00	5	$125,286
120 of 120	7.00	10	$302,896
180 of 180	7.00	15	$554,681
240 of 240	7.00	20	$911,618
300 of 300	7.00	25	$1,417,620
360 of 360	7.00	30	$2,134,941
Less Phantom Mortgage:			($300,000)
Less 7% Interest for 30yrs:			($630,000)
Add 30 Tax Refunds:			$207,900
Balance after buying their house:			$1,412,841
Pay back the additional loan plus interest acquired for tuition, braces & wedding:			($410,000)
Remaining Cash at 30-yr point:			**$1,002,841**
Plus Their Debt-Free House Valued At:			**$1,300,000**
Their Total Assets:			**$2,302,841**
Their remaining side account pays them:		**$5,850**	*tax-free*
into perpetuity & the million-dollar balance will pass to heirs.			

Well, it certainly paid off. They have a whopping **$2,134,941** in their side account and they only earned 7% over the years. Their home has grown to just about $1,300,000 in the mean time.

Now, if they wish to keep the house, they simply pay the producers $722,600, which is the $300,000 purchase price and $422,600 interest. The interest was calculated at 7% annually, less the tax refunds they would have received if they had a mortgage.

All their family expenses, like tuition and a wedding, were handled by taking out a side loan. If they decide to pay off this loan and its interest, they would need $410,000 of their $1,412,841.

Wow! They're left with a side account balance of $1,002,841 and a paid-off 1.3 million dollar house. This makes for total assets of 2.3 million dollars and their side account will provide them with a monthly income of $5,850 until they are 100 years old. When they do pass away, the full million-dollar account will still be intact and transfer to their kids.

They are definitely **THE WINNERS**!!

Now, let's move ahead 20 more years, and check in with our *Home Free* families to see how they've done …

FAMILY ONE — ZEKE AND LIZ — AGES 79 AND 80

"Happy Birthday, Grandpa!" chimed the voices surrounding Zeke, as he soaked in all the warmth of his smiling and laughing family. The candles on his cake cast a glow bright enough to have doubled as a lighthouse beacon. Happy days such as this were rare events for him, so he wanted to savor every second.

As Liz looked on, a tear appeared in the corner of her eye. She tried her best to hide it, so as not to spoil the day for Zeke.

"How could we have come to this?" she said to herself slowly shaking her head. The sight was almost too much for her.

Here, in this three-room public housing unit they now called home, stood her two children, her son-in-law, daughter-in-law and four grandchildren with one of their spouses. Many had visible beads of sweat rolling down their foreheads. The air was so heavy, so humid; it made them feel as if they were wearing thick bathrobes in August. She wondered if those paper church fans with the wooden handles people used a century ago might still be available on Ebay these days. She shook her head, chuckling at the silly idea. Her emotions began to overcome her.

(continued)

"How could we have been so careless?" she thought, feeling the need to get outside before she broke down in front of everyone. She squeezed between bodies and made it to the door.

Zeke saw the distress on Liz's face and he knew he'd better follow her. After asking Erica to serve the cake to everyone, he excused himself.

Entering the hallway, the odor of boiling cabbage and onions wafted up his nose. He had become accustomed to apartment building cooking smells, so he just tried not to breathe too deeply. He carefully descended the hallway stairs, grasping the loosely attached metal handrail. Outside was no escape from the severe summer heat.

Liz sat on the concrete steps in the shade of the one puny little tree that stood between the front door and the street. He sat down beside her and put his big arm around her frail shoulder.

"Are you alright?" he asked, handing her a tissue. Then he smiled and said, "You know, I'm the one with another birthday. Shouldn't I be upset?"

"Oh, Zeke! What did we do wrong? I hate to admit it, but I'm ashamed to have the kids and grandkids see how we're living now. That shabby little apartment ..." she began to sob again.

"Sweetheart, we just blew our chances. Looking back, I now see that we had so many opportunities that we just ignored. You saw what those other *Home Free* couples did. We could've changed our lives long, long ago if we had only done some planning."

Wiping her eyes, Liz took a deep breath. "We swore we'd never do it, Dear. We have no choice but to ask the kids for help now. You can't work anymore with your back the way it is. And, the medicine! I just don't think we can keep cutting those pills in half."

"Heavens, Liz!" Zeke's smile slid right off his face as he turned away from her and crossed his arms. "How can we go begging to our own kids? We'll look like complete failures! Is that how we want our grandkids to remember us?"

She looked at his curled fingers, injured soldiers from years of battling arthritis. She squeezed his hand lovingly and said, "Gracious, Zeke, you're 80 today! We've worked our entire adult lives, and now, we just aren't physically able to go on!"

(continued)

"We can't afford the prescription insurance and our medicine costs more every year. You know, its probably a good thing the old car just went its last mile, because we can't pay the premium for our auto insurance. I guess I can learn how to take to bus to get to my job." Liz looked hopelessly into his eyes and continued, "That income is our food money. I've got to keep going to work as long as I'm able, even if it's only a few hours a week."

"What else can we do?" she sobbed. "We have nowhere to go. Our sweet kids don't need two old folks under foot in their busy lives. We just can't become a financial drain on our children when they should be preparing for their own futures. Oh, Dear! Oh, Dear! Oh, Dear!" She rocked her body. Her hands shook as she wiped the tears from her eyes. "I am really scared!"

The heat from the sidewalk warmed their cheeks like a roaring campfire. Zeke prayed for just one rare and cooling breeze to make its way between the city buildings to where they sat.

He shook his head and stared toward the sunset, helplessly whispering, "Me, too, Sweetheart. Me, too."

FAMILY THREE — TOM AND SAMANTHA — AGES 77 AND 80

The screen door screeched as the tiny red-haired girl opened it and stepped inside the hot kitchen. She cupped her freckled hand beside her mouth and called, "Grandma Sam! We're here. Where are you?"

She stood patiently waiting, listening for a reply, but there was silence. As the child was about to turn and go outside to search, a plump, smiling Samantha appeared from the next room.

"My goodness, Becky, how you've grown!" she said. "Let me get a good look at you. Come here and give me a big hug."

As she embraced the child, Tom entered from the back porch with Alex and his wife. The yard was filled with chatter from the other family members. The last of them had arrived for their annual Father's Day celebration.

(continued)

"Mother, that bread smells absolutely wonderful!" exclaimed Alex. "When will lunch be ready? That long drive has left me ravenous!"

"Soon, son. Really soon." she assured him. "Why don't you help your father set up the picnic tables in the back yard?"

The big old house had served the Cash family well. When they had paid it off 35years earlier, they'd decided they would always live there. After the *Home Free* series had ended and all their child-rearing costs were behind them, Tom and Samantha had turned their attentions to preparing for retirement.

Since neither of them knew much about investing or the stock market, they decided to locate a financial planner for help. An advertisement on a local radio station led them to a local money manager. He complimented them on their no-debt position, but told them the small savings they had was not going to supply them with enough income in their golden years.

The advisor recommended that Samantha go back to work for additional retirement cash to invest, they should put their current meager savings into some aggressive mutual funds in the stock market to get some "strong growth" (as he called it) and Tom should go back to over-funding his 401K to take advantage of tax-deferred growth.

The advisor said, "We'll select actively managed funds with good recent records. If you follow this plan for the next 8 or 9 years, you should be able to catch up on your savings and have enough to support yourself in your retirement."

"Well, it sounds good to me," said Tom. "As long as we don't go into debt. Since you do this for a living, I'm sure you know more about investing than we do, so we'll trust your advice."

The advisor moved much of their savings into several aggressive funds and he help them set up an automatic investment into those vehicles for the earnings Samantha was receiving from her teaching job at the local community college. Tom's 401(k) received the most matching from investment into his company stock, so he put in as much as was allowed.

Their investments were doing pretty well the first year or so, but the market took major downturns for the next three years

(continued)

running. The impact on their assets was devastating! Even after Samantha's four years of saving and investing all she earned, the market's losing years had left them below where they had started.

The advisor had kept telling them the market would bounce back each year, so they should hold on. In fact, he switched their money into different funds in an effort to get better results. By the end of the four years, they were completely disillusioned with him and the stock market. They were even more upset that they had wasted all those fees the mutual funds had charged. So, they took every dime of their cash and moved it into bank CDs.

Tom was able to keep working for several more years after age 65. His own company's stock had not done well in the market downturn. The 401(k) money he had been salting away, those few years it was allowed, had not achieved much success. Since the stock was way down, even though he had been receiving company matching on some of his deposits, his account wasn't worth much more than the cash he had originally put into it.

So now, at ages 77 and 80, Tom and Samantha have used up almost all of their meager life savings. Today, there's enough to pay for their food, medicine and utilities, but the property taxes keep rising every year. They worry that their cash isn't going to last them much longer.

The house is in dreadful need of repair and painting. The roof has a leak in more than one place. They wear sweaters inside in the winter and use window fans in the summer. They clip coupons, walk to the local library for entertainment and never take the car out except for grocery and drug store visits.

"Dad, have you got a couple of minutes?" asked Alex, as he finished off the last crumb on his plate.

Tom stood up and patted his stomach in satisfaction. "Sure, son," Tom replied. "Why don't we stroll around the block and try to walk off some of this great meal."

The summer sun was intense, so Tom grabbed his gardening hat as they left the back yard. Alex explained to Tom that he, his wife and his sister, Nancy, had been checking into reverse mortgages. They wondered if that kind of borrowing might be the answer to Tom and Samantha's financial situation.

(continued)

"Absolutely not!" Tom yelled out loud. "You know how I feel about debt. Those things have all kinds of expensive rates and fees. What about when your Mom and I are gone? We want you kids to get the house, not some government agency.

We appreciate the trouble you've all gone to. Your Mom and I love you for your concern, but we'll not think of it, son."

"But, Dad!" Alex pleaded. "Won't you even …?"

Tom interrupted, "No, Alex! You know I just don't believe in debt. Now, that's all I've got to say about the issue, so I'd appreciate it if you would just not mention it to me ever again."

As they trudged back, the sidewalk radiated heat like the hood of a running car. They spent the rest of the afternoon sitting under the shade tree in the back yard, enjoying each other's company.

That evening, Tom sat with Samantha on the back porch. All the family had gone, leaving a strange quiet. The stars above twinkled in the clear night air.

"Well, Tom, dear. It's just you and me, again. That meal for ten pretty much took our food money for the week, so I'll try to stretch those leftovers as long as I can," Samantha said in a reassuring voice.

"Sam, you are one in a million," Tom replied. "You're surely a master at making a dollar go a long way these days. I don't know how we'd get by without your money-stretching magic."

Tom reached over to take her hand. "How do other people seem to have so much more? What did we miss, sweetheart? We did everything right. We followed the wisdom our fathers passed on to us. We always worked hard. We've been in the same house most of our adult lives. We avoided mortgages. We always paid cash. We tried to provide the best for our kids."

Samantha chimed in, "We keep healthy habits, exercise and eat right. Tom, we've got lots of good years ahead of us. I just don't understand how we could be sitting here now not knowing how we'll keep this house running or even feed ourselves."

Tom took a deep breath, looked up into the starry night and whispered, "I only hope we don't run out of money before we run out of time."

FAMILY TWO — MATT AND JULIA — AGES 79 AND 80

"Papa! Papa!" squealed the five-year-old voice as the front door to the cabin flew open. The calls, along with the sound of little footsteps, echoed up into the loft above, where Matt was sitting at his hobby desk, working on his handmade fishing lures.

"Teddy!" he called down, "Papa's up here. You don't suppose my favorite great-grandson would like to go out in my boat and do a little fishing with me, today? Do you?"

Julia stood at the front window, watching the angular beams of sunlight trickle through the immense growth of giant pines. Her heart began to pound in anticipation and the corners of her mouth began to curl as she saw the gang of chattering and smiling visitors file up the stone path.

As they entered, the wonderful aroma of homemade oatmeal cookies engulfed them, on its way up into the beautiful hand-hewn rafters above. This was the 15th annual Best Family gathering at their mountain cabin. There wasn't a single one of the twelve of them, which now included great-grandchildren, who would even think of missing this week of sharing, encouragement, remembering, recharging and family love.

Amy placed her hand on her chest and took a deep breath. She gazed out through the massive windows at the sun glistening on the sparking, blue lake below. "Mom, I never get tired of this awesome view! You and dad are so lucky to be at this fabulous place whenever you want."

"Your cookies smell unbelievable!" said Ben as he bent down to embrace his mother, pick her up and swing her around. "Are they ready to scarf down now? I'm up to the challenge, you know."

Matt descended the stairs holding Teddy's hand. The child simply bubbled with excitement. "Mommy, look at the new fishing rod Papa made for me! Can we go fishing right now? Please? Please? Please?"

"Let's wait until we get unpacked and settled first, Buddy," said Vicky, their granddaughter, to her son. Then turning to Julia, she asked, "Grandma, do you want us in our normal bedrooms this year, like always?"

(continued)

Julia replied, "Of course, dear. We want you to feel like you're at home when you're here. We're just so happy you're all with us! I know we are going to have the greatest week ever!"

A few years after the *Home Free* series had ended, Matt and Julia had sold their big home, putting the proceeds into their S.A.F.E.T.Y. Fund™, along with the money they had paid to buy the house from the reality show. Then they purchased their mountain cabin on the lake for their summer home and a place in Arizona for their winters, getting large mortgages on both while Matt was still working. Then, they retired shortly after that.

Now, twenty years have passed since the show ended and life has proven to be very good for them. At ages 79 and 80, they have visits in most all seasons from their family. The clear mountain air lures them to remain active and take lots of walks and hikes. Julia enjoys gardening and reading, while Matt spends hours fishing and working on his hobbies. In addition to the travel between their two homes, they try to take a pleasure trip each year to a different destination. "Eventually, we'll see the world," they say. They both volunteer at the local community center every week. They have lots of choices, lots of freedom and enjoy their lives immensely.

As they relax on their expansive deck looking out at the lake, they watch Amy and Ben with their spouses, their grandkids and great-grandkids all sitting on the boat dock with their feet dangling into the water. With the mountain breeze blowing in her hair, Julia turns to Matt, with a tear in her eye.

"What's wrong, sweetheart?" he asks, with a concerned wrinkle in his brow and tilt to his head. He puts his arm around her shoulder and squeezes it lightly.

"Oh, Matt. It was so important for us to create these lasting, loving memories for our kids. I truly believe we did that, and a whole lot more. Now we've created an atmosphere where Amy and Ben can be wrapped in that warm, fuzzy blanket of family memories that extends out to every member of their two families. All in all, I think we made the right choices. How else could we have made it to this wonderful joyous time in our lives?"

He smiled and nodded his head in agreement.

(continued)

"You know, Dear," Matt said tenderly as he took Julia's chin and turned her face toward his. "You may not think I recall, but I have memories of a day when we sat on a bench with the sound of a college band drum beating in the background. Do you ever think of that day?"

Julia's jaw dropped in amazement. "I can't believe you remember that conversation! You never cease to amaze me."

He went on. "We talked about what our family would be like and the things we both wanted. I was scared out of my wits even saying that kind of stuff out loud back then. Well, we made it happen, sweetheart. We pulled it off in a big way. In fact, I think we achieved even more than I had ever dreamed."

Julia squeezed his hand and leaned over, placing her head against his. As they gazed out at the remarkable sunset over the lake, Matt whispered, "We truly couldn't ask for more. No ... we truly couldn't ask for more."

So, What Did The *Home Free* Reality Series Teach Us?

Don't be lured into following old traditional wisdom and pay down or pay off your mortgage. You see what happened to Tom and Samantha by following those old ways. While they did end up with a fairly safe position, in the end, they were nowhere near the level of wealth achieved by Matt and Julia, the winners.

Obviously, don't put off taking care of building your life's wealth. Poor Zeke and Liz will never achieve a relaxing and secure retirement and will be working as long as they live. They just never got around to implementing their H.E.R.O. Solution™ plan.

Each of these contestants had the same income, same household size and approximately the same expenses in their lifetimes. Isn't it interesting to see how three families can end up with such dramatically different results?

You don't need television show producers or a nationally televised reality series to give you a house to live in for free. You can do exactly what Matt and Julia did with your own home.

How?

Implement the H.E.R.O. Solution™ and create a S.A.F.E.T.Y. Fund™ for yourself. The simple Real Wealth Vision™ steps necessary are laid out in this book for you to follow. Get an interest-only mortgage, take full advantage of tax deductions and harvest your tax-free equity as it grows to get it working in a tax-favored environment. Your S.A.F.E.T.Y. Fund™ will far exceed your puny little mortgage over time and, in the end, if you recycle your H.E.R.O. Solution™ a few times, your worry-free plan to millionaire status may even **exceed** Matt and Julia's results.

Good Luck with your H.E.R.O. Solution™ Plan!
        You're almost *Home Free* —
        And you'll soon create a constant flow of
        wealth and security to last for the rest of our life.

In the Introduction section of this book, I predicted that, once you understood the concepts presented, a fresh new day in your life would dawn:

Now, close your eyes. Stop and breathe in the fresh ocean air. Listen to the seagulls and the sound of the waves rolling onto the beach. Feel the cool pleasant breeze at your back. Stretch your arms up high and open your eyes to gaze into the fabulous morning sky. Wiggle your toes in the sand and feel its warmth beneath your feet.

Go ahead. Place your heel into the first footprint that has appeared on the beach of life directly in front of you. Roll forward to your toes and repeat with your other foot. You get the picture. Once you get going, you may even break into a jog. The steps will come easily and naturally. Your experience has been life changing. You've become unstoppable as you start down the path laid out ahead.

There'll be no going back, now that you've been shown the secrets of the H.E.R.O. Solution™ and you possess Real Wealth Vision™. Your future of personal wealth is inevitable.

Your Next Steps Are As Easy As 1, 2, 3 ...

To follow the footsteps of the wealthy, which now lie in front of you, and to set up your personal H.E.R.O. Solution™ plan, the steps are now as easy as 1, 2, 3 ...

> *A journey of a thousand miles begins and ends with one step.*
> — Lao-Tsu

ONE: Go to our website at *www. StopSittingOnYourAssets.com*. There you can see how to locate H.E.R.O. Solution™ advisors in your area who can answer any questions you may have. You'll be able to request your own personalized H.E.R.O. Solution™ plan and sign up to receive the FREE *H.E.R.O. Solution™ Newsletter*. If you don't have Internet access, you may call 866-404-HERO.

TWO: Harvest your equity using the details of your personal H.E.R.O. Solution™ plan to get your unproductive assets to work. This personalized plan will assure you get the right kind and amount of mortgage for your own situation. Sometimes it may be more beneficial to temporarily get a home equity loan rather than a full refinance of your first mortgage balance. This must be evaluated by a H.E.R.O. Solution™ advisor, so don't just go out and do this step without assistance.

THREE: Carefully place your liberated equity into your S.A.F.E.T.Y. Fund™ to protect it and get it working in a tax-favored environment. This step should be done according to your H.E.R.O. Solution™ plan to assure you receive favored tax treatment per IRS guidelines with the guidance of a

H.E.R.O. Solution™ advisor. Again, don't just dump the proceeds of a self-guided, cash-out refinance into just any insurance policy or some other investment on your own. You could invalidate any tax benefits or place your critical cash into an improper or risky vehicle.

RELAX! Your H.E.R.O. Solution™ plan is in place and will propel you down the road of life toward assuring your many years to come are rich and secure ones. Every three to five years, or whenever life-changing events occur, you should plan to meet with your H.E.R.O. Solution™ advisor to check in on your financial situation and stay on track.

Actuary — Intensively educated professional statisticians in the insurance industry. Their knowledge is used to predict future events based upon past occurrences.

Annuity — Savings account or investment with a life insurance company.

Arbitrage — The purchase of securities in one market to make gains on the sale in another. Also known as "riskless profit."

C.O.F.F.E.E. Crisis™ — Trademarked acronym for *Cost of Forfeiting Future Equity Earnings.*

Compound Interest — Interest calculated on both the principal and the accrued interest.

Conforming Loan — A mortgage amount that is at or below the lending limits set each year by the agencies, FNMA and FHLMC.

Deed of Trust — A legal document conveying property to a trustee, often used to secure an obligation such as a mortgage. It is the legal document used in lieu of the mortgage document in some states.

DEFRA — Deficit Reduction Act of 1984 established more stringent rules and added mathematical tests to assure the cash value component of a universal life insurance contract remains a tax-favored instrument per IRS guidelines.

Dow Jones Industrial Average — (DJIA) An indicator of stock market prices, based on the share values of 30 blue-chip stocks listed on the New York Stock Exchange.

Equity — The difference between the current market value of the property and the amount the owner still owes on the mortgage.

Equity Index — (AKA Fixed Index) A fixed insurance contract or annuity in which the gains paid on the cash value are based on the performance of a published stock market index. Not a variable insurance product. Cash value is protected and not invested in the stock market.

FIFO — Acronym for *first-in-first-out*. Tax treatment of amounts withdrawn from an insurance policy cash value. Amounts deposited or earned earliest must be selected and taxed first when withdrawn.

Fixed Index — (AKA Equity Index) A fixed insurance contract or annuity in which the gains paid on the cash value are based on the performance of a published stock market index. Not a variable insurance product. Cash value is protected and not invested in the stock market.

H.E.R.O. Solution™ — Trademarked acronym for *Home Equity Riches Optimizer* or *Home Equity Retirement Optimizer*.

Index — A statistical average or measure of change in a securities market, such as a group of stocks.

Insurance Contract Loan — Money removed from an insurance contract in the form of a loan against the cash value. Repayment and/or monthly payments are not due in the lifetime of the insured but can be repaid at any time while the policy is in force.

Interest-only Mortgage — Loan in which only the interest accrued on the current balance is due, monthly. No principal payments are required during the interest-only period of the loan.

LIFO — Acronym for *last-in-first-out*. Tax treatment of amounts withdrawn from an annuity. Amounts earned or deposited most recently must be selected and taxed first when withdrawn.

Mortgage — A temporary, conditional pledge of property to a creditor as security for performance of an obligation or repayment of a debt.

Mutual Fund — A regulated investment company with a pool of assets, such as stocks or bonds. Its performance is a reflection of the total return of the assets it holds.

Pre-Tax Dollars — Money on which income taxes have not yet been paid.

Principal — A sum of money not including the gains earned or interest owed. In a mortgage, it is the amount of the debt without interest. In a depository account, it is the amount deposited without the gains earned.

Real Wealth Vision™ — The "super-power" vision and ability to see the REAL Wealth you can achieve by utilizing the idle equity in your REAL estate.

Refinance — To pay off an existing mortgage and acquire a new one.

S.A.F.E.T.Y. Fund™ — Trademarked acronym for *Side Account Faithfully Earning Tax-favored Yields.*

S&P 500® — Standard and Poor's market index containing 500 stocks designed to be a leading indicator of U.S. equities. Many consider it to be the definition of the market.

TAMRA — Technical and Miscellaneous Revenues Act of 1988 (IRC Section 7702) set guidelines for the controlled funding of premiums into a universal life insurance policy to assure retention of IRS tax-favored status.

Tax-Deferred — Payment of income taxes postponed to some future date.

Tax-Favored — Money allowed to grow and/or be accessed without loss to taxation.

Tax-Free — Income or capital gain taxes are not and will never be due.

Tax-Postponed — Payment of income taxes delayed or deferred to some future date.

Term Life — Basic, low-cost policy providing life insurance only. Protection is for a defined length of time and no cash-value component exists.

TEFRA — Tax Equity and Fiscal Responsibility Act of 1982 and 1983 established a minimum corridor between the cash value and death benefit that must be maintained to qualify as life insurance and receive IRS tax-favored treatment (IRC Section 101) including tax-free inside build-up of cash values.

Universal Life — The low-cost protection of term life insurance as well as a savings component. Face value, premiums and/or amounts paid to cash value may be adjusted within contract limits.

Variable — Life insurance contract or annuity in which the cash value is not guaranteed or protected from loss. Principal is actually invested in the stock market.

Whole Life — Insurance contract in which the face value and payments are established upfront and are fixed throughout the whole-life of the insured. Contains a cash-value component.

ACKNOWLEDGMENTS

If my father were still with us, he would have been so proud and would have given this book to everyone he knew and everyone he met. Knowing how he desired to help others, he would have wished to spread the word about better planning and preparing for retirement so that others could avoid his devastating pension experience. Each day, I continue to be inspired by his integrity, kindness, selflessness, compassion and natural sense of dry humor. He was a rock of love and support that always was and will forever be my foundation. Dad, I couldn't have done this without you.

No book would have been possible without my mother, Joyce Snow, whose constant encouragement in my life made me believe that all things are possible. Her boundless love, unending energy and complete selfless dedication to others have always existed as my ideal of a perfect earthly existence. Mom, there are mansions waiting for you that all us other mere mortals here can only dream about.

Thank you to my family for their patience and support during the long months I spent at my laptop; my amazing husband and partner, Tim, my beautiful daughter, Robin, and my brilliant sons still at home, Tom and Sean. Thanks, also, for the reviewing and content contribution from Robin and Tim. Robin, thanks for filling in for me and holding down the fort during my travels. There aren't very many daughters who can sit at a desk just a few feet away from their mother all day, every day. You are truly my right hand. Thanks to my astonishing, talented sister and champion, Sherri, and my extraordinary niece, Angie, for their long hours of proofreading. Your loving input was invaluable. To Brett, my incredible son who lives hundreds of miles away with his stunning wife, Farah, and two of the most marvelous kids on the planet, Ethan and Madison, I thank you all. Brett, you lovingly fill your namesake's shoes as my source of consistent encouragement, caring and strength.

I would like to thank all the financial professionals, tax specialists and attorneys who understand the importance of this unique approach to personal planning and have forged the path by creating the plans I discovered in my research. Without the fresh approaches and imaginative minds of these individuals none of these strategies would have been possible. Not only did you make a difference in the lives of our shared clients, but you will continue to have a dramatic impact on the ultimate financial peace and security of countless others through this book. Additionally, I wish to thank those who wrote about many of these topics in their own books, periodicals and online columns which further validate many of the individual component strategies used in this book in the areas of creating your own banking system, creative use of insurance products and strategic tax planning. It was extremely fulfilling to discover that other professionals support and endorse my conclusions. Thanks, also to the thousands of past clients whose personal financial data was used in my research. While your privacy was protected at every turn, your contribution of real numbers for statistical evaluation was priceless.

My gratitude also goes out to Mark Victor Hansen for your enthusiasm and encouragement, and for introducing me to

Ellen Reid, my shepherd throughout this book production process. Ellen, thank you for your professionalism as you truly took my work from manuscript to completion with finesse. Your experience, marvelous suggestions and guidance were invaluable. Thanks, also to Laren Bright, for your copywriting genius. The teamwork and synergy of our collaboration, together with Ellen, took the mediocre to the marvelous. Three heads truly are better than one!

I offer a huge chunk of gratitude to Bill Ebersole, for your editing expertise and input. I'm waiting for that great American novel that I know you have in you. Thanks, also, to Jim Pockross, author of *Confessions of a Real Estate Mini-Mogul*, for your editorial input and words of wisdom. Of course, I must thank Michele DeFilippo for your beautiful design work on the interior and for making my cover ideas become reality.